JOYCE'S *ULYSSES*

OXFORD STUDIES IN PHILOSOPHY AND LITERATURE

Richard Eldridge, Philosophy, Swarthmore College

PUBLISHED IN THE SERIES

Ibsen's *Hedda Gabler*: Philosophical Perspectives
Edited by Kristin Gjesdal

Shakespeare's *Hamlet*: Philosophical Perspectives
Edited by Tzachi Zamir

Kafka's *The Trial*: Philosophical Perspectives
Edited by Espen Hammer

The Oedipus Plays of Sophocles: Philosophical Perspectives
Edited by Paul Woodruff

Jane Austen's *Emma*: Philosophical Perspectives
Edited by E. M. Dadlez

Murasaki Shikibu's *The Tale of Genji*: Philosophical Perspectives
Edited by James McMullen

Dostoevsky's *Crime and Punishment*: Philosophical Perspectives
Edited by Robert E. Guay

Joyce's *Ulysses*: Philosophical Perspectives
Edited by Philip Kitcher

JOYCE'S *ULYSSES*

Philosophical Perspectives

Edited by Philip Kitcher

OXFORD
UNIVERSITY PRESS

OXFORD
UNIVERSITY PRESS

Oxford University Press is a department of the University of Oxford. It furthers
the University's objective of excellence in research, scholarship, and education
by publishing worldwide. Oxford is a registered trade mark of Oxford University
Press in the UK and certain other countries.

Published in the United States of America by Oxford University Press
198 Madison Avenue, New York, NY 10016, United States of America.

Library of Congress Cataloging-in-Publication Data
Names: Kitcher, Philip, 1947– editor.
Title: Joyce's Ulysses : philosophical perspectives / edited by Philip Kitcher.
Other titles: Oxford studies in philosophy and literature.
Description: New York, NY : Oxford University Press, 2020. |
Series: Oxford studies in philosophy and literature | Includes index. |
Identifiers: LCCN 2019055800 (print) | LCCN 2019055801 (ebook) |
ISBN 9780190842260 (hardback) | ISBN 9780190842253 (paperback) |
ISBN 9780190842284 (epub) | ISBN 9780190842291
Subjects: LCSH: Joyce, James, 1882–1941. Ulysses. | Joyce, James,
1882–1941—Criticism and interpretation. | Literature—Philosophy.
Classification: LCC PR6019.O9 U65945 2020 (print) | LCC PR6019.O9 (ebook)
| DDC 823/.912—dc23
LC record available at https://lccn.loc.gov/2019055800
LC ebook record available at https://lccn.loc.gov/2019055801

1 3 5 7 9 8 6 4 2

Paperback printed by Marquis, Canada
Hardback printed by Bridgeport National Bindery, Inc., United States of America

*To the Columbia students
in my courses on Ulysses and on Finnegans Wake,
who have put up with my enthusiasm for Joyce,
and sometimes come to share it.*

CONTENTS

CONTENTS

SERIES EDITOR'S FOREWORD

At least since Plato had Socrates criticize the poets and attempt to displace Homer as the authoritative articulator and transmitter of human experience and values, philosophy and literature have developed as partly competing, partly complementary enterprises. Both literary writers and philosophers have frequently studied and commented on each other's texts and ideas, sometimes with approval, sometimes with disapproval, in their efforts to become clearer about human life and about valuable commitments—moral, artistic, political, epistemic, metaphysical, and religious, as may be. Plato's texts themselves register the complexity and importance of these interactions in being dialogues in which both deductive argumentation and dramatic narration do central work in furthering a complex body of views.

While these relations have been widely recognized, they have also frequently been ignored or misunderstood, as academic disciplines have gone their separate ways within their modern institutional settings. Philosophy has often turned to science or mathematics as providing models of knowledge; in doing so it has often explicitly set itself against cultural entanglements and literary devices, rejecting, at least officially, the importance of plot, figuration, and imagery in favor of supposedly plain speech about the truth. Literary study has moved variously through formalism, structuralism, post-structuralism, and cultural studies, among other movements, as modes of approach to a literary text. In doing so it has understood literary texts as sample instances of images, structures, personal styles, or failures of consciousness, or it has seen the literary text as a largely fungible product, fundamentally shaped by wider pressures and patterns of consumption and expectation that affect and figure in non-literary textual production as well. It has thus set itself against the idea that major literary texts productively and originally address philosophical problems of value and commitment precisely through their form, diction, imagery, and development, even while these works also resist claiming conclusively to solve the problems that occupy them.

These distinct academic traditions have yielded important perspectives and insights. But in the end none of them has been kind to the idea of major literary works as achievements in thinking about values and human life, often in distinctive, open, self-revising, self-critical ways. At the same time readers outside institutional settings, and often enough philosophers and literary scholars too, have turned to major literary texts precisely in order to engage with their productive, materially and medially specific patterns and processes of thinking. These turns to literature have, however, not so far been systematically encouraged within disciplines, and they have generally occurred independently of each other.

The aim of this series is to make manifest the multiple, complex engagements with philosophical ideas and problems that lie at the hearts of major literary texts. In doing so, its volumes aim not only to help philosophers and literary scholars of various kinds to find rich affinities and provocations to further thought and work; they also aim to bridge various gaps between academic disciplines and between those disciplines and the experiences of extra-institutional readers.

Each volume focuses on a single, undisputedly major literary text. Both philosophers with training and experience in literary study and literary scholars with training and experience in philosophy are invited to engage with themes, details, images, and incidents in the focal text, through which philosophical problems are held in view, worried at, and reformulated. Decidedly not a project simply to formulate A's philosophy of X as a finished product, merely illustrated in the text, and decidedly not a project to explain the literary work entirely by reference to external social configurations and forces, the effort is instead to track the work of open thinking in literary forms, as they lie both neighbor to and aslant from philosophy. As Walter Benjamin once wrote, "new centers of reflection are continually forming," as problems of commitment and value of all kinds take on new shapes for human agents in relation to changing historical circumstances, where reflective address remains possible. By considering how such centers of reflection are formed and expressed in and through literary works, as they engage with philosophical problems of agency, knowledge, commitment, and value, these volumes undertake to present both literature and philosophy as, at times, productive forms of reflective, medial work in relation both to each other and to social circumstances and to show how this work is specifically undertaken and developed in distinctive and original ways in exemplary works of literary art.

Richard Eldridge
Swarthmore College

NOTE ON TEXTS AND REFERENCES

References to Joyce's works of fiction will typically use the following styles to cite the following editions:

Dubliners—New York: W. W. Norton, 2006 (Norton Critical Edition). References by story title and line number. Thus, "Eveline: 3" refers to the third line of "Eveline."

A Portrait of the Artist as a Young Man—New York: W. W. Norton, 2007 (Norton Critical Edition). References by part and line number. Thus "III: 636–7" refers to lines 636–7 of part III.

Ulysses—New York: Vintage, 1986 (Gabler Edition). References by episode (Joyce's preferred term for what many readers recognize as chapters) and line number. Thus "16: 60–68" refers to lines 60–68 of episode 16 ("Eumaeus").

Finnegans Wake—New York: Penguin, 1999. References by page and line number. Thus "455: 29" refers to line 29 of page 455. (Fortunately, the pagination of most editions of the *Wake* is the same. In particular, British printings [e.g., Faber and Faber] agree with their American counterparts [Viking, Penguin].) The 1975 Faber edition is often viewed as the most accurate, although the differences with the 1999 Penguin (essentially the original edition of 1939) are relatively minor.

There are two exceptions to this scheme. The Gabler edition has been criticized and is rejected by some scholars. Martha Nussbaum and Garry Hagberg have preferred to use the Modern Library edition (whose pagination is that of the Random House edition of 1961). In their chapters, citations are to the page numbers of the Modern Library edition.

CONTRIBUTORS

Garry L. Hagberg is the James H. Ottaway Professor of Philosophy and Aesthetics at Bard College, and has also been Professor of Philosophy at the University of East Anglia. Author of numerous papers at the intersection of aesthetics and the philosophy of language, his books include: *Meaning and Interpretation: Wittgenstein, Henry James, and Literary Knowledge; Art as Language: Wittgenstein, Meaning, and Aesthetic Theory;* and *Describing Ourselves: Wittgenstein and Autobiographical Consciousness.* He is editor of *Art and Ethical Criticism* and *Fictional Characters, Real Problems: The Search for Ethical Content in Literature,* co-editor of *A Companion to the Philosophy of Literature,* and Editor of the journal *Philosophy and Literature.* His most recent edited volumes include *Wittgenstein on Aesthetic Understanding; Stanley Cavell on Aesthetic Understanding;* and *Narrative and Self-Understanding.* Hagberg is presently completing a new book on the contribution literary experience makes to the formation of self and sensibility, *Living in Words: Literature, Autobiographical Language, and the Composition of Selfhood.*

David Hills is Associate Professor of Philosophy (Teaching) at Stanford University, having previously taught at Harvard; University of California, Los Angeles; The University of Pennsylvania; University of Michigan, Ann Arbor; and University of California, Berkeley. He has written and spoken widely on aesthetics, philosophy of mind, philosophy of language, and the history of modern philosophy, especially Kant and Wittgenstein. He prepared a bibliography on Metaphor for Oxford Bibliographies in 2018 and is at work on two books: one on metaphor and another on Kant's *Critique of the Power of Judgment*.

Philip Kitcher is the John Dewey Professor at Columbia University. He has written widely on many philosophical topics. With respect to literature, he has published articles on Robert Musil and on the Oedipus plays of Sophocles. He also has two books in this area: *Joyce's Kaleidoscope: An Invitation to Finnegans Wake* (Oxford University Press, 2007) and *Deaths in Venice: The Cases of Gustav von Aschenbach* (Columbia University Press, 2013). He is a Fellow of the American Academy of Arts and Sciences, a member of the American Philosophical Society, and an Honorary Fellow of Christ's College, Cambridge.

Vicki Mahaffey is the Clayton and Thelma Kirkpatrick Professor at the University of Illinois, Urbana-Champaign, and Professor Emerita at the University of Pennsylvania. A current elected member of the Board of Trustees of the International James Joyce Foundation and a former Guggenheim Fellow, she is the author of *Reauthorizing Joyce; States of Desire: Wilde, Yeats, Joyce and the Irish Experiment; Modernist Literature: Challenging Fictions,* and the editor of *Collaborative Dubliners: Joyce in Dialogue*. She is in the process of completing a monograph called *The Joyce of Everyday Life*.

Martha C. Nussbaum is Ernst Freund Distinguished Service Professor of Law and Ethics at the University of Chicago, appointed in the Law School and the Philosophy Department. She is the winner of the 2018 Berggruen Philosophy Prize and the 2016 Kyoto Prize in Arts and Thought. Her most recent books are *The Monarchy of Fear* (2018) and *The Cosmopolitan Tradition* (2019).

Sam Slote is an Associate Professor at Trinity College Dublin and lives in the Liberties in Dublin. He is the author of *Joyce's Nietzschean Ethics* (Palgrave, 2013) and is the co-editor, with Luca Crispi, of *How Joyce Wrote 'Finnegans Wake'* (Wisconsin, 2007). His *Annotations to James Joyce's 'Ulysses'*, cowritten with Marc Mamigonian and John Turner, will be published by Oxford University Press in 2020. In addition to Joyce and Beckett, he has written on Virginia Woolf, Vladimir Nabokov, Raymond Queneau, Antonin Artaud, Dante, Mallarmé, and Elvis.

Wendy J. Truran is a Visiting Lecturer in writing and communications at the Georgia Institute of Technology, Atlanta GA. Her scholarship focuses on modernist structures of feeling and affect, and she is one of the founding editors of *Capacious: Journal for Emerging Affect Inquiry*. She has published on May Sinclair and is co-editing an Edinburgh Critical Edition of Sinclair's *The Creators: A Comedy*. She also has forthcoming work on W. B. Yeats.

JOYCE'S *ULYSSES*

Introduction

PHILIP KITCHER

In 1998, a prestigious jury of scholars and writers selected *Ulysses*
as "the finest English-language novel" of the twentieth century.
Judgments of this kind often raise eyebrows—and not only because
of suspicions about the timing of the pronouncement: Shouldn't it
have come at least two years later? Nevertheless, despite the legendary difficulty of *Ulysses* (as well as its famous troubles with censors),
the verdict aroused little surprise. Joyce's second novel occupies a
stellar position in the modernist canon, widely recognized as changing the ways in which the art of fiction is understood.

At Columbia, where I teach, undergraduates flock to courses on
Joyce, classes focused on *Ulysses*, often because they want to pen-
etrate a novel widely viewed as baffling. As they quickly learn, part
of the problem they face results from the vast gulf between the education they have received and the curriculum in which Joyce was
immersed. Twenty-first-century students know all sorts of things,

Thanks to Vicki Mahaffey and to an anonymous reader for Oxford University Press for their
helpful suggestions, which have enabled me to improve earlier versions of this introduction. I am especially grateful to Richard Eldridge for two sets of extraordinarily constructive
comments.

Joyce's Ulysses. Philip Kitcher, Oxford University Press (2020). © Oxford University Press.
DOI: 10.1093/oso/9780190842260.001.0001

particularly in the natural and social sciences, about which their late nineteenth-century counterparts were completely ignorant. The Irish boys who went to Clongowes Wood and Belvedere received by way of compensation an extraordinarily rich introduction to languages and to the humanities. The allusions of *Ulysses* draw effortlessly on that humanistic education, expressing familiarity with thinkers and writers beyond the contemporary undergraduate's ken. Among them are philosophers, and not only canonical figures like Plato, Aristotle, and Aquinas but others whose treatises most professors no longer read.

James Joyce was steeped in philosophy. Yet, in comparison with other great modernists—Proust, Mann, and Musil, for example—he has received little attention from contemporary philosophers in the English-speaking world.[1] Proust's discussions of time, personal identity, self-knowledge, and love have given rise to numerous illuminating books and articles, establishing his philosophical *bona fides*.[2] Mann and Musil have provoked a smaller number of philosophical explorations, although they seem to have proved more philosophically inspiring than Joyce.[3]

My judgment will surely excite resistance, for philosophers *have* weighed in on Joyce in two different contexts. First is a genre

---

1. European philosophers have shown substantially more interest. An obvious example is Jacques Derrida.
2. See, for a small number of outstanding examples, Richard Moran, "Kant, Proust, and the Appeal of Beauty," *Critical Inquiry* 38, no. 2 (Winter 2012): 298–329; Martha Nussbaum, *Upheavals of Thought* (Cambridge, UK: Cambridge University Press, 2001), chapters 9 and 10; Robbie Kubala, "Love and Transience in Proust," *Philosophy* 91, no. 4 (2016): 541–57; and, especially, Joshua Landy, *Philosophy as Fiction: Self, Deception, and Knowledge in Proust* (New York: Oxford University Press, 2004). It's also worth remembering the role Proust plays in motivating Derek Parfit's much-discussed account of personal identity; see Derek Parfit, "Personal Identity," *Philosophical Review* 80, no. 1 (1971): 3–27.
3. The ambiguities of Hans Castorp, the protagonist of *Der Zauberberg*, have been brilliantly elaborated by Alexander Nehamas, *The Art of Living* (Berkeley: University of California Press, 2000), chapter 1. Philosophical themes in Musil are the topic of an issue of *The Monist* 97, no. 1 (2014), edited by Bence Nanay.

exploring the aesthetic theories supposedly present in Joyce's novels.[4] The words Joyce assigns to Stephen Dedalus in (the surviving fragment of) *Stephen Hero*, in *Ulysses*, and especially in part V of *A Portrait of the Artist as a Young Man* have sometimes been used as starting points for attempts to elaborate an aesthetic theory allegedly advocated by Stephen's creator. To my mind, and I suspect most people trained in philosophy would agree, ventures of this sort are profoundly misguided.

The idea that *any* of Joyce's fiction conforms to some mix of ill-defined principles whose supposed roots lie in Aristotle and Aquinas is *prima facie* puzzling. Stephen Dedalus is not, of course, James Joyce, and the portraits Joyce offers are those of a *young* man: the mature author might be expected to have followed the Apostle Paul's example, putting "away childish things," and thinking far more deeply about the nature of art. Joyce depicts Stephen as a talented and precocious thinker, not yet fully formed, whose "philosophizing" is a superficial imitation of figures he admires, writers who have contributed to a discipline in which he is at best half-trained. Like Stephen's villanelle, the "aesthetic theory" simultaneously reveals the young man's promise and his shortcomings. To treat either of them solemnly, as a scholarly contribution or an inspired lyric, is to fall victim to a sly Joycean joke.

The alternative would be to think that Joyce was confused about what it is to practice philosophy. When Stephen arrogantly declares that Aristotle "has not defined pity and terror," a lack he will make up, philosophical readers are primed to scrutinize his definitions.[5] Are the terms employed sufficiently clear and precise to enable justified applications—and are the applications Stephen goes on to make

---

4. For examples, see A. D. Hope, "The Esthetic Theory of James Joyce," *Australasian Journal of Philosophy* 21 (1943): 93–114; David E. Jones, "The Essence of Beauty in James Joyce's Aesthetics," *James Joyce Quarterly* 10, no. 3 (1973): 291–311.

5. *A Portrait of the Artist as a Young Man*, V: 1082.

warranted? On a charitable reading, they might be seen as preliminary efforts, susceptible to further work and careful refinement. At best, the judgments he offers his interlocutor (Lynch) are impulsive leaps requiring much more detailed explanation and defense. Stephen's ambition overrides his patience. He treats an initial insight as if it were a philosophical account. As in the case of the villanelle, where the mastery of form is clear and the poetic content amorphous, it's easy to recognize promise and latent talent, and also the lack of mature development.

Similarly, with respect to Stephen's performance in the National Library. "Scylla and Charybdis" reveals his awareness of what definitions are supposed to accomplish and his difficulties in navigating the metaphysics supposedly fundamental to his approach: "Unsheathe your dagger definitions. Horseness is the whatness of allhorse" (9: 84–5).

Definitions are supposed to be sharp—all the better to be used in a dueling disputation, of the kind on which Stephen is about to embark. Yet, if we need an account of "-ness" terms, what is "whatness" doing in this definition? How do we understand "whatness"? Should the "definition" really be "Horseness is the what of allhorse"? And what exactly would that mean? To take any of what follows seriously is to overlook a feature of the episode about which Joyce takes great pains to remind us: it is a *performance* (9: 465, 484, 761–2, 846–7, 981–2, 1066–8). Stephen is singing for his supper, hoping to earn anointment from the deans of Irish literature. The poignancy of the scene lies not only in his failure, but in his own awareness that what he offers is bullshit (in the precise sense offered by Harry Frankfurt),[6] or, in a less anachronistic idiom, that he is prostituting himself (9: 1104–13).

---

6. Harry Frankfurt, *On Bullshit* (Princeton, NJ: Princeton University Press, 2005).

The second genre, far more valuable, consists in efforts to help contemporary readers by distilling the central ideas of the philosophers to whom Joyce often alludes.[7] Scholars who have studied Aristotle, Aquinas, Giordano Bruno, and Vico can illuminate passages in *Ulysses* and *Finnegans Wake* by explaining how Joyce engages with (and often plays with) themes sounded by these thinkers. Commentaries of this sort expose Joyce's links to the history of philosophy. They do not, however, reveal him as an interesting philosopher in his own right.

* * *

One way to begin an excavation of Joyce as philosopher is to explore the route that led a young man with an extraordinary humanistic education, already marked as a promising writer by his regular success in winning prizes ("exhibitions") in national competitions,[8] from the relatively conventional prose and verse of his student days to the recasting of the novel undertaken in his two last masterpieces. No short account can do justice to the complex sequence of experiences, social interactions, and reflections that formed the mature novelist, but a letter from Trieste to his brother provides a useful thread to follow. Writing to Stanislaus, Joyce indicates his early dissatisfaction with the nineteenth-century version of the genre. Reading Oliver Goldsmith, he felt "a moment of doubt as to the excellence of [his] literary manners"; he was prompted to ask about the durability of the Victorian novel, even in its late (Hardyesque) form; and, beyond that, led to a disturbing skeptical

---

7. Two excellent instances of this genre are Donald Phillip Verene, *James Joyce and the Philosophers at Finnegans Wake* (Evanston IL: Northwestern University Press, 2016) and the currently unpublished (second) Ph.D. thesis (written for the Faculty of English at University College, Dublin) of Fran O'Rourke, emeritus professor of philosophy at UCD, on Joyce's debts to Aristotle and Aquinas.

8. Richard Ellmann, *James Joyce* (New York: Oxford University Press, 1959), 47–57, *passim*.

question: "Is it possible that, after all, men of letters are no more than entertainers?"[9]

Joyce's answer was a resounding "No". For all the importance of humor in his fiction, to ignore the efforts of *Ulysses* and *Finnegans Wake* to illuminate, even transform, human lives is possible only for the tone deaf.[10] Yet what kinds of insight can a novel bring? And how, exactly, does it convey them?

A constant theme across Joyce's four published prose works is the bleakness of the lives Ireland allows most of her inhabitants. The figures in *Dubliners* are confined by the meanness of a subservient city, almost to the point of paralysis; nor are they significantly liberated when they return in *Ulysses*. In *A Portrait of the Artist as a Young Man*, Stephen Dedalus vows to fly by the nets that his country has set to trap him; when readers encounter him again in *Ulysses*, his ignominious failure is evident. *Finnegans Wake* brilliantly encapsulates the Dubliners' predicament. They scrape along to "sneeze out a likelihood that will solve and salve life's robulous rebus." But they must always serve:

Behove this sound of Irish sense. Really? Here English might be seen. Royally? One sovereign punned to petery pence. Regally? The silence speaks the scene. Fake!
So This Is Dyoublong?
Hush! Caution! Echoland![11]

---

9. Richard Ellmann, ed., *The Letters of James Joyce*, volume 2 (London: Faber and Faber, 1966), 99; letter (fragment) to Stanislaus Joyce of July 19, 1905.

10. Commentators rightly attend to the comedy of the two late novels. There's an unfortunate tendency, however, to respond to *Finnegans Wake* as if it were some compendium of brilliant jokes, completely overlooking the many melancholy moments when the laughter stops.

11. *Finnegans Wake*, 12:32, 12:36–13:5.

Paid in debased coinage, required to express themselves in the master's tongue, offering a mute, hypocritical obeisance, Dubliners are forced to wonder if they belong in their own city. They have to tread quietly, carefully echoing the attitudes of their rulers.

Coming of age as Parnell's political fall (and subsequent death) had dashed hopes for home rule, belonging to a family whose fortunes spiraled ever downward, Joyce was both encouraged by the revival of Irish literature and disappointed by its lack of connection with the social confinement he witnessed. Major figures in the revival movement—George Russell (A.E.) and Yeats—recognized his promise and offered encouragement.[12] Yet, as his scatological broadside, *The Holy Office*, makes clear, their retreat to ethereal realms where the body and its needs were absent irked him: Aristotle needed to be brought to the tavern and the brothel; someone must relieve the "arses" of the socially timid poets.[13] Joyce nominated himself for the task.

For literature to move the hearts and open the minds of twentieth-century people, it could not lose itself in the "dreamy dreams" of the established writers who had generously reached out their hands to him.[14] Literary reform required a refusal to blink in the face of the squalor, suffering, and hypocrisy of early twentieth-century life.[15]

12. Letters from Russell to Yeats, from Russell to Joyce, and from Yeats to Joyce make their interest in the twenty-year-old writer clear. See *Letters of James Joyce*, 2:11–12, 13, 14, and 15.
13. Ellsworth Mason and Richard Ellmann, eds., *James Joyce: The Critical Writings* (New York: Viking, 1959), 149–52. Joyce wrote *The Holy Office* in 1904, but it appeared in print only the following year. Martha Nussbaum's study in this volume reveals the persistence of these themes in Joyce's work.
14. Ibid. The "Scylla and Charybdis" episode captures the tensions between the young Joyce and the writers who had initially befriended him. By 1912 warmer relations were beginning to be restored. See Joyce's account of a meeting with Yeats in London, when "for a wonder" the poet was "polite" (*Letters*, 2:298). Given Joyce's earlier review of Lady Gregory and the scathing tone of *The Holy Office*, Yeats' cooler attitude in the intervening years seems eminently understandable.
15. Of course, Joyce was also critical of turn-of-the-century movements of political resistance. The waddling "Citizen" and his attendant courtiers in Barney Kiernan's substitute impotent

Famously Joyce found inspiration in a writer from another small nation. Toward the end of his schooldays he discovered Ibsen. Reading Ibsen, first in translation and later (after teaching himself Norwegian) in the original, he committed himself to a rigorous honesty. His first publication (a review of *When We Dead Awaken*) expressed his admiration: Ibsen had begun "an epoch in the history of drama."[16] Joyce was inspired by the scathing denunciations of bourgeois hypocrisy and Ibsen's sympathy for women whose lives are cramped by conventions and social expectations.

An obvious next step would have been to follow in the master's footsteps, to write Ibsen-inspired drama in English. Perhaps Joyce initially thought of pursuing that course. By 1900, he had written a play, which he sent to Ibsen's translator, William Archer. The response was not encouraging. While acknowledging Joyce's talents as a writer, Archer thought the dramatic effort unsuccessful, wondered whether Joyce really wanted to write for the stage, and concluded with apologies for being "a wet blanket."[17]

I don't know if Archer's lack of enthusiasm turned Joyce away from the stage (at least for the time being) or whether it simply reinforced a prior conviction that prose fiction was his métier. The influence of Ibsen is apparent in the work that follows, in *Dubliners'* unmasking of stunted forms of life, and in the first (long) attempt to chronicle the efforts of a talented youth to resist the cramping and distortion of an unhealthy social environment. The surviving fragment of *Stephen Hero* celebrates the dramatist's "haughty, disillusioned

---

spleen for genuine action; Molly dismisses the Gaelic Revival movement as the insignificant twittering of "sparrowfarts" (18: 878–81)—her judgment is foreshadowed in the early pages of "A Mother"; at best, as "Ivy Day in the Committee Room" shows, post-Parnellian politics is impoverished, nostalgic, and sad.

16. Mason and Ellmann, *James Joyce*, 48–67, at 48. For Ibsen's impact on the young Joyce, see Ellmann, *James Joyce*, 55.

17. *Letters*, 2:8–9, letter of September 15, 1900.

courage"[18]—and it embodies the precise and unflinching description of situations and events that Joyce had learned from Ibsen. Yet, sometime around 1908, bogged down and dissatisfied with his long manuscript, he decided on a complete rewriting. *Stephen Hero* metamorphosed into *A Portrait of the Artist as a Young Man*.

With good reason. The brilliant—and disturbing—delineations of disappointment, humiliation, and hopelessness that distinguish *Dubliners* reveal how standard third-person narrative, pursued with rigorous honesty and "disillusioned courage," can be powerful on the small scale of the short story. On the larger canvas of the projected *Bildungsroman*, monotony sets in, and the narrative voice undergoes a long diminuendo. The breakthrough of *Portrait* consisted in vocal variation. Stephen's voice is dominant, but it varies with the stages of his development. Moreover, it is punctuated by the voices of others, members of his family, teachers, priests, university friends. A long sequence of reports has been replaced by intimacy, achieved in the nuances of characteristic modes of expression used by different people and by Stephen at the different periods of his career. *Saying* gives way to *showing*.[19]

The miniatures of *Dubliners* jar readers into new reactive emotions, prompting them to see familiar things anew and to reflect on their entrenched beliefs, even on the language they casually employ. Readers inevitably come to the pages of fiction with complexes of psychological states, intricate webs of judgments, predilections, tastes, emotions, and aspirations. Fiction illuminates us by inviting

18. James Joyce, *Stephen Hero* (New York: New Directions Press, 1959), 41. The first five hundred or so pages of Joyce's manuscript seem not to have survived. According to Herbert Gorman, *James Joyce* (New York: Farrar and Rinehart, 1940), Joyce burned most of the manuscript in 1908. No hard evidence supports this claim, but scholars are agreed that the chances of finding the missing pages are extremely small.

19. It is interesting to ask how Joyce learned to make this transition. I *conjecture* that his Ibsen-inspired attempt to depict unsparingly a version of his own younger self in *Stephen Hero* eventually brought home to him the limitations of his approach.

reconsideration, sometimes by forcing us to reflect on our taken-for-granted connections. By showing us something we had not anticipated, we are given the opportunity—or are required—to reweave our *synthetic complexes*.[20] We also observe the linkages made by individual characters, the idealized synthetic complexes with which they approach their experiences, and the ways in which those complexes are refined and transformed in the encounters attributed to them—and our subsequent reflections aid us in our own revisions.[21]

Joyce transcended the Ibsenite approach with which he had aimed to reform prose fiction by inventing a vibrant multivocality.[22] *Ulysses* and *Finnegans Wake* represent the full flowering of his technical advances. His last two novels reveal how fiction can bring home to readers a rich chorus of voices, a dazzling array of perspectives. So, with respect to the material of most concern to him, he was able to replace saying by showing. He could entertain—but also become far more than an entertainer. He could move readers' minds on important matters.

* * *

Which matters? Does the illumination he provided bear on *philosophical* issues? Is there "real philosophy" *in* Joyce's fiction? A few scholars have thought so. Two of them are contributors to this volume.[23] Another was the late distinguished philosopher Donald

---

20. I introduced this term in *Deaths in Venice* (New York: Columbia University Press, 2013). Pages 11–26 and 179–91 propose an account of how works of art can have genuinely cognitive import, offering more detail than I can provide here. It is still not enough, and I hope to remedy the deficiency in future work.

21. Joyce's precursors had assembled techniques of their own for achieving similar effects—the novels of Flaubert, George Eliot, Tolstoy, and Henry James testify to that. But in his three novels, he radically expanded the writer's arsenal.

22. For further development of this theme, see chapters 5 and 6 in this volume.

23. Martha Nussbaum, "The Transfiguration of Everyday Life: Joyce," in *Upheavals of Thought*, chapter 16; Samuel Slote, *Joyce's Nietzschean Ethics* (Basingstoke, UK: Palgrave Macmillan, 2013).

Davidson.[24] Having heard that Davidson had sometimes given lectures on *Ulysses*, I hoped his legacy might include unpublished material that could be included (or developed) here. Sadly, it was not to be.[25]

Why is the philosophical side of Joyce so neglected by Anglophone philosophers? If the answer is that there is very little to that side—Joyce turns out to be philosophically uninteresting—then the project of this volume is misguided, and you (the reader) would be justified in asking for your money back. I don't think that's so. Rather, the difficulty lies in the *scope* of the philosophical issues exercising Joyce, and in their entanglement with intricate *literary* issues surrounding his fiction.[26]

While European thinkers have long embraced the possibilities of fiction as a vehicle for exploring central philosophical questions— think of Dante and Petrarch, Goethe, Schiller and Hölderlin, Sartre and Camus—Anglophone philosophy, particularly since the "linguistic turn," has tended to insist on strict separation. As Iris Murdoch (someone you might have thought to be sympathetic to "philosophy in literature") sternly told Bryan Magee, when philosophical ideas enter novels they cease to be "real philosophy" and become the "plaything" of the novelist.[27] Recent Anglophone interest in finding philosophy of real value in literary works owes an enormous debt to Stanley Cavell, and particularly to his widely acclaimed explorations of philosophical themes in Shakespeare.[28] Given Joyce's ambition to

24. Donald Davidson, "James Joyce and Humpty Dumpty," *MidWest Studies in Philosophy* 16 (1991): 1–12.
25. As Marcia Cavell informed me, any notes that Davidson used haven't survived.
26. Hence the importance of understanding *how* Joyce reformed the novel and *why* he chose to develop the genre as he did.
27. See "Iris Murdoch on Philosophy and Literature: Section 3," YouTube, https://www.youtube.com/watch?v=maGN8--MhIQ; Murdoch does concede one example of a "philosophically interesting novel," Sartre's *La Nausée*.
28. The most seminal contributions are chapters 2 and 3 of Stanley Cavell's *Disowning Knowledge* (Cambridge, UK: Cambridge University Press, 2003): "The Avoidance of

do for the novel what Shakespeare had achieved for English drama,[29] perhaps *Ulysses* and *Finnegans Wake* should be viewed as invitations (or challenges?) to philosophers to emulate Cavell's magisterial discussions.[30]

The core of Joyce's philosophical interests lies in the oldest problem of philosophy—Socrates' question "How to live?" Yet Joyce comes to the question from a very different angle from that taken by the ancient thinkers who set up academies in which the high-born males of the *polis* might seek answers. From the beginning, Joyce is not solely concerned with the elite, with gifted young high-born men who might aspire to "forge in the smithy of [their souls] the uncreated conscience of [their] race." Indeed, he takes pains to identify the *obstacles* to living well, the "nets" that might trap the talented, past which they must "fly." Stephen Dedalus does not inhabit some protective environment, suited to helping him discover and develop his gifts, offering a smooth path to fulfilling his destiny. The life around him is typically mundane, sometimes squalid, blotched and flawed, palliated with lies and half-truths, acquiescing in a resented

Love" and "Othello and the Stake of the Other," both reprinting material Cavell had written earlier.

29. Joyce's wish to measure himself against Shakespeare pokes through the text of *Ulysses* in "Scylla and Charybdis." John Eglinton remarks, "When all is said Dumas fils (or is it Dumas père?) is right. After God Shakespeare has created most." It seems impossible not to hear a Joycean whisper—"And after Shakespeare, Joyce has created most." Thomas Mann's preoccupation with Goethe expresses a similar rivalrous admiration.

30. Precisely because I see Cavell as having begun an important movement within Anglophone philosophy—one continued by writers like Martha Nussbaum, Robert Pippin, Susan Wolf, Alexander Nehamas, Richard Eldridge, Joshua Landy, Garry Hagberg, Moira Gatens, Richard Moran, Bence Nanay, and others—I have chosen not to invite self-described "Continental philosophers" to contribute to this volume. Cavell not only taught many of us how to undertake serious philosophical investigations through the study of literary texts, but he also showed how the supposed split between "analytic" and "Continental" philosophy should be transcended. There are many interesting thinkers on both sides of the alleged divide. The time has surely come for full recognition of the absurdity of viewing the English Channel as a significant philosophical boundary—also for Cavell-inspired philosophers to come to terms with Joyce.

subjugation, threatened always with paralysis. In counterpoint to Nietzsche's youthful declaration (occurring twice in *The Birth of Tragedy*) that "only as an aesthetic phenomenon are existence and the world justified," Joyce begins from the assumption that life in Dublin (or anywhere else in the modern world), at least on the face of it, is strikingly lacking in aesthetic qualities. Commonplace at best, frequently sordid and superficially repulsive, twentieth-century human existence will have to be justified (if it can be justified at all) by digging deeper. Any contemporary answer to Socrates' question will require a "transfiguration of everyday life."[31]

Joyce might be seen as standing Socratic inquiry on its head. Instead of asking (portentously) for the nature of the Good Life (or the Happy Life, the Fully Human Life, the Meaningful Life, or whatever),[32] he asks how people might do better than live the miserable, grubby, confined, and paralyzed lives to which their social and cultural environments often condemn them. *Dubliners* is naturally read as a review and commentary on forms of paralysis and confinement. If it ever points to any possibility of living better, that comes only with the final story, *The Dead*, with the warmth the Misses Morkan and their niece share with their guests—the conviviality to which Gabriel Conroy condescends—and the stirrings of generosity Gabriel eventually attains, after his blind and apparently blundering responses to Gretta's revelation lead him, miraculously it seems, to an

31. As Martha Nussbaum insightfully explains. See the chapter cited in n23 and chapter 1 in this volume. Joyce continued to hold that literature should not flee reality by weaving "dreamy dreams." An enduring lesson from Ibsen was that modern life becomes bearable only through confronting and working through its initially repellent aspects.

32. When contemporary philosophers return to the Socratic question, there's a common tendency to vary the adjectives, perhaps to avoid stylistic monotony. Yet the valences of the characterizations plainly differ. Moreover, it seems that some versions of the question are better suited to some human circumstances than they are to others. To my mind, inquiring into the meaningful life for a Paleolithic hunter-gatherer or for many oppressed people since is fatuous and insensitive.

unexpected state of incipient understanding. The prose poem of the final two paragraphs points to the possibility of a new depth in the Conroy marriage but gives no assurance that it will be realized.

A Portrait of the Artist as a Young Man poses Joyce's inversion of the Socratic question for a life in prospect. Like his creator, Stephen Dedalus is recognizably brilliant, a child and adolescent for whom the future seems to offer wonderful possibilities. His attempts to find his way begin in soaring visions—the epiphanies Joyce so memorably characterizes. One facet of the novel's artistry lies in the sudden crash as one part gives way to the next. From the ecstatic vision of life as "simple and beautiful" and "all before him," when Stephen, reconciled to God, contemplates the breakfast food laid out in the family kitchen, part IV opens abruptly with the deadening monotony of his self-appointed devotional routine.[33] From the sight of the bird-girl whose image passes "into his soul for ever," part V returns Stephen to the kitchen, to the "watery tea," the "crusts of fried bread," the "pawn-tickets," and the grime on his face and neck.[34] The exaltation of his last three diary entries[35] prepares us for the swift descent to come. In the struggle between life and aesthetic rapture, life wins.

Ulysses opens with the fall of Icarus. The Stephen we meet in its early chapters is directionless, and aware of the fact.[36] His wanderings through Dublin during the long day do not lead him home, or even toward anything. He leaves through the back gate ("an obsolescent unhinged door") of a garden in Eccles Street—and goes out of fiction.[37]

---

33. James Joyce, A Portrait of the Artist as a Young Man, Norton Critical Edition (New York: Norton, 2007), 127, 128–32; III: 1554–62; IV: 1–154.
34. Ibid., 150, 151–2; IV: 854–90.
35. Ibid., 223–4; V: 2777–92.
36. James Joyce, Ulysses, Gabler Edition (New York: Vintage, 1986), I: 739–40; II: 404; III: 158–9, 488–90, 503–5.
37. Ibid., XVII: 1218.

Of course, Stephen is not the principal wanderer of *Ulysses*. That honor belongs to Leopold Bloom, a man "in the middle of life" who (like Stephen) has "lost the straight way."[38] If *A Portrait of the Artist as a Young Man* takes up the (inverted) Socratic question for a life in prospect, *Ulysses* focuses on re-finding one's path after it has been lost. On June 16, 1904, Bloom has to come to terms with that fact.

One way to approach *Finnegans Wake* is to see it not as addressing some quite different set of themes but as continuing the investigations of its three predecessors. The *Wake's* perspective is retrospective. It looks back on a life nearing its end, trying to make sense of it and to vindicate it, despite the scars and stains and deformations it inevitably contains. As one of the documents attributed to ALP informs us, her husband "had to see life foully the plak and the smut" (FW 113: 13–14). Her later voice recognizes an alternative: to close the eyes, "so not to see," contemplating instead "a youth in his florizel, a boy in innocence." Sadly, however, "all men has done something" and are thus burdened with "the weight of old fletch" (FW 621: 29–33, with omissions). Looking with clear eyes easily provokes her bitter, penultimate verdict: "How small it's all!" (FW 627: 20). Only the force of positive memory—the type of memory Bloom and Molly share of the afternoon among the rhododendrons on Howth Head—enables an honest affirmation.[39]

Approaching the *Wake* from this angle gives substance to Joyce's chosen image for the book, provided in the "Quiz Show" chapter, as a "collideorscape" (FW 143: 28). His meandering question (FW 143: 3–27) envisages an elderly man apparently engaged in serious reflection, shaking a kaleidoscope again and again, in efforts

---

38. Stephen quotes the opening line of Dante's *Inferno* in meditating on Shakespeare's loss of direction in his personal life (9: 831). The line is applied to Bloom's predicament (14: 859). Stephen's language connects Bloom and Shakespeare (compare 9: 651–2 and 11: 907–8).
39. See FW 628: 6–16, and compare with *Ulysses*, 8: 899–916; 18: 1571–81.

to produce some satisfying pattern. The constant threat is that the ugly elements will spoil it all, that what once appeared beautiful "pales as it palls" (FW 143: 24). So too *Finnegans Wake* continues to engage with the detritus of a life, working through the material, obsessively chewing over the same stories, in search of a satisfying conclusion.[40]

If I am right, Joyce's mature fiction is much concerned with a reworking of the oldest, most central philosophical question, Socrates' "How to live?" Joyce hopes to understand how to avoid the factors that confine our lives, how we might find some direction when we inevitably go astray, how we might come to terms (honestly) with our inevitable faults, missteps, and misdeeds. To pose good philosophical questions, however, is compatible with not having anything interesting to offer by way of answers. Perhaps philosophers have found so little to discuss in Joyce because the explorations of his novels prove disappointing? Let us see.

* * *

Ulysses, I suggest, pursues three strategies for answering the philosophical questions Joyce raises. The first of these consists in an extraordinary "revaluation of values," puncturing conventional emotional responses to mundane human activities. The second reflects on our sensory reactions to the world around us and on the ways that unscrutinized assumptions distort the perceptual judgments at which people frequently arrive. The third considers our interactions with our fellows and the difficulties that restrict us to a single point of view. Each of the three strategies can be viewed in liberatory mode— as a means of resisting the confinement of human lives; each can also

40. I defend this approach (one way of reading Joyce's final masterpiece) in *Joyce's Kaleidoscope: An Invitation to Finnegans Wake* (New York: Oxford University Press, 2007). For an extended interpretation of question 9 of the Quiz Show, see my "Collideorscape: *Finnegans Wake* in the Large and in the Small," *Joyce Studies Annual* (2009): 188–211.

be seen as a means of coming to terms with the apparent defects in our past—as a way of achieving that elusive, clear-eyed vindication.

Passages that have moved some readers (including at least one as sophisticated as Virginia Woolf) to wrinkle their noses in disapproval and that have excited censorious judgment (not only from official censors) show very clearly how activities not normally within the scope of novels—digesting food, farting, urinating, defecating, masturbating, and the like—need not be provocations to disgust. Bloom's perfect bowel movement (4: 510), like his later breaking of wind (11: 1290–94), is a hero's response to the challenge posed by Blazes Boylan. Molly's post-copulatory assessment of Boylan's performance, with its pluses (18: 149–50, 583–8, 732–3, 1510–12) and minuses (18: 122–3, 152–7, 1369–77), set in the context of her enforced decade-long abstinence from vaginal intercourse, undercuts shallow revulsion against female adultery. Re-educating the emotions of his readers, Joyce teaches us to view "the plak and the smut" differently. Demolishing the taboos society has erected to haunt us, he transfigures everyday life.[41]

Typical perceptions of our environments are also structured by the expectations instilled in us by socialization. Joyce recognized the "Myth of the Given"—he knew that, in perception, we inevitably bring prior categories to organize the stimuli we receive.[42] The dominance of prejudices and expectations is forcefully evoked in "Proteus," where the push of external stimuli is slight in comparison

---

41. Joyce's pursuit of this strategy is brilliantly explained and defended in the final chapter of Nussbaum's *Upheavals of Thought*. As I'll suggest later, her contribution to this volume further extends the work of that chapter.
42. The idea that there is no naïve perception, no pure observation language, is often taken to stem from Hegel. I doubt that Hegel's *Phenomenology of Spirit* (one of the most difficult philosophical texts) was Joyce's source and suspect that he discovered the point for himself. Contemporary discussions of the "Myth of the Given" (and the "theory-ladenness of observation") begin with Wilfrid Sellars' classic "Empiricism and the Philosophy of Mind," in *Science, Perception, and Reality* (London: Routledge and Kegan Paul, 1963), 127–96.

to the weight of the material, assembled from an extraordinary range of erudite and experiential sources, used in reworking it. The grip of Stephen's learning is so strong that he hardly sees at all.[43]

Bloom's perceptions, by contrast, are more sensitive to the stimuli he receives, categorized at a more familiar, less esoteric level. Readers first meet him in the kitchen in Eccles Street, with a review of his responses to the tastes and smells of food. He feels the air on his skin and the unevenness of the breakfast tray, sees the glowing coals in the fireplace, and observes the shape of the kettle. Then, in a sequence of ever closer exercises in listening, he hears more finely differentiated sounds in the cat's mewing (4: 1–32).

Two features of this introduction to the novel's main figure are significant. First, Joyce treats the senses ecumenically. From the beginning, Bloom is characterized as a man of five senses, all of them alert. Although vision dominates discussions of human perception, Joyce does not treat it as our sole mode of access to our surroundings. Indeed (the second point) he does not even give it pride of place. If any sensory modality is *primus inter pares* it is, apparently, hearing. Bloom's most acute perception comes as he opens his ears to the cat. So, readers are prepared from the beginning for the sonic richness of Bloom's world, for the snatches of melody that run through his consciousness, for the individuality of accents and voices, for the auditory power of "Sirens," "Cyclops," "Nausicaa," "Oxen of the Sun," "Circe," and "Penelope."[44]

---

43. Indeed, if he broke his glasses on June 15, 1904, the power of visual stimuli would be even more restricted. Part I of *A Portrait of the Artist as a Young Man* made it clear how little Stephen can do without glasses, and myopia usually does not improve with age. For more discussion of this point, see chapter 6 in this volume, especially n17 and the text to which this note refers.

44. Not only was Joyce afflicted with extremely poor vision, but he was also a trained singer. Nora Barnacle, impressed with a performance she heard in their courtship, when Joyce shared the stage with the legendary tenor John McCormack, is supposed to have contended (probably not seriously) that Joyce should have pursued a musical career rather than writing novels. (It is hard to square this with the comment on Gide attributed to her

Ulysses thus invites us to emulate Bloom, attending more closely to the sounds, smells, tastes, and textures of our environments, and opening ourselves to alternative ways of categorizing what we perceive. Joyce takes up epistemological questions, issues about our knowledge of the world around us, not in the traditional philosophical vein, as responses to skepticism.[45] Rather, reflections on perception are pursued to prepare release from the conventions that so often dominate our organization of sensory experience. The novel teaches us to hear, taste, smell, touch—and see—better, thus opposing the factors that confine and cramp human lives and allowing new possibilities of eventual vindication.

The third strategy charts a similar course for the human realm. Central to *Ulysses* is the idea of attending to *different* voices, to understanding the world from alternative *human* points of view. Throughout Joyce's fiction, the value of a life is gauged by its relations to others. The deadening confinements of *Dubliners*, whether they appear in the social pathologies of Lenehan and Corley, in the collapse of Farringdon's sense of himself, in the icy isolation of Mr. Duffy, or in the sad self-deception of Maria, are exposed in the poverty of the connections to others to which those confinements restrict them. If Stephen Dedalus learns anything during the many pages he inhabits, it is to pose the right question: "What is that word known to all men?" (3: 435; 15: 4192–3). If Bloom and Molly (like Gabriel and Gretta Conroy before them) have any hope of re-finding "the straight way," it must lie in renewing their marriage.

---

after her husband's death: "When you've been married to the greatest novelist in the world, it's hard to keep track of the little fellers.") The priority of hearing over vision figures in some of the clashes of *Finnegans Wake* (see, for example, the fable of the Mookse and the Gripes, especially FW 158: 13–15).

45. As, in fact, Stephen (unprofitably) does in the opening sentences of "Proteus." For more on Joyce's opposition to the priority of vision among the senses, and, in particular for the importance of touch, see chapter 3 in this volume.

Ethical life, as Joyce understands it, shies away from command-
ments and principles. It is grounded in extensive forms of human
sympathy, not the shallow camaraderie on display in the Committee
Room or among the organizers of Irish Revival Concerts or in the
offices of the *Freeman* newspapers or in the Ormond Bar or at Barney
Kiernan's. Once again, our early encounters with Bloom offer a
model. As he strolls along Sir John Rogerson's quay, he observes a
boy smoking "a chewed fagbutt" and considers offering moral advice.
"Tell him if he smokes he won't grow. O let him! His life isn't such a
bed of roses" (5: 6, 7–8). Bloom is distinguished by his ability to take
many perspectives and to allow their influence on and integration in
a reflective conclusion. Among all the other characters who popu-
late *Ulysses*, only one shows even a fraction of his capacity for human
sympathy: Molly, in her post-copulatory musings.

The possibility of a wide range of ways of ordering and valuing the
same experiences is not brought home to readers merely by display-
ing the sympathetic excursions of Bloom's consciousness. It is woven
into the fabric of *Ulysses*, in the different narrative voices and the multiplicity of styles.[46] To hear those voices and to grasp the point of the
styles is to *perform* the move Joyce takes as central to living better.
We escape the confinement of our social milieu by breaking bonds
that limit our sympathies. We understand our lives as worthwhile by
recognizing, in our faults and in our follies, the ways in which they
absorb the joys and sorrows of others and touch the human exis-
tences around us.

---

46. Here I extend a seminal insight of David Hayman, who sees a distinctive narrator (the
"Arranger") behind the cornucopia of styles present, especially in the later sections of the
novel: David Hayman, "Cyclops," in Clive Hart and David Hayman, eds., *James Joyce's
Ulysses, Critical Essays* (Berkeley: University of California Press, 1974), 243–75. For discussion of the point, see chapters 5 and 6 in this volume, where David Hills and I offer
different reactions to Hayman's proposal.

With respect to all three strategies the humor of *Ulysses* plays an important role. Joyce famously wanted to know whether or not his readers laughed, and Nora reports hearing his laughter as she lay in bed while he wrote in an adjoining room. Even though *Ulysses* and *Finnegans Wake* are often funny, the temptation to over-emphasize the comic, to detach it from other aspects of the novels, ought to be resisted. Neither work should be viewed as some strange rival to anthologies of the world's best jokes.[47] Both are comedies—in two different senses. They share with theatrical comedies an abundance of light-hearted moments. Yet, just as Shakespearean tragedy makes room for comic interludes (in the aftermath of Duncan's murder Macbeth's porter answers the importunate newcomers at the castle gate), so too Joycean comedy allows for moments of intense seriousness. Joyce follows Shakespeare in recognizing how the somber and the absurd can live cheek by jowl. His second debt is to the style of comedy present in Dante and Balzac, to comedy as including all facets of human life. That broad embrace must contain the times, perhaps the many times, when laughter overtakes us.

Humor can be deployed, as Martha Nussbaum lucidly shows, to destabilize the prejudices and taboos constraining our emotional reactions.[48] Similarly it can ridicule the conventions we unthinkingly bring to perceptual experience. Perhaps the primary Joycean use of the comic lies in expanding our sympathies. Readers may laugh *at* the social conventions and absurdities that bind, and even at those whose words and actions uphold them (Father Conmee, for example; 10: 26–32, 69–72, 88–92, 103–6, 141–52, 191–2). The humor directed toward those who are bound—not only Bloom, Molly, and

---

47. As noted earlier (n10), commentators, especially on the *Wake*, sometimes fall victim to this temptation. They then tend to denounce attempts to discern more serious themes in Joyce's later fiction. My own previous work on *Finnegans Wake* (see references in n41) errs in the opposite direction, underplaying the humor.
48. See chapter 1 in this volume.

Stephen but also the pupils at Mr. Deasy's school, Simon and Dilly Dedalus, Tom Kernan and Ben Dollard, even the bilious narrator of "Cyclops"—is very different. We often laugh *with* the characters whose lives are subject to confinement. Awareness of their follies is tinged with the sympathy Bloom exhibits on the quay: they do not lie on beds of roses.

I conclude that Joyce presents important philosophical questions and also offers interesting discussions of them. Why, then, the relative lack of philosophical interest? Partly, I suspect, because the English-language tradition has tended to shy away from issues where clarity and rigor of argument seem hard to achieve. Among the courageous philosophers who have revived concern for Socrates' question, other authors (or other artistic genres) have proved more attractive.[49] More importantly, in my view, exposing Joyce's approaches to that question involves attending to issues about narration, and different styles of narration, issues that have been treated with great subtlety by literary scholars. Fathoming Joyce's philosophical significance requires engaging with a critical tradition about which even well-read philosophers are usually ignorant.

My initial claim was carefully qualified. Not much *philosophy in literature* with *Joyce as its focus* has been written by *Anglophone philosophers*. Having understood why that is so, it's possible to

---

49. The contemporary writers I have in mind are Stanley Cavell, Bernard Williams, Harry Frankfurt, Alexander Nehamas, Martha Nussbaum, and Susan Wolf. The range of literary references in the writings of Cavell and Nussbaum is enormous—and, in Nussbaum's case it includes Joyce. Williams' explorations of philosophical questions in opera are rightly admired. As already noted, Nehamas has written masterfully about Mann; he has also explored the philosophical significance of paintings in Alexander Nehamas, *Only a Promise of Happiness* (Princeton, NJ: Princeton University Press, 2007) and used many examples from literature in examining the place of friendship in human lives in *On Friendship* (New York: Basic Books, 2016); although he refers to Joyce, other writers are more relevant to his concerns. Susan Wolf's wide interests in literature and film, and their significance for how we think about our lives, do not include Joyce; as she once confessed (apologetically) to me, she dislikes Joyce.

appreciate how many interesting philosophical discussions and *aperçus* can be found in the English-language critical study of Joyce's fiction, particularly in writings concerned with Joycean narration. The books and articles of Richard Ellmann, Dorrit Cohn, Wayne Booth, David Hayman, Clive Hart, and especially Hugh Kenner are especially valuable in this regard. It is no accident that several of the following chapters are greatly indebted to the insights of these scholars.

* * *

In chapter 1, Martha Nussbaum builds on her earlier work, not only her study of how *Ulysses* transfigures the everyday but also her probing discussions of the emotions and of their place in ethical and political life. She retains her previous conviction that people experience disgust far more frequently than they should, and that the consequences are often morally troubling (leading to prejudices against particular groups). Yet the complete rejection of disgust, identified by Nussbaum with Walt Whitman's embrace of all existence, is, she claims, impossibly cosmic, insensitive to the feelings of those who care "about each individual life in all its dailiness."[50] Leopold Bloom, she argues, reveals an appropriate *via media* between Whitmanian acceptance and stoical tolerance of the harms to which culturally induced disgust typically gives rise. Bloom shows us ways of distancing ourselves from our routine disgust-projections. We can raise interesting questions about the objects standardly taken to excite disgust, or we can explore different perspectives on them, or we can treat them with humor. As Nussbaum shows, in his attitudes toward decay and death (particularly in "Hades") and in confronting the disgust manifested in the knee-jerk anti-Semitism of his fellow Dubliners, Bloom deploys these strategies to great effect.

50. See chapter 1 in this volume, p. 39.

In chapter 2, Garry Hagberg is concerned with Joyce's account of perceptual experience. As he correctly points out, much philosophical psychology (and much philosophy) is dominated by a simple empiricist picture. We imagine ourselves looking at a medium-size stable object, placed before us in a good light. Physical processes stimulate the optic nerve, furnishing the conscious mind with sensory data. *Ulysses*, Hagberg argues, shows the naiveté of this model. Through exploring the consciousnesses of Stephen and Bloom, Joyce offers a more adequate view of perception, anticipating insights of American pragmatism and of Ryle and (the later) Wittgenstein. The resulting complex picture enriches our understanding of consciousness in ways philosophers need to absorb. Yet the recognition of perceptual experience as structured by prior categories provokes worries about the objectivity of our perceptions. By comparing the forms of consciousness depicted in "Circe" and in "Ithaca," Hagberg points to a way of avoiding the error of an extreme subjectivism.

Like Hagberg, Vicki Mahaffey and Wendy J. Truran find insights about perception in *Ulysses*. They, too, oppose the dominance of simple models of perceptual experience, but with a different target. Vision, they maintain, is over-emphasized. In chapter 3 they celebrate an alternative sensory modality: touch. To see clearly requires a distance between subject and object. Touch, by contrast, connects. Part of the achievement of *Ulysses*, they suggest, consists in its ability to touch readers and to lead them to "see feelingly." Contrasting Stephen's recurrent failures to touch and be touched with Bloom's partial successes, they focus on the moments of revealing touches in the novel—the kiss on Howth Head, the nighttime kiss bestowed on Molly's rump, the feel of the blind stripling's hand—to illustrate the ways in which Bloom has known how to learn through touch and how he has also lost touch. Joyce, as they interpret him, offers an account of perceptual experience centered on learning about the human world and relating us to one another. The perceptions that matter, we might conclude, are those connecting human lives.

The last three chapters focus on reality, as it is represented in fiction, as it is organized in our thought and feeling, and as we resist its potential confinement of our lives. All three are concerned with the multiple perspectives Joyce offers his readers. In chapter 4, Sam Slote starts by considering the relation between the city described in *Ulysses* and the actual Dublin of June 16, 1904. Using Joyce's well-known (notorious) habit of assigning the names of real people to some of his characters, Slote asks how seriously readers should take the identification. Does *Ulysses* describe a possible world (a fictional world) that overlaps the actual world in certain respects? He shows how the novel, like any novel, is incomplete in important ways, and how it invites the imagination of its readers to try to fill in the details. Indeed, on the assumption of authorial omniscience, even the apparent tensions and inconsistencies are sources for ventures in reconciliation, thus leading to even more elaborate and widely divergent alternatives. Add to this the textual variants, stemming from misprints, editorial choices, multiple drafts, and Joyce's fluctuating judgments, and the possibilities proliferate even further. In the end, Slote concludes, the incompleteness and the ambiguity proliferated throughout *Ulysses* invite readers to the kinds of deeper reflections that can transform their understandings—of themselves and of the actual world in which they live.

Hugh Kenner's recognition of the multivocality of *Ulysses*[51] inspires David Hills to reflect in chapter 5 on Joyce's opposition to a single vision. The novel's most obvious narrative devices are third-person narration, interior monologue, and free indirect discourse (where some contextual clue enables us to attribute a description to the perspective of some particular character). But if these exhausted

51. Hugh Kenner, *Joyce's Voices* (Berkeley: University of California Press, 1978).

the resources deployed, *Ulysses* would contain many puzzling passages. By suggesting imaginative readings of some of them, Hills argues that the usual understandings of interior monologue and—especially—free indirect discourse need to be refined and extended. Joyce wants the competing senses of things associated with different characters to jostle and contest each other freely within the confines of individual scenes. So he uses interior monologue to construct subtle forms of "virtual backtalk"; he also introduces what Kenner dubbed "Uncle Charles Style." The result is an expanded technical repertoire for addressing a distinctive personal problem, arising in the modern, urban context. How are we to define ourselves in the presence of many alternatives, some useful suggestions from tradition, others thrust upon us by those who think they know better than we do what is significant for us? Joyce's three central figures—Bloom, Molly, and Stephen—struggle to find their way by trying out models from the past, models whose value is initially unclear to them. In doing so they must cope with construals of their actions, some friendly, some hostile, from fellow Dubliners who presume to understand, at least as well as they do, what is proper for them. Joyce's narrative innovations bring these struggles home to his readers, as we hear the deliverances—and clashes—of different voices.

Hills and I concur in recognizing Joyce's perspectivism—although I see it as outstripping the limits of free indirect discourse and of recognizable "voices." Like Hagberg, I see a link to themes in Classical Pragmatism, in particular to a version of the thesis that we construct the world of experience that does not collapse into relativism. The aim of chapter 6 is to show how Joyce's perspectivism transfigures the everyday, and how taking alternative perspectives can subvert conventions and expand our sympathies. So for me, as for Nussbaum, the stylistic devices and the critique of strong realism they advance help us to see how to live better than we do. Thus (I hope) Joyce makes progress with Socrates' question.

These six chapters surely do not address all the ways in which *Ulysses* pursues the three strategies I have attributed to Joyce in his efforts to tackle the oldest problem of philosophy. Very probably they overlook entirely many other philosophical facets of the novel. I hope, nevertheless, that they will enable philosophers in the English-speaking world to appreciate Joyce's philosophical significance and inspire attempts to articulate that significance more precisely and more fully than has so far been done.

BIBLIOGRAPHY

Cavell, Stanley. *Disowning Knowledge*. Cambridge, UK: Cambridge University Press, 2003.

Davidson, Donald. "James Joyce and Humpty Dumpty." *MidWest Studies in Philosophy* 16 (1991): 1–12.

Ellmann, Richard. *James Joyce*. New York: Oxford University Press, 1959.

Ellmann, Richard, ed. *The Letters of James Joyce*. Volume 2. London: Faber and Faber, 1966.

Frankfurt, Harry. *On Bullshit*. Princeton, NJ: Princeton University Press, 2005.

Gorman, Herbert. *James Joyce*. New York: Farrar and Rinehart, 1940.

Hayman, David. "Cyclops." In Clive Hart and David Hayman, eds., *James Joyce's Ulysses, Critical Essays*. Berkeley: University of California Press, 1974, 243–75.

Hope, A. D. "The Esthetic Theory of James Joyce." *Australasian Journal of Philosophy* 21 (1943): 93–114.

Jones, David E. "The Essence of Beauty in James Joyce's Aesthetics." *James Joyce Quarterly* 10, no. 3 (1973): 291–311.

Joyce, James. *A Portrait of the Artist as a Young Man*. Norton Critical Edition. New York: Norton, 2007.

Joyce, James. *Stephen Hero*. New York: New Directions Press, 1959.

Joyce, James. *Ulysses*. Gabler Edition. New York: Vintage, 1986.

Kenner, Hugh. *Joyce's Voices*. Berkeley: University of California Press, 1978.

Kitcher, Philip. "Collideorscape: *Finnegans Wake* in the Large and in the Small." *Joyce Studies Annual* (2009): 188–211.

Kitcher, Philip. *Deaths in Venice*. New York: Columbia University Press, 2013.

Kitcher, Philip. *Joyce's Kaleidoscope: An Invitation to Finnegans Wake*. New York: Oxford University Press, 2007.

Kubala, Robbie. "Love and Transience in Proust." *Philosophy* 91, no. 4 (2016): 541–57.

Landy, Joshua. *Philosophy as Fiction: Self, Deception, and Knowledge in Proust.* New York: Oxford University Press, 2004.

Mason, Ellsworth, and Richard Ellmann, eds. *James Joyce: The Critical Writings.* New York: Viking, 1959.

Moran, Richard. "Kant, Proust, and the Appeal of Beauty." *Critical Inquiry* 38, no. 2 (Winter 2012): 298–329.

Nehamas, Alexander. *The Art of Living.* Berkeley: University of California Press, 2000.

Nehamas, Alexander. *On Friendship.* New York: Basic Books, 2016.

Nehamas, Alexander. *Only a Promise of Happiness.* Princeton, NJ: Princeton University Press, 2007.

Nussbaum, Martha. *Upheavals of Thought.* Cambridge, UK: Cambridge University Press, 2001.

Parfit, Derek. "Personal Identity." *Philosophical Review* 80, no. 1 (1971): 3–27.

Sellars, Wilfrid. "Empiricism and the Philosophy of Mind." In *Science, Perception, and Reality.* London: Routledge and Kegan Paul, 1963, 127–96.

Slote, Samuel. *Joyce's Nietzschean Ethics.* Basingstoke, UK: Palgrave Macmillan, 2013.

Verene, Donald Phillip. *James Joyce and the Philosophers at Finnegans Wake.* Evanston IL: Northwestern University Press, 2016.

Chapter 1

Between Detachment and Disgust

Bloom in Hades

MARTHA C. NUSSBAUM

"Come forth, Lazarus!" And he came fifth and lost the job.

—Leopold Bloom, in *Ulysses*, "Hades" episode

Most of us view our end with at least some fear, at least some of the time. Even when we're not thinking consciously about death, a sentiment of an obscurely burdensome sort dogs our mental life—a "large mountain sitting on our chest," as the Roman philosopher Lucretius shrewdly said. And really, we'd be fools not to fear death.[1] Life is good.[2]

I am very grateful to Philip Kitcher for his extremely insightful comments on an earlier draft, and to Molly Brown for excellent research assistance. Because I am convinced that the Gabler edition is less adequate that the original Modern Library edition, and was issued primarily in order to renew copyright, I cite the pagination of that edition (New York: Modern Library, reset 1961).

1. Fear needn't always be conscious; we are motivated by an unconscious fear of death every time we cross the street, and thus fear is not always characterized by trembling or shivering; as Aristotle said, it simply requires awareness (at whatever level) that there are bad things impending and that we are powerless to ward them off. (We don't have to have a psychoanalytic doctrine of repression to acknowledge the hidden workings of fear; many other beliefs direct our actions without being the objects of conscious reflection: belief in gravity, in the solidity of objects, etc.) Of course there are also other emotions one might have toward death, such as rage, but rage seems less rational than fear since, it presupposes some fantasy of a just world, which most people do have in some form, but irrationally.

2. There are, of course, exceptions, particularly cases of unbearable pain. But people do strive to live despite great affliction. And even when some worthwhile goal, such as saving others,

Funerals are occasions for grief, if the dead person was close. But they are also reminders of our own mortal condition and invitations to contemplate it. Especially when the dead person was not close, a funeral service and an ensuing trip to the graveyard are often meditative times, providing powerful signals about our own future, stimulating fear or bringing hidden fear to the surface. They create, all too often, a volatile emotional condition in which we may be susceptible to some of fear's less savory neighbors, other painful emotions (anger, envy, disgust) that may pollute our relationship with others. But the reminder of a shared fate might also have more benign consequences (as Rousseau thought), encouraging a kind of egalitarian compassion, an awareness of a common human condition that transcends class and wealth and even religion, bringing people together.

One emotion that is especially likely to be present at a burial is the emotion of disgust—disgust in the first instance toward the corpse and the general scenario of stench and decay. Disgust toward rotting corpses is very likely rooted in our evolutionary heritage; few smells are more powerfully aversive. Corpse-disgust has led to many beautification rituals in many cultures—in Christian Europe and North America, to the creation of an elaborate industry of cleanup and cosmetic adornment that never quite makes us forget what lies beneath or within.

The psychological literature on disgust has said relatively little so far about this particular type of disgust, although the corpse is always mentioned as a central example of a primary disgust-object.[3] When we do examine this case, we find, I believe, that it is

---

leads a person to die willingly, that does not mean that the person lacks fear. As Aristotle notes in his discussion of courage, good people are perhaps even more likely to feel fear than a bad person since they are convinced that their lives are valuable.

3. Extensive references to Rozin's work and the rest of the psychological literature are given in my *Hiding from Humanity: Disgust, Shame, and the Law* (Princeton, NJ: Princeton University Press, 2015); I will not replicate them here.

especially complicated, a case of "primary disgust" that also embodies a number of learned stigmatizing reactions toward the human body. I myself have typically mentioned but then avoided this case in my writings dealing with the disgusting.[4] And the little I have said, I now believe, has been partly false. In speaking about disgust toward aspects of one's aging body, I have suggested that a possible and admirable human response would be to follow Walt Whitman's "I Sing the Body Electric" and simply learn not to feel disgust toward the stench and decay associated with death.[5] I now feel that my former view, and Whitman's, are far too simple. If we love our lives and fear our end, as seems not only human but rational, disgust toward corpses is a permanent possibility and perhaps some of it is impossible to avoid. What I believe we can avoid, however, is a further step, where fear and disgust lead to self-evasive projections in which we impute disgust-properties to other people and groups, marginalizing and subordinating them.

On this topic, I now believe, there is no finer teacher than *Ulysses*—both Bloom the character and the literary strategies of its writing. Pondering the "Hades" episode has made me rethink my ideas about disgust, and the purpose of this chapter is to describe the illumination that we gain, or so I think, from following in Leopold Bloom's footsteps as he attends Dignam's funeral. Despite its reception as a disgusting book—containing "secret sewers of vice," as one early review said—the novel combats not only sexual disgust, as has often been observed, but also the more tenacious and malign form

---

4. See my *Hiding from Humanity; From Disgust to Humanity: Sexual Orientation and Constitutional Law* (New York: Oxford University Press, 2010); *Aging Thoughtfully: Conversations about Retirement, Romance, Wrinkles, and Regret* (with Saul Levmore) (New York: Oxford University Press, 2017); and the introduction and my two papers in *The Empire of Disgust: Prejudice, Discrimination, and Policy in India and the U.S.*, ed. Zoya Hasan, Aziz Huq, Martha C. Nussbaum, and Vidhu Verma (Delhi: Oxford University Press, 2018).
5. See Nussbaum, *Aging Thoughtfully*.

of disgust that turns us against the body's mortality, while avoiding the human absurdity of Walt Whitman, when he urges us to love our bodies by loving and even seeking death. Instead, the task seems to me to be to avoid disgust (and its malign consequences) while disliking and even fearing death. The way Bloom manages this delicate tightrope walk gives us a detailed paradigm of balanced and generous humanity, while the anti-Semitism of many other Dubliners gives us a stern warning about the bad social attitudes to which death-inspired projective disgust can lead.

I begin by summarizing the status quo ante (including my own previous writing on love and sex in *Ulysses*). I then turn briefly to the novel's portrayal of anti-Semitism in Dublin, as grounded in a profound insecurity of poverty and squalor whose root is somehow connected to the fear of death. I then follow Bloom as he rides in the funeral procession, attends Dignam's funeral mass, and accompanies the other mourners to the grave.

THE PROBLEMATIC OF DISGUST (AND A FLAW IN MY EARLIER REASONING)

We human animals have invented strategies to distance ourselves from our animality and mortality. Disgust is a key emotion that polices this boundary. Although it is easy to think that disgust is a visceral reaction to certain smells, feels, and sights, important experimental work by Paul Rozin has shown that it is distinct from sensory distaste: whether people react with disgust or not depends on what they think they are smelling. (For example, if people think that they are smelling cheese, they typically do not report disgust, whereas if they smell the very same smell but are told it is feces, they are disgusted.) The "primary objects" of disgust (using, now, my own terminology) are bodily excretions and fluids (apart from tears), corpses of humans and animals, and animals that are smelly, sticky, oozy, thus similar to the disgusting bodily fluids. The way Rozin puts it is that the objects of disgust are all "animal reminders," reminders of what we share with other animals. But of course this is too simple, since we also share strength and speed with animals, and sometimes beauty. Disgust's primary objects appear to connect with our aversion to decay and mortality.[6]

What is the content of primary object disgust? One might think that it is danger: the avoided objects are seen as threatening to ourselves or our projects. Rozin's research, however, shows that this thesis has problems, even though disgust very likely evolved in close connection to the sense of danger. People do not feel disgusted by many objects known to be dangerous: poisonous mushrooms are an obvious case in point. And they feel disgust at many objects they know not to be dangerous at all, as is shown by experiments with sterilized cockroaches, sterilized fly swatters, etc. Nor is the content of disgust a simple wish to avoid: it appears to be a refusal to ingest or to make physical contact with the disgusting item, and the central idea appears to be one of contamination or sullying rather than danger. If you take this object in, or let it rub off on you, you will be debased to the level of a mortal animal, the thought seems to be. (It's for this reason that I entitled my book on disgust *Hiding from Humanity*: we are somehow evading recognition of what we are.)

Let's think further about the corpse. (As I've said, Rozin unfortunately does not devote any time to this example.) First of all, it's possible that a long-rotting corpse might be sensorially distasteful under all descriptions. I'm not sure that you could convince someone that it was anything nice, in the style of the feces-cheese experiments. But it's certainly right that the standard experience of disgust at rotting animal and human corpses is mediated by thought. Small

6. See Nussbaum, *Hiding from Humanity*, chapter 3.

children poke at corpses without appearing to be disgusted. The idea of refusing contamination by death is surely a salient part of the adult experience, whether or not distaste and a sense of danger (by transmission of disease) is also present. If death touches you, it taints you. An underlying fear of death seems to help the emotion of disgust into being.

So a first normative question should be: Is this phobic/disgusted reaction to the dead body something to be encouraged? And this question is really, in turn, two questions: Should we discourage the fear of death, which surely underlies fear/disgust toward the corpse? And if we do not discourage the fear of death, or discourage it only a little, can and should we break the link between the fear of death and corpse-disgust? (Leopold Bloom breaks this link, as we'll see.)

The damage done by primary object disgust, however, seems small by contrast to the damage of what I call "projective disgust." This is a disgust in which disgust-properties—stench, ooziness, stickiness, in general animality—are projected onto some group of humans, usually a marginal or less powerful social group, as a further stratagem in the war against the disgusting. If those disgusting humans stand between us and our animal mortality, we are that much further from being animal and mortal ourselves. Projective disgust takes many forms, but it typically involves some type of refusal of bodily contact, especially (at least in theory) sexual contact, refusal to share drinking water, swimming pools, and other fluid locations in which bodily substances mingle. Projective disgust is a major element in racism, in caste discrimination, in European anti-Semitism, in the subordination of women, in homophobia.

Projections are historically contingent, and in the post-Victorian era depicted in the novel there are specific obsessions, which the literature on Joyce and other writers of the period meticulously charts—in particular the type of phobic disgust toward the unchaste female body and female sexuality that inspired most attacks on the novel as disgusting.[7] I've dealt with Joyce's implicit response to those attacks in earlier work on Joyce, arguing that he makes a move that is not just of local cultural interest, but of very broad human interest, turning the Platonic ladder of love upside down and encouraging the reader to take delight in bodies and especially the unchaste woman.[8] (Joyce, after all, is living in Trieste-Zürich-Paris and writing for an international audience, including an Irish diaspora, although shaped, of course, by a specific Irish upbringing, of which he is severely critical.) We are not stuck with the projections dominant in our society. We can always ask, as do both Joyce and Whitman, "What would a healthy society do with these projections? How would such a society encourage men and women to live together in a healthy way?"

All cases of projective disgust have something to do with death and the corpse, in the sense that a fear of being animal and mortal underlies the entire enterprise of projection. But there are two cases in which the relationship between death and projective disgust is more intimate, less mediated by removable cultural constructs: disgust toward people with disabilities and disgust toward the aging body. Let me focus only on the latter here. Wrinkles and sagging skin are often found off-putting and even disgusting, in something like the way that the other projective disgust-formations operate. But there is

---

7. Relevant studies include Diarmaid Ferriter, *Occasions of Sin* (London: Profile Books, 2009) (focusing on the stigmatization of women, frequently poor, who have sex outside marriage, as well as the deplorable living conditions of poor Dubliners); Michael G. Cronin, *Impure Thoughts: Sexuality, Catholicism, and Literature in Twentieth Century Ireland* (Manchester, UK: Manchester University Press, 2012) (arguing that a study of fiction gives us insight into the regulation of sexuality in Ireland); and John McCourt, ed., *Joyce in Context* (Cambridge, UK: Cambridge University Press, 2009) (an edited collection with several essays pertinent to our theme, particularly Marian Eide's "Gender and Sexuality," Vike Martina Plock's "Medicine," L. M. Cullen's "Dublin," and Matthew Campbell's "Nineteenth-Century Lyric Nationalism").

8. Martha Nussbaum, *Upheavals of Thought: The Intelligence of Emotions* (New York: Cambridge University Press, 2001), chapter 16.

a difference. Racial and caste disgust are just a fiction. The bodies of the two races and of the many castes smell exactly the same, engage in exactly the same bodily functions. The idea that one group is "animal" and the dominant group is not is a fiction bizarre on its face, but so deeply internalized in society that people have strong physical reactions toward those onto whom society projects disgust-properties. But the signs of aging really are signs of nearness to death. That is not just a fiction. And the shrinking from these signs seems to be more universal and less mediated by culture than in our other cases.[9] Furthermore, while a body of African origin, beneath cultural projections, is no different from a white body, a corpse is very, very different from a living person. That difference is no fiction.

Culture enters into this realm too: specific religious and cultural customs of burial and care of the corpse shape emotions of both fear and disgust. One custom that should be mentioned is the Christian tendency to delay burial for a longish time, often a week, in such a way that the corpse is bound to decay quite a lot and to bloat with gas, phenomena the curious eye of Bloom will ponder. Christians also favor elaborate clothing and makeup where open caskets are preferred (especially in Roman Catholic funerals), and elaborate caskets as well (in most denominations). Jewish burial, by contrast, takes place within twenty-four hours, when decay is minimal, in order to honor the dead. The shroud is simple and white, the casket a simple plain wood, and there are no open caskets. Thus Jews have no need of the elaborate funeral parlor industry that Christian culture employs to anoint and beautify the corpse. And accounts of Jews who are appointed to "watch over" the corpse (a ritual requirement) characterize the experience as positive—meaningful and connected rather than disgusted.[10] By contrast, the whole open casket thing can often

---

9. See Nussbaum, *Aging Thoughtfully.*
10. I owe this observation to Saul Levmore.

seem a ghastly charade, a pretense that this is the person, all dolled up there, but of course by now severely decomposed or else embalmed (forbidden under Jewish law). Open-casket corpses are pretty disgusting, even (or maybe especially) when embalmed.

Here's what I said about disgust toward the aging body: we should just get rid of it. It is a phobic projection like racism, and it does social harm. Instead, we should celebrate all the functions of the body, as does Whitman in "I Sing the Body Electric"—the insides as well as the outsides. (I focused on a colonoscopy, an event often found disgusting but capable of being rendered beautiful by love of the body.)

Up to a point, all this still seems right to me. First of all, we should struggle to rid ourselves and our societies of any form of projective disgust linked to social discrimination. It would be a great gain simply to eradicate racial and sexual disgust, disgust toward people with disabilities, and disgust toward the bodies of aging people. And we can use love of previously unloved parts of the body in the struggle against disgust. The Whitman project of loving the insides, like the feminist project of loving the specific insides of the female body (in the famous feminist book *Our Bodies, Ourselves*) is an appealing insurgency in our world of widespread age discrimination. Second, we should even greatly moderate primary object disgust, so that it is not intense and is not accompanied by considerable anxiety. (These are probably related: most bodily disgust is intense only in the presence of anxiety.) The disgust and the anxiety do no good, and they can lead to great harm. Children can learn to put their feces in the toilet rather than on the dining-room wall without being taught that feces are disgusting (a view young children do not have). If during toilet training a mild disgust toward feces does appear, it never becomes intense or troubling, unless the training goes wrong, imparting anxiety. Again, the *Our Bodies, Ourselves* movement taught women that they (and others) could love the female body, its menstrual periods, its association with birth, rather than shrinking from these things in disgust. That disgust was valueless and harmful. It would be better not to have any of it. Similarly, though we have to contend against the hospitals, with their greedy love of anesthetizing people, we can reclaim our colons with Whitmanian love and curiosity. Being disgusted by one's own colon is useless and potentially harmful.

Maybe we should modify this just a little: cleanliness and good manners are encouraged by other people's mild disgust at bad bodily smells. If bad breath, flatulence, and body odor did not disgust others, we might lapse into very slovenly habits, and anyone who finds the enforced intimacy of the airplane a trial has to be grateful that for the most part people try to maintain their bodies in a state that will not disgust others. (Even when one is perfectly happy with one's own smells and with the smells of people one loves, that is less often the case with strangers, particularly of the rude and overbearing persuasion.) So perhaps it is good to make a very small place for primary object disgust in society—but not for the sort that is ramped up by anxiety and phobic self-avoidance.

That much, in my earlier work, seems right (with the modification I just introduced). I stopped short, however, not really facing the corpse, or death. The colon is a major functioning part of a living human body. Blood is coursing through it; digested food is processed through it. There is no reason not to love it, or at least to view it with sympathetic curiosity as a part of oneself. A corpse is not part of oneself. And while there are many who have said, over the ages, that we should strive to lose our fear of death, I don't agree. I think some degree of fear toward death is the necessary correlate of the love of life.[11] I also don't see why love of life has to be bounded at a particular place, so that we would say, "Now I'm done, and death is fine." There

---

11. As I said earlier, this doesn't mean shivering fright, nor does it mean that other emotions cannot also be prominent.

may indeed be times when death is preferable to continued suffering, but that does not mean that life isn't better (subtracting the terrible suffering). If one can imagine some people thinking of death as
a peaceful end to suffering in that way, it is not because death is really
peace at all; it is because in this special case nothing is best—and in a
kind of self-delusion people often imagine that nothing (being dead)
is not really nothing, but a peaceful existence of the self. So it is likely
that, fearing death and thinking life good, one will always shudder
at the presence of a corpse. As Bloom says, each time you go to a
funeral, you're just a little closer.

That shudder is on the border of disgust. It may not cross the line.
Much depends on the person, the funeral customs, the relationship
of the dead person to oneself. But there's always a perilous line there,
and it's easy to cross it, particularly in the Christian world, where one
is surrounded by advanced decomposition, covered over with an
equally disgusting odor of perfume and flowers.

Whitman, however, disagrees. He urges the same attitude of
love and wonder toward our future dead selves that he urges toward
our living colon. We should welcome death and even seek it rather
as a lover, "lovely and soothing death."[12] He urges us to see how
the matter that constitutes us now soon goes into the earth: how
the young men dead in the war nourish the "leaves of grass" above
the earth. We're all part of one process. He insists on this even in a
poem ("When Lilacs") that is one of the supreme examples of an
elegy for a particular loved individual (Abraham Lincoln). But this
detached perspective is, I think, too detached by far. It loses the
sense that individual lives have meaning. The cosmic perspective
is no consolation to someone who cares about each individual life
in all its dailiness. As D. H. Lawrence memorably said of Whitman,

12. Whitman, "When Lilacs Last in the Dooryard Bloom'd," l. 135.

"Even if you reach the state of infinity, you can't sit down there."[13] The embrace of death is the embrace of a world in which individuals as such have no meaning. Some people may attain this perspective; most will not succeed, and the attempt may have a boomerang effect, leading to a heightened kind of aggression, as our unassuaged fears catch us by surprise. In any case the goal itself seems not humanly worthy.

One extreme position, then, would be to stick to culturally typical disgust toward the corpse, which may easily lead to baneful projections, as we'll shortly see. The other extreme would be to flee into Whitman's cosmic and not fully human detachment. Somewhere in the middle, though perhaps closer to the Whitman side, is our human task: to cut back on revulsion and a disabling type of fear, without a flight into utopian pretense and stoicism. I'll be arguing that Leopold Bloom is indeed "The Man in the Gap."[14]

Our question is about how to live, and how parents and cultural leaders should try to shape the attitudes prevalent in a culture. But it raises as well a related question about the writer of fiction: How should such an author speak to us about our bodies and our fears of their propensity to decay? Authors, of course, have many purposes, and one is surely to reveal the dark side of many human practices. This practice raises some worrisome questions, given the power of fiction to shape habits of imagining. Should we, for example, applaud

---

13. See D. H. Lawrence, "Whitman," in Sculley Bradley and Harold W. Blodgett, eds., *Leaves of Grass*, Norton Critical Edition (New York: W. W. Norton, 1973), 842–50, at 846. See also Denis Donoghue's essay in the same volume.

14. See *Ulysses*, 297, where this epithet comes just before "The Man Who Broke the Bank at Monte Carlo." These epithets are part of the hilarious long list of the "tribal images of many Irish heroes and heroines of antiquity" imagined as adorning the belt of the Irish nationalist dubbed "the Citizen" in Barney Kiernan's bar. The list contains some real Irish heroes, but lots that are false and absurd, such as Patrick W. Shakespeare, Brian Confucius, Murtagh Gutenberg, and Cleopatra. Even a Jew makes the list: "the Mother of the Maccabees." The expression "Man in the Gap" appears to be a paraphrase of Ezekiel 22:30. Contrast p. 408, where the same expression is given a different (sexual) twist.

the author of a novel of violent pornography, on the grounds that this author reveals something true about some common (mainly male) patterns of imagining? The worry is that these patterns of attention are not static: the imitation co-creates the reality. So one question for the writer is how to reveal our bad habits where disgust is concerned, without giving them aid and comfort. The answer to this question surely involves thinking about how the reader may be distanced from problematic characters and led to see the world through the eyes of a character or characters whom we can trust to see the world in a way not warped by hatred or even crassness. Henry James' prefaces discuss this question at great length. He concludes that the novelist needs to include a character who reveals the human world in a reasonably rich, accurate, and responsive way, one who is "finely aware and richly responsible." He was well aware that authors have often tried to play this role themselves inside their texts, but he objected to what he called the "muffled majesty of authorship," which he associates in particular with George Eliot, on the grounds that this strategy introduces, in effect, an above-it-all character (viz. George Eliot) who is not fully human but enjoys a godlike moral omnipotence. So he preferred, as does Joyce, to show the world of the work through a flawed human being.[15]

This leads us to a second, and related, question: What attitude toward the disgusting and the fearful should an author encourage us to see as attractive and reasonably good? Plato was not wrong in thinking that by attaching certain bad patterns of emotion to characters whom we are encouraged to admire and with whom we are encouraged to identify, fiction can deform us. So let's suppose a

---

15. There may of course be an unreliable narrator who is clearly seen by the reader as such, but such projects are fraught with uncertainty and usually work best in a shorter fiction, such as James' *The Aspern Papers*. It is actually too simple to say that the novel shows us the world through Bloom's eyes; on the multiplicity of perspectives, see Philip Kitcher's chapter in this volume.

novelist wants to create a character who is appealing and lovable—
not exemplary in a remote way, like the George Eliot voice in Eliot's
novels, but recognizably "our friend," as Henry James liked to put
it. How should the inner discourse of that character be rendered
where the disgusting is concerned? The author could observe literary proprieties that forbid language expressive and evocative of
disgust. But then the character would be on the stoical, distanced
end of our possible relation to our humanity and would end up not
being representative of our humanity. We'd have a hard time seeing ourselves in such a character (much though the chaste habits
of Victorian fiction may lead us to forget the problem). Whitman's
poetry, with its odd combination of clinical detachment and rap-
turous death-Eros, lies at this stoical end, where death and decay,
at least, are concerned. Or, the other extreme, the author could
let it all hang out, so to speak, observing no delicacies of any sort
(as perhaps in James Kelman's 1994 Booker prize–winning novel,
How Late It Was, How Late, in which the word "fuck" was said to
occur some five hundred times in the mind of its criminal and drug-
addicted lower-class Scottish protagonist). That might be a fine
strategy if, as in Kelman's case, the aim is realistic representation
with no normative element. There would remain our first question,
but it seems safe to say that Kelman's hero does not solicit identification and does not lead the reader to prefer his indelicate language. The Kelman strategy would be very problematic, however,
in a novel one of whose purposes is to work on our imagination
in ways that may broaden our humanity, using for this purpose a
technique of identification with a central character or characters.
Following my tentative argument, we might conjecture that such an
author would seek honesty and dailiness, so we could say, "Oh yes,
I've done that so many times," while yet seeking to encourage habits
of generosity rather than narrowness, humane curiosity rather than
phobic animosity. Enter Leopold Bloom.

BLOOM AND THE DISGUSTING

Throughout the novel, Bloom is portrayed as lacking various types of disgust that form part of the daily repertory of many of the characters—and of many of Joyce's readers. His general approach to life combines zest with delicacy. He takes bodily functions as a matter of course, a part of life, but he has good manners and doesn't offend: a delicate line to walk in Joyce's Dublin, and indeed in our own places and time as well. He is first introduced to us as loving food: "Mr. Leopold Bloom ate with relish the inner organs of beasts and fowls" (55)—and there follows an entire paragraph about his favorite foods, including mutton kidneys, "which gave to his palate a fine tang of faintly scented urine." No shrinking, here, from bodily products. After breakfast, he enjoys a leisurely defecation in the outhouse while reading the newspaper, not disgusted by "his own rising smell" (69); still, he makes sure that the neighbor isn't watching him from the window above, and he takes care not to soil the trousers he is wearing to the funeral (68). Much later, in the much-maligned Gerty McDowell scene, he masturbates in a public place, so to speak—but discreetly concealing himself from others.[16] (The narration in this episode is itself delicate and indirect, metaphorical albeit clear.) Needless to say, he utterly lacks Dublin's zealous moralized disgust toward "loose" women.[17]

As for Molly, he doesn't mind her "tossed soiled linen" (62) or her "soiled drawers," her "twisted gray garter" (63). It seems that he typically satisfies himself on top of her round bottom, those

---

16. Not, however, it appears, from Gerty: "His hands and face were working," this from her perspective (365).
17. See also p. 290, where his attitude to an aging prostitute is one of distaste ("Looks a fright in the day") but at the same time tolerant compassion ("O well, she has to live like the rest").

"adipose posterior female hemispheres, redolent of milk and honey and of excretory sanguine and seminal warmth"—not disgusted, that is, by traces of her menstrual period, her excretion, or even the remains of Boylan's semen.[18] And here too, there are love and delicacy without disgust. "He kissed the plump mellow yellow smellow melons of her rump, on each plump melonous hemisphere, in their mellow yellow furrow, with obscure prolonged provocative melon-smellonous osculation" (734–5). The wordplay itself, whether Joyce's or Bloom's we can hardly say, makes the act, otherwise potentially problematic (because apparently non-reciprocal), delightful.

As I've argued in *Upheavals of Thought*, the relationship between Poldy and Molly exemplifies a love that is human, imperfect, and not desirous of any ascent away from the flawed reality of human love. Indeed, as I argued there, we can see in the novel as a whole a deliberate rejection of philosophical strategies of the "ascent of love" that begin with Plato. When we turn to death and the corpse, then, we expect a related reconciliation of human realism with immersed vulnerability.

As a further preparation for the "Hades" episode, we are invited to observe Bloom's tenderness toward non-human animals, part of his nondisgusted attitude toward things bodily. In his kitchen, he understands what their cat means by arching her back: she's asking him to scratch her back. "Mr. Bloom watched curiously, kindly, the lithe black form" (55). In "Lotus-Eaters" he sees a "wise tabby, a blinking sphinx" (77), and thinks immediately of a story about Mohammed: that he cut a piece out of his coat to avoid waking a

---

A similar tolerant repudiation of moralism is on p. 71, as he watches a poor boy smoking: "Tell him if he smokes he won't grow. O let him! His life isn't such a bed of roses!"

18. See p. 734, where an "approximate erection" is among the "visible signs of antesatisfaction," and, after fondling her buttocks, a "proximate erection" is among the "visible signs of postsatisfaction."

sleeping cat. This love of animals, and curiosity about how they feel, is part of the "Hades" episode too: the funeral coach passes a home for abused dogs, and this makes Bloom think of his father's dog Athos. "Dogs home over there. Poor old Athos! Be good to Athos, Leopold, is my last wish. Thy will be done. We obey them in the grave. A dying scrawl. He took it to heart, pined away. Quiet brute. Old men's dogs usually are" (90). Kindness to animals, animals' love of humans, mourning, loss, all these run together in Bloom's mobile mind.[19]

Just before the "Hades" episode begins, Bloom's thoughts link simple bodily pleasure with religious skepticism. He goes to the bath, thinking of the enjoyment he will have there:

> Enjoy a bath now: clean trough of water, cool enamel, the gentle tepid stream. This is my body.
>
> He foresaw his pale body reclined in it at full, naked, in a womb of warmth, oiled by scented melting soap, softly laved. He saw his trunk and limbs riprippled over and sustained, buoyed lightly upward, lemonyellow: his navel, bud of flesh: and saw the dark tangled curls of his bush floating, floating hair of the stream around the limp father of thousands, a languid floating flower. (86)

This passage could be right out of Whitman, but for its gentle dailiness, its particularity, and its love of life (not death). The Dublin-shocking idea that this is a correct application for the most sacred phrase of the Mass is not thought in order to mock or undermine; it's just true.

Bloom may not be disgusted, but he is, as a Jew, an object of disgust. But is Bloom actually a Jew? The literature on the novel

19. See also p. 315 ("Because the poor animals suffer").

often raises this question. In some ways Bloom is distant from his own tradition. His mother was not Jewish, so under (non-Reform) Jewish law he doesn't count as a Jew. He is uncircumcised, as we learn in the Gertie McDowell episode. He is an agnostic. He remembers the general outlines of the Passover ritual, including the song usually sung at its conclusion, about one creature eating another,[20] but he knows only scattered words of Hebrew and is ignorant of some very important ones.[21] And although he prefers mutton kidneys, he eats a pork kidney when he has to—when, that is, he realizes Thursday is not a good day to get fresh mutton kidneys and he doesn't want to do without any kidney at all (55, 56). His Jewish father committed suicide when he was rather young, so he hasn't had much in the way of Jewish instruction. He is married to a non-Jew (apparently), and his infant son, Rudy, was given a Christian burial.[22]

Still, it's evident that Bloom identifies himself emotionally with his Jewishness at many crucial times. He feels alien among Christians, perhaps because they give him the cold shoulder, and he is pleased when he can identify fellow Jews: for example, he recognizes Dlugacz the pork butcher (named after Joyce's Trieste friend Moses Dlugacz) as a fellow Jew by the mailing the butcher has received from a Zionist organization in Berlin, which cites the name of Moses Montefiore

---

20. "Sounds a bit silly until you come to look into it well" (122).
21. See p. 378, where he can't remember "mezuzah": "And the tephilim no what's this they call it poor papa's father had on his door to touch."
22. Rudy is in the Catholic cemetery where Bloom's mother is also buried (111); Molly knitted the "little wooly jacket" in which he was interred (778). However, it is not clear whether Molly is, in the technical sense, a non-Jew. Her mother, Lunita Laredo, is said to look Jewish, and Joyce kept revising the passages of the novel's ending concerning her right up until publication. For a summary of the evidence in the novel and for Joyce's various revisions, see Jonathan Quick, "Molly Bloom's Mother," *ELH* 57 (1990): 223–40. It would be a neat Joycean joke to make Molly, who identifies as a Christian, really Jewish through the rule that the maternal line determines Jewishness, while Leopold, so Jewish-identified, does not officially count as a Jew.

to ask for subscriptions to Agendath Netaim, a model farm in Palestine—and which the butcher then uses to wrap Bloom's pork kidney. "Thought he was," concludes Bloom (59). Throughout the novel Agendath Netaim[23] keeps recurring in Bloom's mind, and he views it with both skepticism and warmth. Above all, Bloom strongly identifies with his father's history as an exiled persecuted Jew, and we'll see that this memory is recent and vivid for him when he attends Dignam's funeral.

The most telling moment of Bloom's Jewish identification occurs in Barney Kiernan's bar, where, facing down the anti-Semitism of the Citizen, he declares, "I belong to a race . . . that is hated and persecuted. Also now. This very moment. This very instant" (332) "Are you talking about the new Jerusalem? says the citizen. I'm talking about injustice, says Bloom." Bloom then proclaims a catalogue of distinguished Jews, ending with "And the Saviour was a jew and his father was a jew. Your God." Martin Cunningham points out that Christ had no father, so Bloom corrects himself: "Well, his uncle was a jew . . . Your God was a Jew. Christ was a Jew like me" (342).[24]

To which, in one of the novel's most hilarious moments, the Citizen responds, "By Jesus, says he, I'll brain that bloody jewman for using the holy name. By Jesus, I'll crucify him so I will" (342).

And shortly thereafter, as a brawl ensues, Bloom achieves a comic apotheosis as "ben Bloom Elijah" (345).

---

23. Although Agendath is not a real Hebrew word, and there was no such settlement, there was an Agudath Netaim organized at Constantinople; the Berlin address is also fictional, in that the building at Bleibtreustrasse 34 did not exist until 1908, but then it was indeed occupied by a Palestine Industries Syndicate.

24. However, when he recounts the episode to Stephen later on, he acknowledges that he really doesn't count as a Jew: "He called me a jew and in a heated fashion, offensively. So I, without deviating from plain facts in the least, told him his God, I mean Christ, was a Jew too, and all his family, like me, though in reality I'm not" (643).

DUBLIN ANTI-SEMITISM AS DISGUST PROJECTION

Joyce represents more than one type of anti-Semitism in *Ulysses*.[25] The ideological anti-Semitism of Mr. Deasy ("England is in the hands of the Jews" [33]) comes equipped with a developed theory of political decline; the views of the participants in Dignam's funeral are cruder and more visceral. But through the variegated types run some common, all too familiar threads. Jews are associated with money, and they dominate the Irish through the power of their money. They control banks (Deasy) and, on a more daily basis, poor Dubliners' access to credit (the funeral-goers). They are repeatedly found physically repulsive, "dirty," in a way that's a little hard to understand, given that they are supposed to be so affluent.[26] What interests me

25. An excellent treatment of Jewishness and Jews in the novel is Neil R. Davison, *James Joyce, Ulysses, and the Construction of Jewish Identity* (Cambridge, UK: Cambridge University Press, 1996), an exhaustive survey of the sources for ideas about Jews that Joyce could have drawn on, and then a detailed analysis of these motifs in the novel. An older contribution, well worth reading, is Phyllis Joyce Cohen Levy, "The Image of the Jew in James Joyce's *Ulysses*," master's thesis, University of Richmond, 1968, paper 283 in the UR Scholarship Repository, https://scholarship.richmond.edu/masters-theses/283/.

26. The trope of the "dirty Jew" records a millennia-long association of Jews with the "low-ness" of the body. For a detailed analysis, see Martha Nussbaum, "Jewish Men, Jewish Lawyers: Roth's 'Eli, the Fanatic' and the Question of Jewish Masculinity in American Law," in Saul Levmore and Martha Nussbaum, eds., *American Guy: Masculinity in American Law and Literature* (New York: Oxford University Press, 2014), 165–201. But it is fascinating to see that the phrase "dirty Jew" as anti-Semitic insult became ubiquitous precisely in the late nineteenth and early twentieth centuries, so much so that Zola alludes to it as a persistent source of anti-Semitism in his intervention in the Dreyfus case. For a complete rundown of the epithet in this period, see Josh Lambert, "A Literary History of the Dirty Jew," *JBooks*, http://jbooks.com/interviews/index/IP_Lambert_DJ.htm. In addition to the Citizen's reference to "bugs," his sidekick, the episode's narrator, says (observing the Citizen's dog sniffing Bloom), "I'm told those Jewies does have a sort of a queer odour coming off them for dogs" (304). Mr. Deasy, more indirect, suggests that his own personal crusade against the foot-and-mouth disease (an obvious type of dangerous decay and "dirt") is being thwarted by the Jews (27–8). Bloom (despite the evident cleanliness of his habits) is connected with dirt by others: Miss Douce and Miss Kennedy call him "greaseaseabloom" and "the greasy nose" (260), and they laugh hysterically about his "greasy eyes." There's a reluctance to touch him, a sense that his body is strange: even Stephen experiences "a

particularly about the "Hades" episode is the connection of this idea of dirt to the perceived squalor of the impoverished Irishmen's own (sense of their) daily lives. The "dirty Jew" is a projection of one's own decaying life onto the banker's body.

Two themes that surface with monotonous regularity in the portrayal of male Dubliners are poverty and alcoholism. More or less every male, with the exception of Bloom, regularly gets drunk—and his moderation is a major source of his apartness and alienation in the "Cyclops" episode. The Dedalus family is dirt-poor (note this locution, which embodies a common mental association). Martin Cunningham's alcoholic wife makes his life a misery. Dignam himself died relatively young of heart disease, which Bloom imputes to "[t]oo much John Barleycorn" (95), remembering his "[b]lazing face: redhot." Liquor, says Mr. Dedalus with a sigh, is "many a good man's fault" (103). The Citizen, of course, is a loquacious drunk with a taste for barroom violence. These Dubliners feel their own lives poor and dirty, and they all (except Bloom) owe a lot of money to Jews. "We've all been there," says Martin Cunningham of indebtedness to the Jewish moneylender—and then, looking Bloom in the eye, adds, "Well, nearly all of us" (94). Lucretius insightfully says that people feel that poverty is like "lurking around the gates of Hades." This sense of squalor as half-death, in Dublin, leads to a familiar type of disgust projection in which the source of unease in the self (one's nearness to death through poverty) is cast out and projected onto the other, so that the Jew becomes dirty and squalid.

Consider the Citizen's aggressive remark hurled in Bloom's direction: "Those are nice things, says the citizen, coming over here to Ireland and filling the country with bugs" (323). While Bloom "lets

strange type of flesh" when he touches Bloom (660), although his focus is less on dirt (and Stephen himself offends by his bathless state) than on softness, "sinewless and wobbly and all that," thus connecting to another anti-Semitic trope of the Jewish man as feminine.

on he heard nothing," let us ponder this fascinating remark. The Jew is foul, a bringer of disgusting "bugs." This idea of disease and blight surely can't but hark back to the Great Famine (1845–52), a major rallying point for Irish nationalists. The blight was not actually caused by "bugs" but by two types of plant rot or virus. However, "bugs" are a handy summary of the devastating infestation. Now of course Jews had been thrown out of Britain (including Ireland) completely in 1290, and were recalled by Cromwell only in 1655, and they began to have considerable influence only in the nineteenth century. The first non-converted Jew to sit in the British Parliament was Lionel de Rothschild in 1858. So the era of Jewish ascendancy coincides exactly with the years of the Famine, and the Citizen appears to be connecting the two: Jews are disease and sources of Irish death. The remark even suggests that they aim to kill off the Irish. How?—presumably by financial exploitation and impoverishment.

As a disgust-projection, this one wears its falsity on its face. So far as hygiene goes, as we see from the beginning, the Bloom house is clean and well-kept, with an outhouse at some distance from the kitchen. Metaphorically too it is "clean," financially solvent though not affluent. So the reader can say that Bloom is the one with the fewest "bugs." Bloom has a love of hygiene, with his pleasure in his bath and his attraction to nice-smelling soap—whereas Molly knows that most men in Dublin "never dream of washing it from 1 years end to the other" (776). Bloom tends to shrink from dirt: thus it is no surprise that he won't kneel on the church floor in his good suit, without first putting a newspaper under his knee (103). Dirt is everywhere, and a wet, smelly sort of dirt at that: the inside of the funeral carriage is mildewed, making Mr. Dedalus wrinkle his nose, and its seat is covered with crumbs left over from someone's "picnic party" (89).

This sense of (Christian) Dublin as disease-ridden and poverty-stricken—unclean, smelly, decaying, lingering around the gates of death—suffuses the novel. But in "Hades" we see a further emotional dimension, as the men attending Dignam's funeral connect their sense of their own squalor with the Jews' financial power over them.

Bloom's fellow passengers in the funeral coach clearly see him as a Jew. Their remarks about moneylending make this abundantly clear. And the ride in the smelly coach occasions a sharp outburst of anti-Semitic disgust. Mr. Dedalus is in general highly prone to disgust-filled outbursts connected to his own poverty and the perilous state of his family. He calls Stephen's friend Buck Mulligan "a contaminated bloody doubledyed ruffian" whose "name stinks all over Dublin" (88)—presumably wishing that Stephen would redeem the family fortunes and that Mulligan is a poverty-perpetuating influence, leader of "a lowdown crowd." Thinking of Stephen's fondness for the Goulding part of the family, which he connects with waste and drunkenness, he refers to Cissie Goulding as "papa's little lump of dung, the wise child who knows her own father" (88), linking sexual and excretory disgust. And even the weather is described with a disgust metaphor—"as uncertain as a child's bottom" (90). That's the frame of mind Daedalus is in when the carriage goes past Reuben J. Dodd, the Jewish moneylender.[27] They all recognize the "tall blackbearded figure bent on a stick" (93) immediately, and Martin Cunningham nudges Mr. Power, saying, "Of the tribe of Reuben." Mr. Power snidely remarks, "In all his pristine beauty." So they all react to Dodd as ugly, foreign, obscurely revolting, but it is Dedalus who bursts out violently, "The devil break the hasp of your back!" And, shortly after, Dedalus bursts out, "Drown Barabbas! . . . I wish to Christ he did" (94). They all understand that his violent outburst is connected to debt: that's when Cunningham says, "We have all been there"—exempting Bloom. (In real life Joyce's father, the prototype

---

27. See Davison, *James Joyce, Ulysses, and the Construction of Jewish Identity;* Don Gifford with Robert J. Seidman, *Ulysses Annotated*, revised and expanded edition (Berkeley: University of California Press, 1988), 6.264–5n. The real Dodd was not actually Jewish.

of Mr. Dedalus, owed money to the real-life Reuben J. Dodd.) Bloom tries to distract the company by narrating a supposedly funny (true) story about Dodd's son jumping into the river. (With tact he does not mention the well-known fact that the son was rescued by a Jewish boatman named Moses Goldin.)[28] Targeted indirectly by projective disgust, he reacts kindly and generously.

ANXIETY ALMOST WITHOUT DISGUST: BLOOM VISITS THE DEAD

When Bloom sets out for Dignam's funeral, he has just had a sharp reminder of the grief his father's death occasioned. In "Lotus-Eaters," shortly before the start of the "Hades" episode, seeing a poster for the drama *Leah*, he immediately names the author, (Solomon) Mosenthal, and recalls his father's enthusiasm for the play, which concerns issues of apostasy and anti-Semitism, and remembers his father speaking to him the speech in which the blind Abraham recognizes his (apostate) son Nathan by his voice, touches his face, and says, "I hear the voice of Nathan who left his father to die of grief and misery in my arms, who left the house of his father and left the God of his father." His father then said to him, "Every word is so deep, Leopold" (76).[29] This recollection leads Bloom to a painful memory of his father's suicide. "Poor papa! Poor man! I'm glad I didn't go into the room to look at his face. That day! O dear! O dear! Ffoo! Well perhaps it was best for him" (76). This is an especially intense example of grief in Bloom's mental life. It is followed by an odd utterance, "Ffoo," which is probably a deep sigh.

28. See Davison, *James Joyce, Ulysses, and the Construction of Jewish Identity*; Gifford and Seidman, *Ulysses Annotated*.
29. See the companion for a plot summary: 5.194–5n.

During the carriage ride, this memory of grief recurs, as the dog hospital reminds Bloom of Athos and thus of his father's dying wish. Not long after that, the conversation in the carriage turns to suicide, as Mr. Power opines that "the worst of all . . . is the man who takes his own life" (96). Martin Cunningham tries to head him off, but Mr. Dedalus takes Power's side, but Cunningham insists, "It is not for us to judge." Bloom, in closed-lipped silence, thinks of Cunningham: "Sympathetic human man he is. Intelligent. Like Shakespeare's face." Silent grief separates him from most of the Christians. And the second great grief of Bloom's life has already been summoned to mind, just a moment before: they pass the funeral of a child, in its "tiny coffin" (95), and Bloom thinks of the funeral of his son, Rudy, dead a few days after birth: "A dwarf's face mauve and wrinkled like little Rudy's was. Dwarf's body, weak as putty, in a whitelined deal box" (96). Bloom thinks that it's just nature, but he also feels guilty and thinks of a common superstition: a healthy child is caused by the mother, an unhealthy child by the man. His sense of his own compromised masculinity (which has made future children unlikely) intensifies his sadness.

As they approach the funeral mass and the interment, then, Bloom feels intense grief, mingled obscurely with self-blame, depression (he thinks he will probably never have another child),[30] and guilt. A related source of anxiety swirls around with these: anxiety about Molly's affair with Boylan, which keeps recurring in his mind: references to the Zerlina–Don Giovanni duet, and then the sight of Boylan himself in his "white disc of a straw hat" (92) as the carriage passes by. Boylan is a reminder of death, because he represents Bloom's sense of sexual failure and the death of his male line.

So far, though, we see no disgust: Rudy's little disabled corpse is seen with compassion and sadness. The visit to the funeral, however,

---

30. The novel itself leaves this question unresolved.

exacerbates his death-anxiety—or is it death-sorrow? As they walk out into the cemetery, Bloom thinks of the way people forget the dead after a short time, and about how all of them are dying one by one, "dropping into a hole one after the other" (111). He thinks of the plot he bought "over there," and is reminded of "Mamma poor mamma, and little Rudy" (111). How many are buried there! "All these here once walked around Dublin. Faithful departed. As you are now so once were we" (113). And as he prepares to leave the cemetery, he reflects: "Enough of this place. Brings you a bit nearer every time . . . Poor papa too" (114).

Does Bloom feel disgust toward corpses during the funeral mass and the burial? Almost, but not quite. When he sees the coffin upset on the road, with Dignam's corpse suddenly falling out "stiff in the dust," he has a sharp sensory distaste that verges on disgust:

> Red face: grey now. Mouth fallen open. Asking what's up now. Quite right to close it. Looks horrid open. Then the insides decompose quickly. Much better to close up all the orifices. Yes, also, With wax. The sphincter loose. Seal up all. (98)

Even here, however, we see Bloom's mobile curiosity and sense of humor. His ability to imagine decay does not really disgust him, it just makes him approve of cleanly funeral practices. And in an instant his thoughts move on to science:

> Would he bleed if a nail say cut him in the knocking about? He would and he wouldn't, I suppose. Depends on where. The circulation stops. Still some might ooze out of an artery. It would be better to bury them in red: a dark red. (99)

I'll return to this important passage, which illustrates a standing Bloomian technique for keeping disgust at bay. For now, our answer is no: Bloom does not even feel primary disgust. Even later, when he alludes to "bad gas" from the presence of corpses (103), his curiosity is scientific: Why does the priest look so puffy? And his answer is that it's like the way Molly gets swollen up with gas after eating cabbage. "Must be an infernal lot of bad gas round the place." Out in the grave-yard, later, he thinks of corpses, and then, seeing a rat, he thinks about animals eating the corpse, which is "meat gone bad" (114). Even here, though, he right away moves to curiosity: Is cheese, then, the "corpse of milk"? And when he imagines flies drawn by the smell of Dignam, what he imagines is how, from their point of view, Dignam's smell is not disgusting: "They wouldn't care about the smell of it. Saltwhite crumbling mush of corpse: smell, taste like raw white turnips" (114).

Far less, then, does he experience a projective disgust toward other people in a manner motivated by his corpse-anxieties. There is one near-exception. In the graveyard much later, as he ponders the way in which "corpse-manure" fertilizes the soil, his thoughts turn to maggots. "Soil must be simply swirling with them. Your head it simply swurls. Those pretty little seaside gurls" (109). The thought of mag-gots in the soil leads him—apparently through the word "swirls"—to the thought of Boylan with his characteristic odd pronunciation and his characteristic jaunty song about the seaside girls. And of course the association is not made just through the word "swirls." Boylan figures in his mind as a quasi-maggot, and he enjoys thinking of him that way. That's perhaps a brief disgust-projection, though it quickly turns into a joke, and it's not surprising that this brush with projective disgust occurs in the location of his primary anxiety. But he goes no further even in thought: he extricates himself from that emotional morass quickly, in a manner that I'll soon study.

Bloom, then, is not at all Whitmanian. He views death as tragic, not "lovely," and the loss of loved individuals is not atoned for by any thoughts of cosmic wholeness. He feels deep grief, and a more global sadness. Still, he is also very different from the anti-Semitic

Dubliners: he doesn't feel the grip of primary disgust, and he does not convert his sadness and anxiety into projective disgust. How does he avoid this all-too-common slippage? Bloom, we notice, has three strategies—three movements of the mind by now habitual with him, that make him able to sustain his gentle and kindly attitudes in the midst of sadness and corpse-manure.

The first Bloomian strategy is scientific curiosity. Again and again in this episode, we see Bloom on the verge of yielding to either disgust or grief, but he then starts asking questions, and the very act of asking questions cheers him up. The idea of corpse fluids leads to a question about when and how completely circulation stops: Would blood still drip out? The thought of bad gas leads directly to curiosity about how gases make people look puffy. Later Bloom, sad, thinks of how the heart is the seat of emotions—and then reflects that it is also a physical pump (105). Out in the cemetery, he starts thinking about whether corpses buried standing up would come up above the earth at some point, and whether the blood coming out of them "gives new life" (108). The rat and flies make him ask what a corpse actually tastes like to a fly.

Bloom's scientific strategy verges on Stoicism, since at those moments he distances himself from his personal emotions and the ordinary human meaning of things. There are times in the novel (e.g., in the "Ithaca" episode) when this Stoic or Spinozistic strategy almost pulls him out of his ongoing human relationships—not surprisingly, at a time of maximum anxiety, returning home to confront the aftermath of Molly's adultery. Here, however, curiosity is a cheering antidote to grief.

Bloom's second strategy, or, rather, a perpetual reflex of his mind, is to ask how another person experiences the world. At every threat point, his mobile emotions simply look at the world through other eyes. In the carriage, he is deterred from retaliatory disgust at the anti-Semitism of the others by thinking about Martin Cunningham, his difficult life with a drunken wife. In the church, although feeling isolated during the Latin Mass, he asks himself how the participants react: "Makes them feel more important to be prayed over in Latin" (103). He imagines the boring life of the server, who has to shake holy water "over all the corpses they trot up" (104). Out in the graveyard, he thinks of the kindly caretaker and what sort of life he must have in that gloomy occupation (107–8). He thinks of Dignam's son, recognizing a kindred sorrow: "Poor boy! Was he there when the father?" (103). He's curious even about the rat and the flies: How do they see the world of corpses, and what does a corpse smell and taste like to them? (Instead of recoiling from those creatures in disgust, he asks sympathetically what their lives feel like.) When the coffin finally goes down, Bloom suddenly thinks: "If we were all suddenly someone else" (110). Molly is familiar with this capacity: "yes that was why I liked him because I saw he understood or felt what a woman is" (782).

But empathy by itself is morally neutral: a torturer can use empathy to inflict maximum pain and humiliation on the victim. So we must add that Bloom's empathy is combined with kindliness. He basically wishes well to those whose perspective he assumes—even those rats and flies.

Bloom is a kindly man, but he is not superhuman. He extends empathy only when he believes the person in question is a person of good will (Martin Cunningham, the caretaker), or at least without ill will (the server, those rats and flies). He does not extend empathy to the Citizen later, or, in this episode, to Boylan, since they are, from his perspective (and the reader's), people of ill will. The furthest he goes is in his sympathy with Mr. Dedalus, who, albeit an anti-Semite, has frustrated hopes for his son that Bloom understands all too well. So Bloom draws a line in his sympathy. But a crucial difference between Bloom and the Dublin anti-Semites is this: when he encounters perceived ill will, he does not retaliate with projective disgust. Instead he turns his thoughts to the perspective of people of good will. Let's look more closely now at his close brush with disgust when he thinks of Boylan as a maggot:

> But they must breed a devil of a lot of maggots. Soil must be simply swirling with them. Your head it simply swurls. Those pretty little seaside gurls. He looks cheerful enough over it. Gives him a sense of power seeing all the others go under first. Wonder how he looks at life. Cracking his jokes too: warms the cockles of his heart. The one about the bulletin. Spurgeon went to heaven 4 A.M. this morning. 11 P.M. (closing time). Not arrived yet. Peter. The dead themselves the men anyhow would like to hear an odd joke or the women to know what's in fashion. A juicy pear or ladies' punch, hot, strong and sweet. Keep out the damp. You must laugh sometimes so better do it that way. Gravediggers in *Hamlet*. Shows the profound knowledge of the human heart. (109)

Bloom definitely does not ask how Boylan sees the world. (According to Molly there is not much there anyway.) So there's no faux or even true heroic virtue. But he also doesn't dwell with disgust on Boylan, who is in reality a better candidate for that emotion than the rats and flies, since he does contaminate Bloom's bed, leaving his semen on the sheets, not to mention crumbs of Plumtree's Potted Meat (780), and with ill will. Instead, in a beat, Bloom shifts his perspective to the caretaker: it takes the reader a moment to figure out the referent of "he." Bloom has some very insightful thoughts about what keeps the man cheerful, and how the jokes cheer both him and others. And then he's launched into a characteristically Bloomian comic fantasy about the dead enjoying jokes and gossip—only to finish with a thought about the need to relieve the tension of death with laughter. Boylan, and negative thoughts, are left far behind.

Here we are at Bloom's third strategy for banishing disgust: humor. There are many types of humor. Some of these are in league with disgust. Bloom's humor, here and elsewhere, is itself kindly, fantastical, leavening life with a sense of the incongruous, prominently including word-play. This may be the funniest account of a graveyard in English literature, and without the dark side of *Hamlet,* Act V. It skewers pompous solemnity in a way that brings relief.[31] Here's a quintessential example:

Mr Kernan said with solemnity:

—*I am the resurrection and the life.* That touches a man's inmost heart.

—It does, Mr Bloom said.

Your heart perhaps but what price the fellow in the six feet by two with his toes to the daisies? No touching that. Seat of the affections. Broken heart. A pump after all, pumping thousands of gallons of blood every day. One fine day it gets bunged up and there you are. Lots of them lying around here: lungs, hearts, livers. Old rusty pumps: damn the thing else. The resurrection and the life. Once you are dead you are dead. That last day idea. Knocking them all up out of their graves. Come forth, Lazarus! And he came fifth and lost the job. Get up! Last day! Then every fellow mousing around for his liver and his lights and the rest of his traps. Find damn all of himself that morning. Pennyweight of powder in a skull. Twelve grammes one pennyweight. Troy measure. (105–6)

---

31. When the great classical scholar Kenneth Dover, a lover of Joyce, died, one of the eulogists had the thought of reading from this episode but was rebuffed by the official, who felt this did not befit a solemn occasion. What a pity. Kenneth certainly would have liked a good joke or two.

This passage brings together all of Bloom's three strategies. He addresses religion first, with scientific realism, then with joking wordplay—and finally with empathy for those sad souls on the supposedly glorious day of bodily resurrection.

By now it is superfluous to mention that all of Bloom's mental strategies for deflecting disgust while retaining love, and grief, and moderate fear, are also those of Joyce, in his construction of the novel. He moves the reader around inside different people's minds with generous curiosity (though admittedly we barely enter the non-mind of Blazes Boylan),[32] and the minute we're inclined to hate someone he inspires either sympathy or a laughter that is open-hearted rather than mean. We can't hate Mr. Dedalus in the "Hades" episode—for we see his sad life, his frustrated hopes for his son. And the "Cyclops" episode, which contains ugly anti-Semitism and fear of violence, is one of the funniest in the book. We are so busy laughing at the glorious mock-heroic wordplay that—while understanding clearly the moral badness of this sort of blinkered nationalism—we don't really hate the Citizen, or even his vicious dog, Garryowen. And as for Boylan—although Joyce never really lets the reader see his inner world, he does deploy Molly's humor to defang our partisan resentment (on behalf of Bloom) against

the ignoramus that doesn't know poetry from a cabbage that's what you get for not keeping them in their proper place pulling off his shoes and trousers there on the chair before me so barefaced without even asking permission and standing out that vulgar way in the half of a shirt they wear to be admired like a priest or a butcher or those old hypocrites in the time of Julius Caesar of course hes right enough in his way to pass the time as a joke sure

32. We get only three words: "A young pullet" (228, as he looks down the blouse of the shopgirl); the suggestion is that his mind is small, and not a place we want to explore.

you might as well be in bed with what with a lion God Im sure hed
have something better to say for himself an old Lion would. (778)

Molly's humor is a tiny bit sharper than Poldy's, directed, as often,
at the pretensions and pomposities of the male sex in general (Poldy
excepted); but like the author she is not capable of real hate.

Novels are not ethical treatises, and yet, as Henry James so often
insisted, they can, in their choice of a hero, show us some of our own
possibilities for approaching life. Philosophical and psychological
discussions of disgust have fallen short when it comes to death and
the corpse. We might seem to have few options: either the extreme of
Whitman's Stoical embrace of death or the equally inhuman extreme
of yielding to disgust and the social hatreds it encodes. Bloom, our
friend, shows us another way, with intense sadness and a good deal of
fear, but also with generosity and love.

As he gets ready to leave the graveyard, Bloom recalls Martha
Clifford's inept phrase: "I do not like that other world" (for "word").
He ironically concurs:

I do not like that other world she wrote. No more do I. Plenty
to see and hear and feel yet. Feel live warm beings near you. Let
them sleep in their maggoty beds. They are not going to get me
this innings. Warm beds: warm fullblooded life. (115)

And that—life—is the best response of all to the thought and the
presence of death.

BIBLIOGRAPHY

Cronin, Michael G. *Impure Thoughts: Sexuality, Catholicism, and Literature in Twentieth Century Ireland.* Manchester, UK: Manchester University Press, 2012.

Davison, Neil R. *James Joyce, Ulysses, and the Construction of Jewish Identity.* Cambridge, UK: Cambridge University Press, 1996.

Ferriter, Diarmaid. *Occasions of Sin.* London: Profile Books, 2009.

Gifford, Don, with Robert J. Seidman. *Ulysses Annotated.* Revised and expanded edition. Berkeley: University of California Press, 1988.

Hasan, Zoya, Aziz Huq, Martha C. Nussbaum, and Vidhu Verma, eds. *The Empire of Disgust: Prejudice, Discrimination, and Policy in India and the U.S.* Delhi: Oxford University Press, 2018.

Lambert, Josh. "A Literary History of the Dirty Jew." *JBooks.* http://jbooks.com/interviews/index/IP_Lambert_DJ.htm.

Lawrence, D. H. "Whitman." In Sculley Bradley and Harold W. Blodgett, eds., *Leaves of Grass.* Norton Critical Edition. New York: W. W. Norton, 1973, 842–50.

Levy, Phyllis Joyce Cohen. "The Image of the Jew in James Joyce's *Ulysses.*" Master's thesis, University of Richmond, 1968.

McCourt, John, ed. *Joyce in Context.* Cambridge, UK: Cambridge University Press, 2009.

Nussbaum, Martha. *From Disgust to Humanity: Sexual Orientation and Constitutional Law.* New York: Oxford University Press, 2010.

Nussbaum, Martha. *Hiding from Humanity: Disgust, Shame, and the Law.* Princeton, NJ: Princeton University Press, 2015).

Nussbaum, Martha. "Jewish Men, Jewish Lawyers: Roth's 'Eli, the Fanatic' and the Question of Jewish Masculinity in American Law." In Saul Levmore and Martha Nussbaum, eds., *American Guy: Masculinity in American Law and Literature.* New York: Oxford University Press, 2014, 165–201.

Nussbaum, Martha. *Upheavals of Thought: The Intelligence of Emotions.* New York: Cambridge University Press, 2001.

Nussbaum, Martha, with Saul Levmore. *Aging Thoughtfully: Conversations about Retirement, Romance, Wrinkles, and Regret.* New York: Oxford University Press, 2017.

Quick, Jonathan. "Molly Bloom's Mother." *ELH* 57 (1990): 223–40.

Chapter 2

A Portrait of Consciousness

Joyce's Ulysses as Philosophical Psychology

GARRY L. HAGBERG

In his famous (and in retrospect, one can see almost culture-changing) decision in the United States District Court of December 6, 1933, that lifted the ban on *Ulysses*, Judge John M. Woolsey produced a remarkably incisive passage of literary criticism. In the course of that much longer decision, he wrote:

> Joyce has attempted—it seems to me, with astonishing success—to show how the screen of consciousness with its ever-shifting kaleidoscopic impressions carries, as it were on a plastic palimpsest, not only what is in the focus of each man's observation of the actual things about him, but also in a penumbral zone residua of past impressions, some recent and some drawn up by association from the domain of the subconscious. He shows how each of these impressions affects the life and behavior of the character which he is describing.[1]

---

1. Woolsey's decision is included in James Joyce, *Ulysses* (New York: Random House/Modern Library, [1914] 1961), ix–xiv. References to passages in *Ulysses* are included in parentheses in the text.

Joyce's Ulysses. Philip Kitcher, Oxford University Press (2020). © Oxford University Press.
DOI: 10.1093/oso/9780190842260.001.0001

What Woolsey has captured in brief scope is what I will investigate at greater length in this chapter by situating his observation into a web of relations, both philosophical and literary.

THE EYE AS THE LENS OF A CAMERA: AN INHUMAN MODEL

It has proven easy for philosophers to model all of perception on that of the direct seeing of a physical object; the examples used are not stars, not mile-long coastlines, not mountain vistas, not musicians on a stage, not thunderstorms, not dancers in motion, but rather what philosophers have called "medium-sized dry goods"— the inanimate material object placed on the table directly before us. An empirical version of this is articulated in terms of our perception of a set of sensory impressions that we then assemble into the object we see before us; thus a cluster of Lockean sensations makes up the sensory assemblage that we call the coffee cup. That empirical model has been challenged within philosophy[2] (by the American Pragmatists, among others), but this model has also been challenged within literature. And as I will suggest here, never more completely, convincingly, or powerfully challenged than in the work of Joyce. But by "challenged," what I mean is not that

---

2. In its blunt and simple form this direct-empirical model is now almost entirely abandoned within the philosophy of science because this model significantly underplays the structuring power of the perceiving mind. As I will mention later, the Kantian revolution in philosophy gave this structuring power its due (with in his case fixed and universal categories), as did his successors who argued in favor of this structuring power but against the fixity of categories. However, the influence of this basic model of perception lives on in a number of variations, including a model of aesthetic objectivism (one can see it in the philosophical foundations of New Criticism) where critical judgment is thought to be justifiable by reference to directly perceived "internal" properties of a work of art. Like many philosophical views, its broad influence outlives its refutation by specialists.

the simplified empirical model is invariably wrong or conceptually confused; rather, it is severely partial, and where it purports to capture the essence of human perception in microcosm, misleadingly reductive. Moreover, Joyce's critique, as we shall see, extends well beyond its challenge to the simple empirical model; indeed, it challenges more sophisticated philosophical approaches to perception that in a sense abandon the simple Lockean model but really only by building upon it and not by profoundly supplanting it with a different vision. For example, conceptions of perception common to Wilfrid Sellars, Thomas Kuhn, Norwood Russell Hanson, and their successors emphasize that observation is "theory-laden" and that we see the world through the perspective provided by our categories (where, contra Kant, these categories can shift). But it is still the primary raw sensory content that comes first and is (contingently and after-the-fact) "laden." This view was anticipated by William James (in his "stream of thought" discussion and in his lectures on pragmatism) and generalized by John Dewey. Joyce, as Woolsey so clearly sees, is more extremely, more radically, showing the true complexity of human perception: its perception-defining interconnections, its resonances within the contents of a consciousness, its half- or wholly awakened associations that give a perceptual experience its texture and its historical-autobiographical position or place within the larger experience of a life-in-progress; all of these aspects are inseparably *in* perception, they are *of* perceptual content, and not superadded to it. (Philip Kitcher discusses this more radical position in his chapter in this volume; see pp. 209–11.) Such content is not *added* to human perception, nor can it be subtracted. And in *Ulysses* Joyce shows as well the layered quality of human perception. Woolsey (having employed the word "palimpsest" earlier) writes:

> What he seeks to get is not unlike the result of a double or, if that
> is possible, a multiple exposure on a cinema film which would

give a clear foreground with a background visible but somewhat blurred and out of focus in varying degrees.[3]

A cinematic model of perception could correspond to the simplified empirical or camera-lens philosophical picture, but a multiple-exposure cinematic model could not; it complicates the picture by moving in the direction of Joyce's presentation of human perceptual consciousness (which as we will shortly see is more complex still, because any cinematic model still leaves out the temporal element, the imaginative flooding in of memory images, and the potential swirl of kaleidoscopic associations).

The issue of focus is particularly important here: within consciousness, as Joyce shows in intricate detail, we can direct and redirect our focal attention from blurred background to sharply delineated foreground just as can a movie camera within a scene, which a still photograph cannot. But as we shall see, describing the difference between still photography and the movie camera could lead us to say that what Joyce has shown, generally stated, is that human perception is more like the "perception" of a film camera than a still camera. This would be interestingly wrong: what Joyce has shown is that there lies a vast continuum from simple Lockean perception on one pole to astonishingly intricate and cognitively and affectively saturated perception on the other, with the move from a still-photography model to a moving-image model constituting merely one step in the right direction along that vast continuum.

It was another early Modernist, Virginia Woolf, who wrote that the great difficulty of writing a biography lies not merely in the difficulty of recounting all the important things that happened across

3. Woolsey, quoted in Joyce, *Ulysses*, xi.

the span of a life—that is merely a quantitative difficulty. Rather, she said (exactly correctly in my view) that the special, intrinsic difficulty of biographical writing is always of a qualitative kind, always a matter of what one might call the personal or idiosyncratic "texture" of conscious experience, and so the special difficulty lies in the extraordinarily complex task of capturing the consciousness of the person to whom the recounted external things happened—for the recounting of any event, there is the "what" and the "to whom," where the latter is always far more elusive and demanding. Having found the way to do precisely that is, if too succinctly stated, Joyce's philosophical-literary achievement. It is thus fitting that Woolsey wrote, "*Ulysses* is not an easy book to read or to understand." It is a book that is, indeed, famously difficult (where part of that difficulty is, indeed, the making of a coherent whole of the novel, where the relatively easy or narratively straightforward chapters—e.g., 1, 2, 4, 5—need to be interwoven in a reader's mind with the especially demanding ones such as 3, 11, 14, and 15). But this difficulty, I will suggest, is a natural correlate of the true complexity of the contents of consciousness. To truly and intricately understand another person is to truly and intricately understand perception-defining resonances, associations, experiential linkages, and autobiographical positionings of present perceptions and experiences—that is, to grasp in a nuanced way what things mean *for that person*, where human understanding requires our recognizing the multiform ways in which all sorts of concepts, memories, and aspirations are liable to be linked, as meaning-generators, to the current episode. Woolf's description of this difficulty thus also serves as a description of Joyce's fundamental aesthetic imperative: Joyce's achievement is of a mimetic kind—but where the mimesis is of the inner, not the outer, world. Or perhaps also: where that inner world is captured through the intricate mimesis of a (fictional) outer world through which that inner mind moves.

PHILOSOPHICAL LINKAGES

So before turning to Joyce's psychically mimetic words, what are some of the passages of philosophy that interweave in various ways with Woolsey's profound observation? Let me first return to Gilbert Ryle. If Joyce's achievement is, following Woolsey, as I have suggested, then we need to understand the nature of the mimetic depiction of the contents of the mind. And here, as quickly as earlier, the philosophical picture of the still camera suggests itself: there are mental objects and events, those objects and events have determinate boundaries (temporal and episodic-experiential), and they can be "clicked" in a verbal "snapshot," the outward language describing the inner event in a one-to-one relation. Ryle (in the period of English philosophy just after Wittgenstein's first wave of influence) had become far too sophisticated a thinker about the mind to accept any such oversimplified picture, and he wrote:

> Here I must sound a warning: thinking is not one skill amongst skills. At school we learn geometry, arithmetic, languages, etc. but no special classes are given in thinking alone. All these subjects are exercises in thinking.[4]

One could, in a neo-Wittgensteinian spirit, put this important point in a linguistic way that captures a fallacy to which Joyce, in his writing of the mind, is immune.[5] Because the word "thinking" is a word with a meaning, we too easily believe that it must derive that meaning by reference to the (in this case mental) object it names.[6] That

---

4. Gilbert Ryle, *Aspects of Mind*, ed. Rene Meyer (Oxford: Blackwell, 1993), 149.
5. See Ludwig Wittgenstein, *The Blue and Brown Books* (Oxford: Blackwell, 1958).
6. I offer a discussion of this matter in *Describing Ourselves: Wittgenstein and Autobiographical Consciousness* (Oxford: Oxford University Press, 2008), chapter 4, "The Self, Thinking," 119–53.

ostensive-definition picture has been subjected to a good deal of deserved criticism, but for the present it will suffice to point out the misleading analogy that Ryle has in focus: one can do, and work through in a concentrated way, geometry or arithmetic, where that mental work is bounded in time and experience. On that model, the camera click model of mental mimesis might, within that narrowly delimited frame, serve. But Ryle continues:

> Lots of thinking is unlike long division: it does not involve a continuous stretch of, say, 50 seconds. Someone who has been thinking where to spend his next summer holiday—either in Austria or in Iceland—informs us that there were no special stretches of attending; there were mere isolated pieces with no glue at the ends to stick them together. Thinking is not like the flight of an aeroplane; it is more like the fluttering of a butterfly on a windy day, and often just like its mere sitting on a flower.[7]

"And often just like its mere sitting on a flower": that is, the thought is not presently in flight, but it is poised and ready for flight. In recognizing the phenomenological accuracy of this description, we recognize that thinking is not always either wholly on or wholly off. Thus to have a thought "sitting" is importantly distinct from not having that thought at all. Ryle further describes, again through analogy, this variety of thought:

> To say that I have had a problem on my mind for the past thirty years is to say more than my thinking fluttered about. Compare the compass needle at first swinging wildly but quietening down later to point to the magnetic north. Likewise with my thirty-year

7. Ryle, *Aspects of Mind*, 149.

problem: I had a certain tendency, for thirty years I was interested in it.[8]

Stephen Dedalus certainly thinks, in a distinctively absorbed way, like this. Leopold Bloom, in his different way or within a different sensibility, thinks like this as well.

Consider Ryle's next observation:

> A child listening to a story is listening to every bit narrated to him. But if something related conflicts with something said earlier, he objects (e.g. 'How could the castaway flee from the cannibals on the island if he could not row the boat because of a broken wrist?') The child's thinking suddenly jumped away to something else although there was no problem to be solved. Our question now is: What do we mean by such phrases as 'keeping the thread?' What is it to *concentrate* here and now on something?[9]

Jumping to something else, staying on the topic, scanning for inconsistency while not focusing upon that in the way we focus on a problem in geometry, keeping the thread and yet at the same time interweaving it with others—these cases show that thinking is not mono-dimensional, not always single-layered, not bounded as fixed mental acts that are either "on" or "off." This is Joyce's world, and it is the one that Woolf identified as so especially difficult to accurately portray.

I implicitly pointed to the idea of cognitive saturation earlier— or rather, the cognitive saturation of what we think of as previously unalloyed perceptual content: Joyce did not say this directly or in

8. Ibid.
9. Ibid.

propositionally encapsulated form; he did not use this particular philosophical term, but, unerringly honest to the complexity of the concept of thinking, he most certainly showed it. Ryle, similarly honest to conscious experience and in a philosophical way parallel to literature, continues:

> Consider the following cases. A and B hear a rumbling noise. A says it is a lorry rumbling over the bridge nearby, and B says it is the rumble of thunder. One is right and the other is wrong. The reception of the noises is the same, but the "interpretation" is different. Clearly, there is something more than perception involved here.[10]

We can see here that the grooves of the direct-perception "camera-lens" model are deep, and Ryle at this juncture does not entirely free himself: the phrase "more than perception" suggests that there is in the first instance a direct or simple ocular "snapshot" to which further complexities are then superadded. This additive picture itself represents one step forward along a continuum ranging from the Lockean model to Woolf's nearly uncapturable complexity, but it is hardly the end of the story: Joyce shows that there is very rarely any simple perception in this sense in the first place, so the idea of *adding* to it miscasts the phenomenology that is the nonstop moving target of the mimesis. Ryle has rightly supplanted a simplistic picture, but a still more acute focus will be required. Such focus may be more available to literature than to philosophy as traditionally practiced.

But there are other light-casting philosophical passages into which to situate Woolsey's Joyce. Another philosopher from the post-Wittgensteinian period, Norman Malcolm, offered some

10. Ibid., 150.

remarks on memory and mental content that, with Joyce in view, reemerge as particularly helpful. It is Joyce's Stephen Dedalus who lives in a particularly memory-enriched mental world, and Joyce must have seen clearly that in *Ulysses*, to achieve the depiction of consciousness that was his undergirding intention, he would need to show the interaction between memory-content and what we think of as present or momentary perception. The phenomenon in question is akin to Ryle's perception of lorry or thunder, but now with the source of the inflection coming from within rather than from without. Parallel to the preceding, it is natural to think of this process in additive terms: in visual memory, in Lockean or Humean terms, a visual idea, derived from an originating sense-impression, is added to the present sensory input, yielding a perception that is thereby connected to memory—rather like a snapshot of a previously photographed scene being held up to a scene as presently viewed and then glancing back and forth. And so in verbal memory, one text or utterance is presently perceived with a past text or remembered utterance held up against it, reading, or recalling words, back and forth. But again—and as we shall see Joyce deeply understands—matters of the mind are not so simple. Malcolm writes:

> [T]here is an important difference in meaning between the sentences "I remember hearing Mr. Russell lecture in London" and "I remember that I heard Russell lecture in London" . . . Often we wish to contrast remembering something with remembering that the something occurred or existed: "I remember that there was a huge parade when war was declared, and must have seen it, but I don't remember the parade itself," or "I remember that there was a chap named Robin in my class but I don't remember *him*." These are things we say. On the other hand, we sometimes say "Not only do I remember that there was a lad named Robin

in my class but I remember *him*." When we say these things, what point are we making, what information are we giving?[11]

So sentences such as "I remember hearing or seeing X" record a significantly different phenomenology from those like "I remember that I heard or saw X." What we can go on to do and say in each of these cases is dramatically different—yet they are both unquestionably instances of remembering. When Stephen Dedalus or Leopold Bloom has a distinct association or image or phrase reawakened, they may be experiencing what Malcolm has earlier categorized (following C. D. Broad) as perceptual memory. But in positioning a given experience, a perceptual moment, into a web of associations that serve to make that experience what it is, they often do so in "remembering that" terms. There is here a meaning-generating, significance-determining web of the past into which the present is nested—but an accurate description of this kind of phenomenon will not fit into the "snapshot-comparing" mold. Concerning what points we are making in saying what we do concerning what we remember, Malcolm continues:

> The point is not always the same. But sometimes it is to announce that we cannot *see in our minds* the scenes of the parade or the face of the classmate. This meaning comes out very strongly when we say, "I remember a great deal *about* him but I don't remember *him*." Remembering about him would be factual memory, e.g. remembering that he was captain of the team . . . Remembering all of this and more we might still not remember him in the sense of seeing him, picturing him, "in our minds."[12]

11. Norman Malcolm, *Knowledge and Certainty: Essays and Lectures* (Upper Saddle River, NJ: Prentice Hall, 1963), 205.
12. Ibid.

Remembering is a multi-faceted concept, and its role in inflecting (what we call) present experience is equally complex. It does not reduce to a single essence that lies beneath all cases. Again, Joyce knows this. Can one remember in one sense and not in the other? Do remembering and not remembering overlap upon each other? Breaking the grip of a simplifying philosophical picture, they often do overlap:

> Similarly, one can remember a good deal about a melody (e.g. that is in the key of G, that it is very brisk) without being able to remember the melody itself. Of course, to say that a person cannot remember a melody frequently means that he cannot play, hum or whistle it from memory. Or . . . that he cannot recognize it when he hears it. Sometimes, however, we mean, not this, but that he cannot "hear it in his head," as we say. When . . . it won't come to him, he will often express this by saying "I can't remember it": yet in the sense of recalling many facts about the melody he remembers it quite well, and he may also remember it in the sense that he would recognize it if he heard it.[13]

The past thus does not impinge upon present perception in a single or uniform way (Woolsey intimates as much), and the criteria for what does and does not constitute remembering alter, sometimes bluntly, sometimes subtly, in a contextually sensitive manner. It requires a good deal of detail within a particular context to determine how and when such criteria operate—precisely the fine grain that literature, more than philosophy, provides.

But before turning to Joyce's text, there remain a few further philosophical passages that help to further explicate the significance of

13. Ibid., 205–6.

Woolsey's insight. The first comes from Iris Murdoch's philosophical writing:

> We are not isolated free choosers, monarchs of all we survey, but benighted creatures sunk in a reality whose nature we are constantly and overwhelmingly tempted to deform by fantasy . . . Our sense of form, which is an aspect of our desire for consolation, can be a danger to our sense of reality as a rich receding background.[14]

The fantasy of which she speaks is one of control, of overarching and systematically organized perception of the world around us—monarchs of all we survey. According to that fantasy, our knowledge of the world is a great mosaic of directly perceived objects, all given their place in the encompassing picture we make to ourselves of that world. The empirical picture in large part comports well with, and indeed undergirds, this fantasy (the part it misses is the Lockean insight that we are not and cannot be *complete* masters, because some things come unbidden, forcing us into a perceptual moment for which we did not ask and from which we cannot immediately escape). But the truth for Murdoch—and as we will see, for Joyce—is both darker and more interesting. Sunk in a reality that our need for form would drastically oversimplify, we are always already in a web of words, descriptions, phrases, redescriptions, rephrases, layered perceptions, associations, triggered memories—all in all the conscious repositories of an ever-developing perceptual palimpsest of a kind no inner monarch could control. (It is for this reason that I will suggest that we are all admixtures of, or at least in these perceptual respects profoundly like, Stephen Dedalus and Leopold Bloom—but I will come to that.) And "the rich receding background"? That just is the

---

14. Iris Murdoch, "Against Dryness: A Polemical Sketch," *Encounter* (1961): 16–20, at 20.

penumbra of which Woolsey wrote, and the content, the texture, of consciousness that it was Joyce's great achievement to find a way to represent. This is not the mind's false or reductive or severely partial image of itself; rather, it is the mind's accurate and painstaking self-portrait.[15]

However, in so much as introducing the concept of the mind's self-portrait it is all too easy to fall immediately into grooves of thought long laid down by a fundamentally dualist philosophical model of selfhood that has origins and articulations in religion, in Plato, in Descartes, and (showing the power of that conceptual legacy) presuppositionally in some recent work in cognitive studies.[16]

That model places the mind in a private chamber where its privacy is taken to be ensured by ontology—the mind is one immaterial kind of thing and the material body is another. (This generates the corresponding epistemic distinction, where we are thought to have a kind or type of access to the material realm that we cannot have to the immaterial.) So on that model, cognitive or mental content is always and invariably in the first instance contained within the metaphysically private consciousness of the solitary and bounded

15. R. P. Blackmur captures the complexity and the extreme measure of detail or particularity required to capture a fair likeness of the mind; he writes that Joyce had to "present an inordinate mass of detail," and indeed (and this is precisely correct) that Joyce, to meet the demands of his fundamental aesthetic imperative, is "omnivorous of detail," in his *Eleven Essays in the European Novel* (New York: Harcourt, Brace, and World, 1964), 30–31.

16. Such dualistic presuppositions are often shown where (a) memory is construed on a strict storage-and-retrieval model, where (b) mental imagery is presumed to be the uniform and singular type of entity stored and retrieved, and where (c) a "language of thought" thesis—the idea that we have a pre-verbal language behind our spoken language that mentally pre-identifies such mental content that we then outwardly and only contingently name—is regarded as given fact. For a particularly helpful set of discussions of these issues (some arguing that appeals to cognitive science in discussing aesthetic experience are well placed, and some arguing that in such appeals one often sees a misunderstanding of the philosophical enterprise or a misinterpretation of the scientific experiments or both), see Greg Currie, Matthew Kieran, Aaron Meskin, and Jon Robson, eds., *Aesthetics and the Sciences of Mind* (Oxford: Oxford University Press, 2014).

individual, where self-knowledge is inviolably internal and the unmediated result of hermetic introspection. As one aspect of Joyce's great achievement, that is not the picture he paints. And here again Ryle, who famously wrote of "the Cartesian myth" and "the ghost in the machine," reemerges again as directly relevant to capturing what Joyce has achieved; his observation concerning the circumstantial, contextual, situated, external, and non-immediate character of self-knowledge (these words could serve as descriptions of Joyce's conception of the mind) is worth reconsidering in this context in some detail; his observations here unfold in four stages. First, Ryle writes (with enumerations inserted):

> For example, after listening to an argument, you aver that you understood it perfectly; but you may be deceiving yourself, or trying to deceive me. If we then part for a day or two, I am no longer in a position to test whether or not you did understand it perfectly. But still I know what tests would have settled the point. If [1] you had put the argument into your own words, or translated it into French; if [2] you had invented appropriate concrete illustrations of the generalizations and abstractions in the argument; if [3] you had stood up to cross-questioning; if [4] you had correctly drawn further consequences from different stages of the argument and indicated points where the theory was inconsistent with other theories; if [5] you had inferred correctly from the nature of the argument to the qualities of intellect and character of its author and predicted accurately the subsequent development of his theory, then I should have required no further evidence that you understood it perfectly.

These criteria, fleshed out in particular ways in particular contexts, constitute not only the proof of, but also indeed (and this is Ryle's point) the content of, understanding. But this, so far, concerns our ways of knowing that another possesses legitimate or real understanding. Thus the second stage:

> And exactly the same sorts of tests would satisfy me that I had understood it perfectly; the sole difference would be that I should probably not have voiced aloud the expressions of my deductions, illustrations, etc., but told them to myself more perfunctorily in silent soliloquy; and I should probably have been more easily satisfied of the completeness of my understanding than I was of yours.

That we are more easily satisfied in the first-person case shows something of the asymmetry between the first- and second-person case that Ryle subtly preserves, while drawing more overt attention to the similarities or parallels between our knowledge of others and our knowledge of ourselves. And those similarities come in the form of criteria (1) through (5). And so the third stage:

> In short it is part of the *meaning* of "you understood it" that you could have done so and so and would have done it, if such and such . . . It should be noticed, on the one hand, that there is no single nuclear performance, overt or in your head, which would determine that you had understood the argument. Even if you claimed that you had experienced a flash or click of comprehension and had actually done so, you would still withdraw your other claim to have understood the argument, if you found that you could not paraphrase it, illustrate, expand, or recast it; and you would allow someone else to have understood it who could meet all examination questions about it, but reported no click of comprehension.

With these three stages in mind, Ryle moves to his fourth and final, linking our ways of knowing our own or another's abilities (of the 1-through-5 kinds) to our knowing of our own or another's motives:

> I discover my or your motives in much, though not quite the same way as I discover my or your abilities.[17]

Understanding is not an internally isolated episodic mental occurrence. The ability to see and make connections; to discern relations between the present experienced particular event or thought and a generality or abstraction above it; knowing how to work through cross-questioning from another or from oneself; the ability to articulate and explore further consequences or implications from a present observation or experience or thought; the detection of subtle inconsistencies within oneself and to reconsider accordingly; the capacity to make predictions of oneself and others on inferential bases and to then evaluate those predictions concerning oneself or others morally; fluid movement between doing all this outwardly in conversation and inwardly in silent soliloquy; the gauging in terms of all these elements one's degree or depth of understanding; the unending engagement in expanding, illustrating, recasting, or paraphrasing a thought or description of an experience—all of these are part of the situated, pragmatic, and circumstantially interwoven nature of self-knowledge and, more broadly, human understanding.[18] And central

---

17. Gilbert Ryle, "Self-Knowledge," in Quassim Cassam, ed., *Self-Knowledge* (Oxford: Oxford University Press, 1994), 19–42, at 21–22.
18. Marian Eide, in *Ethical Joyce* (Cambridge, UK: Cambridge University Press, 2002), interestingly observes that, in the scenes in which Stephen Dedalus is teaching the dyslexic student Sargent, an important distinction is in play. "For Stephen, then, it is insufficient pedagogically to demonstrate or impose knowledge. Knowledge arises sympathetically, in a conversation between subjects. That sympathy, however, must also allow for a difference between self and other, between Stephen and Sargent. Stephen cannot assume that he *knows* Sargent's experience but he is responsible for *acknowledging* it" (69). Eide connects this to Stanley Cavell's discussion of the distinction between knowing and acknowledging;

to the conception of mind in play here, "there is no single nuclear performance, overt or in your head" (against what the Cartesian model
would dictate) that serves as the single, trans-contextual, and thus
universal criterion for understanding.

The eye, viewed as a camera lens, does not gain what it knows
by turning inward. Yet, importantly, this is not to say that we should
embrace a blunt behaviorism as a polemical antithesis to the
Cartesian picture; it is not that the inner life is an illusion, nonexis-
tent.[19] This is why Ryle acknowledged and preserved the asymmetry
("in much, though not quite the same way") between our relations
to ourselves and our relations to others and the outside world. And
this too is shown by Joyce: Mulligan is a character we never see from
the point of view of his consciousness (unlike Stephen and Bloom);
Joyce is resolute in presenting him exclusively from the outside. If

a separate examination of Joyce's text could trace this distinction as Joyce shows it functioning at the base of interpersonal understanding—that is, as foundational to the understanding of another mind. For Cavell this distinction operates within a context of recognizing
the scope of interpersonal human understanding yet while remaining aware of the threat
of skepticism concerning other minds. The skepticism that Joyce is working against has
been identified as Humean in its origin; see Richard Barlow, *The Celtic Unconscious: Joyce
and Scottish Culture* (Notre Dame, IN: University of Notre Dame Press, 2017). Barlow discusses the roles that unknowability and the threat of unintelligibility play as *Ulysses* pro-
gresses: "So, unknowability and unintelligibility begin to exert an influence on the latter
stages of *Ulysses*, and Joyce based this on the work of David Hume" (78). Barlow identifies a
particularly interesting shift of focus in Joyce, from Humean skepticism fundamentally concerning causal relations to Joyce's "promot[ing] a system of associative connections" (79).

19. It is important to see, in understanding Joyce's contribution to philosophical psychology,
that it is possible to take an external point of view of oneself in a moment of self-knowledge
without thereby implicitly arguing for behaviorism. Speaking of J. M. Coetzee's memoir,
Boyhood: Scenes from a Provincial Life, David Parker insightfully articulates a connection
to the achievement of Joyce's. Of a passage of Coetzee's, Parker writes, "These moments of
clarity are truly epiphanic in the Joycean sense. The protagonist catches glimpses of himself, not from the self-righteous perspective of the heavily-defended child-self, but as anyone would see him from the outside," in *The Self in Moral Space: Life Narrative and the Good*
(Ithaca, NY: Cornell University Press, 2007), 162. That such a moment is possible and
that its epistemic gain is afforded by taking an external perspective does not eradicate the
psychological asymmetry between the first- and third-person case—a subtle matter that is
perhaps more convincing if shown rather than said.

behaviorism were true, this difference would be neither possible nor intelligible. So conscious experience is still *ours*—but the proper portrayal of this may require an order of complexity that only the very long-form narrative can adequately and non-misleadingly capture. It may not reduce to an "-ism." This is what Joyce has set himself as his task, and this is the world in which Stephen and Bloom live.

PENUMBRA AND PALIMPSEST: *ULYSSES* AND THE COMPLEXITY OF PERCEPTION

As the novel opens (in episode 1, "Telemachus"), in the conversation between Mulligan and Stephen Dedalus, the theme of one mind peering into, partially understanding, and suspecting a characterological issue as it has manifested in action within an external, relational context, is put into play. Remarking on Dedalus' refusal to kneel and pray at the request of his mother on her deathbed, Mulligan says to Dedalus, "There is something sinister in you . . ." (7). The ellipsis is an important part of the sentence; it marks out the open space for further reflection, further observation, further articulation of a personal quality sensed but not yet fathomed or exactingly identified. And there is for Stephen something in Mulligan's remark, something not contained within the words themselves, that leads his mind to turn suddenly and directly to thoughts about his mother. Later, recalling a remark made on the occasion of a visit Stephen had paid to Mulligan after his mother's death, Stephen indicates that he took considerable offense at what Mulligan said. But here Mulligan presses on at length about Stephen's failure to accommodate his mother's final wish, and a second long-form theme is also put into play: Joyce's narrator describes Mulligan as having "spoken himself into boldness" (10). With this description Joyce is intimating his conception of mind: words are not mere external conveyers of prior internal mental content. Rather, by speaking—by moving verbally within what Wittgenstein called a language-game or a circumscribed context of discourse that demarcates the reach of expressive possibility,[20] Mulligan is making himself, in that moment, what he is from (as one might dangerously put it in that it reiterates the dualist categories that need to be overcome) the outside in, and not, consistent with the dualist picture of selfhood, vice versa. And are words mere conveyers of prior inner moral content, or do they themselves, through verbal enactment, bring into existence the moral tone of an exchange? Joyce's Stephen, "shielding the gaping wounds which the words had left in his heart" (10), that is, Mulligan's pressing on aggressively about his refusal of his mother's last wish, makes Joyce's answer to this question clear.

But then also: are spoken words invariably necessary for this kind of constitutive interaction? When the old woman who delivers the milk solicitously asks Mulligan if he is a medical student, Stephen, feeling slighted, "listened in scornful silence" (16). Here also like Wittgenstein, Joyce understood not only the power of words but also the fact that self-constitutive and in its way world-constitutive verbal

20. I offer fuller explanations of the notion of a language-game in Wittgenstein's philosophy and its significance for aesthetic creativity and understanding in *Meaning and Interpretation: Wittgenstein, Henry James, and Literary Knowledge* (Ithaca, NY: Cornell University Press, [1994] 2018), chapter 1, "Language Games and Artistic Styles," 9–44, and "Wittgenstein, Verbal Creativity, and the Expansion of Artistic Style," in S. Greve and J. Macha, eds., *Wittgenstein and the Creativity of Language* (London: Palgrave, 2015), 141–76. Megan Quigley interestingly sees *Ulysses* itself as a novel that houses such a multiplicity of Wittgensteinian language-games that it challenges the reader with the task of following the changes from one to another and finding coherence across those changes—which itself then constitutes an interpretive language-game. Quigley writes, "Within *Ulysses*, the multiplicity of styles creates a novel game with constantly changing rules, where readers struggle to find footing. Eliot proclaimed that Joyce 'had many voices but no "style,"' emphasizing Joyce's unwillingness to commit to a single overriding voice," in *Modernist Fiction and Vagueness: Philosophy, Form, and Language* (Cambridge, UK: Cambridge University Press, 2015), 130. Whether the presence of a single overriding voice is a precondition for having a style is of course one of the aesthetic questions that Joyce in this work asks and—as a Modernist step forward—answers.

interaction is more than strictly *verbal* interaction. And Mulligan learns more, fathoms more, about Stephen from the content of inter-action that is not verbally articulated. Later still, Joyce underscores the point: he says that Stephen saw in Mulligan who had as yet said nothing about it that he was about to ask for the key to his apart-ment. "He will ask for it. That was in his eyes" (21). Perceiving that is not in any sense a matter of direct perception or direct observation-based knowledge. Yet it is undeniably one mode of perception of which every person, when apart from the reductive impulses of philosophical pictures, is aware. A camera lens would not have seen that; Stephen, with a human mind not only saturating but insepara-bly intrinsic to retinal sensation, of course does.

A third and closely related long-form theme put into play early in the work concerns the way in which language carries networks of sig-nificance beyond what any given speaker might intend or realize: this stands broadly parallel to Ryle's ability to show an understanding of an argument in being able to articulate its implications and the range of significance opened by it; meaning-content can be filled in by what we have not yet explicitly cognized but where the space for this supplemental content has been opened by what we have explicitly thought or stated. One could write a full study of the way Joyce devel-ops this theme, but, if one example may stand for very many, we see it early (in episode 2, "Nestor") in Stephen's quiet remark, almost to himself, in response to the schoolmaster Mr. Deasy telling him that young people do not know what money is or recognize its power. Deasy says, "But what does Shakespeare say? *Put but money in thy purse.*" And we get: "Iago, Stephen murmured" (31). Stephen knows the exact source in Shakespeare, he knows the moral condition of the character who uttered it (where, undercutting Deasy's meaning, Iago uses these words with malign intent and is encouraging Rodrigo to be lavish), and thus he knows much more of the range of connota-tion, much more of the word-borne significance of this line, than does Deasy—the person who spoke it. One could say: Joyce is showing that words are, in Wittgenstein's sense, a form of life (rather than merely inert conveyers of mental content).

This theme is centrally important to Joyce's conception of mind, because in this linguistic way consciousness, as expressed in and as created within language, is not hermetically contained, not circumscribed by a speaker's explicit or acknowledged intentional content. It is rather (and here is another step forward in comprehending Joyce's conception) that the speaker of language not only, as with Mulligan speaking himself into boldness, finds words to hold a self-constitutive power, but also that a speaker of language brings her or his mind into contact with, or enters into, something very much larger than what they intentionally carry within. The relation to language is thus, for Joyce, like his conception of the relation of a self to the world: it is a matter of dialogical interaction between (what we too quickly call) the inner and the outer, the self and its relationally webbed or nested context. Throughout the book Dedalus sees that words often themselves know (or if that seems anthropomorphic of words, convey) more than the persons using them. Against what the Cartesian picture would dictate, our relation to language is not invariably an inner-to-outer affair. What Joyce sees here is subtle: the Cartesian thesis could be expressed as "I know exactly and wholly what these words will convey as I use them"; the Cartesian may not know what the words will in practice convey to others, but for the Cartesian the criterion for correct content will always be mentally contained intentional content. So on such a view there could not be a space opened by what we say, space opened by our words and verbal interactions that makes it possible to move into and explore a realm of significance that we at the moment of speaking only partly perceive or that we later better understand. Joyce is showing that such a restrictive picture is false to experience, false to our relation to our speech, false to our psychology.

And the question of our relation to language is not for Joyce separable from the question of our visual perception of (what we call) the external world. Walking alone on a beach (opening episode 3, "Proteus"), Dedalus thinks to himself in this depiction of a stream-of-consciousness the now famous line, "Ineluctable modality of the visible." This could and has been interpreted as his desire to close his eyes (which he does) and wrest his thinking away from the cognitive tyranny of visual experience. This conventional, but I think interestingly incorrect, understanding of these words would suggest that he found his thought dictated to by visual sense-data, and so wants to think in an internal or within his hermetic mind free of that external dictation. But his next words are "at least that if no more, thought through my eyes" (38).

Thought through my eyes. That is, thinking itself reaches out into, and powerfully inflects, visual experience—so powerfully that the very idea of pure or unfiltered visual experience is an empiricist myth. (Given Joyce's intellectual range, we would be right to discern an Aristotelian and neo-Aristotelian account of perception lurking in this passage.) On closer investigation the human eye is not, or is not reducible to, the eye of the camera. The felt tremors or subtle resonances of past experience; the detection of as-yet-unarticulated or semi-hidden content; the desire to more fully fathom; the sensed expansiveness of connotation and implication beyond what one can presently see (as the intertwined analogue to what one can say); the shifting and layered verbal descriptions of what one sees and how that visual content is saturated with cognition of kinds both known and hinted; the way that the visual perception of meaningful places (as they did for Augustine) "whisper" to us—it would be unintelligible to attribute any of these aspects of perceptual experience to a camera. And—Joyce's point here as made in Stephen's words to himself—it would be equally unintelligible to try to understand this line and the following famously

intricate stream of consciousness as it continues through this episode without these enriched aspects of perceptual phenomenology. In addition to many literary and historical allusions occurring
within his mind, and with many sudden turns and juxtapositions of
his thought of a kind to be expected in this educated mind conduct-
ing what Ryle called silent soliloquy, Joyce hits upon an image that
intimates a good deal of his conception of experience: he refers to
"[r]eading two pages apiece of seven books every night" (41). That
is a compact metaphor for the kind of perception, the philosophical psychology, that it is his aesthetic task to portray here. Reading
two pages of a book is *very* different from knowing nothing about
the book. And while it is a world away from knowing the book, it is
certainly not in any respect like knowing nothing of it. Rather, it is
to encounter pages that carry the promise of much larger meaning-
content to be understood far more fully.

Stephen's visual experience is like this: he sees what he sees, but
he also knows that what he sees intimates much more. This is true
because:

(a) he knows that his thought reaches out through his eyes into
the perceived world (there is a Kantian element here, but,
as mentioned earlier, a Kantian element altered strongly in
the direction of William James—like Kant, Stephen sees
through, or within the conceptual frames of, categories, but
like James, the categories are moveable); and

(b) he knows that his thought, as portrayed in this episode so
complexly (hence the famous mentally descriptive micro-
scopic intricacy), is itself of a kind that is connected through
seemingly unending webs of connotation and association;

(c) he knows what Henry James famously said. "Relations end
nowhere," and that, in short, there is *always* more.

And we see here as well that Joyce has found a way to capture what one might call a style of mind (and in this sense too what Woolf was after): While Stephen possesses, and is possessed by, a kind of "magpie mind" (a kind common to both Stephen and his creator), where his quirky erudition yields waves and floods of associations that he is in the habit of letting take control, Bloom perceives the outside world more attentively and thus whose associations, although idiosyncratic, are easier to understand.[21] (The metaphor often used for the phenomenon under inspection here is that of the saturation of sensation by cognitive content as mentioned earlier, but here again we see that Joyce's unsimplified vision is that there is no such thing as uninflected sensation waiting to be saturated or not.) With all of this in mind, one can understand what it means to say that a glance at the world, for Stephen's style of mind, is like reading two pages.

And then what about what we might call the perception of words? "Your postprandial, do you know that word? Postprandial. There was a fellow I knew once in Barcelona, queer fellow, used to call it his postprandial" (43–44). Words, for Joyce, work like his complex conception of visual perception and are inextricably interwoven with it. Rather than a brief dictionary definition, we get a reference to a person once known, and to a place. That evokes a world, a life (again, what Wittgenstein called a form of life), and a way of life, a use of that word both as an enactment of personal style and as an intimation of the larger context within which that word has a life. The word, like what we think of as a single visual sensation, functions much like the two pages.

21. On this point see Philip Kitcher's chapter in this volume, especially pages 218–21. Concerning the differing styles of mind, see Kitcher's discussion of the greater precision of Bloom's perceptual vocabulary and the distinctive way in which, while background associations are still there for him, they are given considerably less free rein; the degree of mental discipline is different.

Like a mind's rapid shift, Leopold Bloom enters the narrative suddenly (in part II: "Odyssey," episode 4: "Calypso"); as quickly as we meet him we encounter a strong variation on the theme of varying depths of understanding (in this case feline to human). Of his cat, Bloom thinks as he looks, "They understand what we say better than we understand them" (55). Joyce has Bloom thinking a Rylean thought about what he would find himself unable to articulate, unable to rephrase or paraphrase, unable to give voice to in terms of the cat's experience. But in this episode what is on display is the quicksilver richness of the mind behind what is being said in a verbal exchange that is outwardly quite simple. That stark contrast, between the richness of mental content and the relative paucity of external talk, can of course reinvigorate the "ghost in the machine" picture—but in a philosophically telling way Joyce does not let it do so.

In answering a question from Molly concerning the meaning of a word in a book while she is still in bed and to whom he has just delivered a tray with tea, Bloom looks to the text: "Metempsychosis, he said, frowning. It's Greek: from the Greek. That means the transmigration of souls." Asked by her to answer the question "in plain words," we get this from Joyce:

He smiled, glancing askance at her mocking eye. The same young eyes. The first night after the charades. Dolphin's Barn. He turned over the smudged pages. *Ruby: The Pride of the Ring.* Hello. Illustration. Fierce Italian with carriagewhip. Must be Ruby pride of on the floor naked. Sheet kindly lent. *The monster Maffei desisted and flung his victim from him with an oath.* Cruelty behind it all. Doped animals. Trapeze at Hengler's. Had to look the other way. Mob gaping. Break your neck and we'll break our sides. Families of them. Bone them young so they

metempsychosis. That we live after death. Our souls. That a
man's soul after he dies. Dignam's soul. (64)[22]

These are the words flying through the mind of a person in a brief
exchange with his wife (he has just said to himself that he knows she
will welcome her lover into that bed later this very day—the very afternoon after he will have attended his acquaintance Dignam's funeral
and after which he will stay out so as not to intrude on the assignation)
about the meaning of a word. But these phrases and rephrases are the
residue, the perception-shaping inflection from his past, into the present moment. "Saturating" what he sees, what he perceives, his mind
moves in the associative space opened by his looking at his wife in their
bed drinking tea and holding up a book of erotica (to which she has
turned, we are later led to think, because of her decade-long frustration)
with a problematic word. And Joyce shows something else in these passages: in his perception (in our perception) Bloom, in imagining the
cruelty of the circus—training young children as trapeze artists from
too young an age; medicating animals; the harshness of the audience;
etc.—about which Molly is reading, does not first see an inert circus and
then superadd moral content to that initial brute perception. Rather, his
perception of, and here his thinking of, the circus is in the initial perceptual experience (and here his thought of it after having seen it) one of
morally laden perception. A camera, of course, does not see that way—
cameras do not strike out in all sorts of directions, making all sorts of
associations. They are, as it were, *focused*. And so—here is the great gulf
that separates his outward speech from his inner world—he steps back
into the conversation (referring to the book) with:

Did you finish it?

22. The terms introduced here form part of a complex that will recur throughout the novel; one
significant part of the art of *Ulysses* is the carefully composed recurrence of literary leitmotifs.

The contrast between the activity of the mind and what is actually said shows how little may be captured in a transcript of a verbal exchange. That itself, within its limits, is a philosophical contribution: we are not stimulus-response mechanisms; we are not robots; our life of meaning is not reducible to (only) what we say—but Joyce is showing and saying very much more than this familiar straightforward point. What is far more telling here, as I mentioned earlier, is not just that, but rather: everything that goes through Bloom's mind in this moment is drawn from, comes from, his circumstantially engaged experience in his past. It is not a matter of metaphysically private mental content (as Wittgenstein has shown, it could not be),[23] but rather an associative and connotative web of his cognitive-affective past that, in a flash, is pressing into his present moment. What is private here is not private in an ontological sense—one could say that what we see depicted herein as the private part of the mind is itself at a foundational level public. In this episode Joyce has many cases of this kind of divide between rapid-fire cognition as it intermingles with what one sees (a development of the theme of Stephen's thought within his eyes); what Joyce depicts with the detail demanded by his subject—the experiencing mind—is Woolsey's penumbra.

But it is in episode 14, "Oxen of the Sun," that Joyce takes another major step forward in terms of the considerations under discussion here. I mentioned earlier that on Joyce's view of the mind the questions of our relation to language, of the constitutive power of language, and of the nature of perceptual experience are not at bottom separable. This episode represents a sustained argument of that

---

23. See Ludwig Wittgenstein, *Philosophical Investigations*, revised 4th edition, ed. P. M. S. Hacker and Joachim Schulte, trans. G. E. M. Anscombe, P. M. S. Hacker, and Joachim Schulte (Malden, MA: Wiley-Blackwell, 2009), sections 243–309 (there are many more sections relevant to this matter).

point. The episode is famous as a grand parodic tour of major style periods of literature from the ancient world to the present, a tour de force of literary mastery that within a given style period stands in the zone between illustration and parody. It is that—but I want to suggest not by any means only that. Rightly understood, the progression of literary styles (the critical tradition on this episode has identified Latinate sturdy elegance, the King James Bible, Bunyan, Pepys, Sterne, Edward Gibbon, and Dickens, among others, leading right up to Dublin street talk to a verbal style bordering for outsiders on the incomprehensible) to which Joyce gives voice here shows the distinctive ways, case by case, that the language we speak—Wittgenstein's form of life—is so interwoven with our perception of the world around us and in which we live that the very idea of a separation of language from world becomes something between very odd and unintelligible. And it is the spectatorial distance on language brought in by parody that makes this all the more visible. One can connect the dots, here listed as (a) through (l), of the following (essentially describing a group of friends drinking, with Leopold joining them) to get a sense of Joyce's trajectory:

(a) Therefore, everyman, look to that last end that is thy death and the dust that gripeth on every man that is born of woman for as he came naked forth from his mother's womb so naked shall he wend him at the last for to go as he came. (379–80)

(b) And the learning knight let pour for childe Leopold a draught and halp thereto the while all they that were there drank every each. (381)

(c) Then spoke young Stephen orgulous of mother Church that would cast him out of her bosom. (383)

(d) Master Lenehan at this made return that he had heard of those nefarious deeds and how, as he heard hereof counted, he had besmirched the lily virtue of a confiding female. (386)

(e) A black crack of noise in the street here, alack, bawled, back. Loud on left Thor thundered: in anger awful the hammer-hurler. (388)

(f) He had been off as many times as a cat has lives and back again with naked pockets. (392)

(g) Our worthy acquaintance, Mr Malachi Mulligan, now appeared in the doorway. (395)

(h) Valuing himself not a little upon his elegance, being indeed a proper man of his person. (396)

(i) Beneficent Disseminator of blessings to all Thy creatures, how great and universal must be that sweetest of Thy tyrannies which can hold in thrall the free and the bond, the simple swain and the polished coxcomb. (398)

(j) Demme, does not Doctor O'Gargle chuck the nuns there under the chin. (399)

(k) But Malachias' tale began to freeze them with horror. He conjured up the scene before them. The secret panel beside the chimney slid back and in the recess appeared . . . Haines! Which of us did not feel his flesh creep? (405)

(l) Hurroo! Collar the leather, youngun. Roun wi the nappy. Here, Jock braw Heilentman's your barleybree. Lang may your lum reek and your kailpot boil! (418)

Each of these brief passages—each like reading two pages of a book—conveys the sense of the world in which those words have a life, and the minds-in-language perceiving that world in a relationally enmeshed way. To say that these are merely different ways of "translating" the experiences described here is to miss the point. One would suggest such a thing, one would invoke the concept of translation, when in the grip of the picture of language as a mere transducer or outward describer of pre-linguistic inward experience—precisely the picture that Joyce's vastly richer conception of language-in-the-mind supplants. But on this point: how so, precisely?

SELF AND SENSIBILITY

One might be tempted at this point to (erroneously) claim that the foregoing considerations concerning the constitutive and evocative power of language imply an extreme form of linguistic relativism, in which, to put it in its most succinct form, saying so makes it so. This would in essence be a nominalist form of relativism, in that the inseparability thesis—that language and linguistic thought are from the instantaneous first moment of perception always already inside that perceptual experience and constitutive of it—would seem to imply that any moment of (humanely rich) perception is as good, as real, as true, as any other. And this view would be tempting precisely because it would seem to be the model, the picture, that would give the richness of human experience and the power of language in constituting that experience the respect they deserve. And so this gives rise to a now-pressing question: If our language inflects experience in the way Joyce has intricately explored, and if it inculcates a way of seeing, a way of describing, a way of layered and complex perceiving in its users, then what are the constraints that would prevent this extreme form of nominalistic relativism? However seemingly (actually mis-leadingly) attractive, we nevertheless sense that we cannot let our respect for perceptual richness cost us the fundamental epistemological distinction between the real and the unreal, or indeed between truth and falsity. It is thus an ingenious philosophico-literary move for Joyce to place the experience of hallucination next (in episode 15, "Circe"), and to place us as readers—now philosophical readers all—into an environment, a complex narrative atmosphere, in which we as readers have to sort out the difference between appearance and reality within that fictional world.

In the course of visiting a brothel, Bloom and Stephen descend into mental states in which their psychically catalogued past transgressions, their fears, their regrets, their losses, and their sexual fantasies take form as varying manifestations before them. Dedalus sees the corpse of his mother rise up to urge him to repent and in a fevered state dashes out; Bloom follows Stephen out of the brothel and extricates him from a quarrel he gets into with soldiers; shortly thereafter outside the brothel Bloom has a vision of his deceased son, Rudy. This episode is a study of the kinds of visions and hallucinations that can overtake one's perceptual field when the mental side of perception takes full control. Blocking out (what we call) the external entirely, this mode of perception, Joyce is showing, is not truly that: it is all projection, no perception. And so—this itself is a remarkable philosophical achievement—Joyce here locates and richly illustrates the opposite pole of a continuum that has Lockean simple sensation at the other extreme. One's location on this continuum in ordinary or undisturbed perception is a matter of degree and circumstance: Joyce has already shown that perception invariably has the resonances, the associations, the connotations, the filters, the connections, the layered combinations of all of these, and everything else discussed earlier. Which are activated in any perceptual moment will, as he has also shown, be a matter of context, sensibility, situation, mood, degree of reflectiveness, and the inflections of memory with the perception of similarities. The extreme relativist's mistake—Joyce is blocking the way into this mistake here—is to believe that because perception is not containable at the Lockean end then it must be contained at the antithesis, at the opposite polemical extreme.

And indeed Joyce shows how subtly different locations on this continuum (in episode 17, "Ithaca") bring out or foreground different aspects of a situation in which two people are present but are, for that difference of location, seeing subtly different things. Bloom, the elder person, and Dedalus, the younger person, discuss a range of issues, and throughout this absorbing episode Joyce, somewhat like gradually increasing the power of a microscope, shows the importance of their experience, their beliefs, and their past for the way they perceive even the most minute things around them. Joyce's technique here is again to reflect the way this tends to work in life. He begins by articulating things they have in common:

> Did Bloom discover common factors of similarity between their respective like and unlike reactions to experience?
> Both were sensitive to artistic impressions musical in preference to plastic or pictorial. Both preferred a continental to an insular manner of life, a cisatlantic to a transatlantic place of residence. Both indurated by early domestic training and an inherited tenacity of heterodox resistance professed their disbelief in many orthodox religious, national, social and ethical doctrines. Both admitted the alternately stimulating and obtunding influence of heterosexual magnetism. (650)

And then Joyce proceeds into first larger, and then increasingly subtle, differences that separate them as he moves outward to increasingly distant peripheries from this center of agreement. They disagree on "the eternal affirmation of the spirit of man in literature" (650). Later, in finer detail, while Bloom perceives a set of events (Bloom climbing over railings and dropping to the basement level to gain entry to his house), "What discrete succession of images did Stephen meanwhile perceive?" (653), followed by an increasingly close description of his perceptual content. But intermingled throughout, Joyce incorporates answers to such questions as "Of what similar apparitions did Stephen think?" (654, the question being occasioned by the ongoing exchange). And then, "What did Bloom see on the [kitchen] range?"

(654), where this question leads to a presentation of (a) what he did, (b) what he thought, (c) what he did because of what he thought, and (d) what he thought because of what he did. The two compare formative educational experience, calculating what would have happened if each had had the experience of the other (these imaginary hybrid personae being named "Stoom" and "Blephen" (666). Differences and similarities within those differences further weave the two together, where their understanding of subtle difference itself engenders further closeness. All of this is relationally intertwining and is also, of course, psychologically ethically mimetic.

But one further aspect of the exchange in this episode is particularly important to Joyce's portrayal of our mental lives. We see by the end of this episode that an interesting symmetry of the understanding of one mind by another has emerged: the longer past is made palpably present to Stephen by Bloom, just as the future, the coming generation, is made palpably real to Bloom by Stephen. In a strictly empirical sense it is plainly evident that neither the past nor the future are here to be perceived. Yet they are, very clearly, made present and thus perceived by each of them. One could say: in this exchange Stephen newly sees the past in the present, while Bloom newly sees the future in his present. And in Rylean terms, they show their understanding by what they are able to articulate, and how they discern the implications of, what they newly perceive.

It was early in the novel (episode 2) that Stephen uttered another famous line from the book: "History is a nightmare from which I am trying to awake." These are of course words that carry meaning in multiple directions simultaneously, complexly in layers and multiply describing. They were spoken and thought in his moment, but the reach of their significance, as one imagines he in that moment understood, is not contained within that moment.

As we have seen throughout this discussion, Stephen is both in the world he perceives and yet trying to transcend the constraining circumstances of his upbringing. He is in a sense both in the world he perceives and yet comparing it to a higher world he imagines. If he perceives his present in that bifocal way so that he seeks avenues for his own transcendence, what does he perceive? He perceives his world—a world not reducible to what the camera lens sees, not reducible to what the strict empiricist picture accommodates. His possible futures are always present.[24] And symmetrically the older Bloom, within his distinctive and—like all of us—unique sensibility, moves through his world with his pasts (plural because describable, connectable, in so many different ways) always present. His memory and the role it plays is the memory that Malcolm described.

Reductive proposals in philosophical psychology have been developed to explain at a most basic level what human action in a field of perception is: a negotiation between the physical environment, the physical-mechanistic human body, and somatic voluntary action. An extension of this view suggests that consciousness can be attributed to any entity that is able to function in a circumscribed physical environment, successfully negotiating survival-enhancing movement among physical objects. Robots can do that—they "see" with the "eyes" of a camera. But as Joyce has shown, the very idea of a basic action, beneath all the complexities of psychological life and over which those complexities are only contingently added after the fact, should be held in rather deep suspicion. Such reductive pictures—manifestations of a misapplied scientific model where that model is itself oversimplified—systematically omit everything that Joyce has shown to be of genuine human interest and everything true of human experience.

---

24. R. P. Blackmur captures this aspect of continual self-transformation, continual self-negotiation, continual new and changing self-assertion as Joyce depicts it in one (perhaps too compressed) sentence: "It is the self struggling with the self to find out the self devours the self through each form it takes" (*Eleven Essays in the European Novel*, 39).

Woolsey saw this, and it changed the possibilities of our cultural representations of ourselves. Woolf saw into the difficulty of describing the human mind; Malcolm saw how to avoid making too simple a picture of memory; and Ryle saw how to set a course for accurately characterizing self-knowledge. But also recall: it was Aristotle who observed that we humans naturally take pleasure in recognizing the representational content of a depiction. In seeing the accuracy and mimetic fidelity of Joyce's brushwork, we recognize ourselves—we are all, if in our unique and unrepeatable ways, Blooms of our own; we are all, if in our uniquely idiosyncratic perceptual styles, inflecting memories, and patterns of association, Dedaluses of our own. P. F. Strawson once called attention to what in these waters still seems fundamental: "In order to *be* a person, one must see oneself and others *as* persons."[25] That distinctive and irreducible mode of seeing—to see ourselves and others *as persons* in all that this entails—is not a simple matter. And as Woolf said, its accurate description presents a profound challenge. But a literary portraitist of consciousness has been here since the advent of modernism to show us how to meet it.[26]

BIBLIOGRAPHY

Barlow, Richard. *The Celtic Unconscious: Joyce and Scottish Culture.* Notre Dame, IN: University of Notre Dame Press, 2017.

Blackmur, R. P. *Eleven Essays in the European Novel.* New York: Harcourt, Brace, and World, 1964.

Currie, Greg, Matthew Kieran, Aaron Meskin, and Jon Robson, eds. *Aesthetics and the Sciences of Mind.* Oxford: Oxford University Press, 2014.

Eide, Marian. *Ethical Joyce.* Cambridge, UK: Cambridge University Press, 2002.

25. P. F. Strawson, "The First Person—and Others," in Cassam, ed., *Self-Knowledge*, 214.
26. Special thanks to Philip Kitcher for an extraordinarily insightful and helpful reading of an earlier version of this chapter.

Hagberg, Garry L. *Describing Ourselves: Wittgenstein and Autobiographical Consciousness.* Oxford: Oxford University Press, 2008.

Hagberg, Garry L. *Meaning and Interpretation: Wittgenstein, Henry James, and Literary Knowledge.* Ithaca, NY: Cornell University Press, (1994) 2018.

Hagberg, Garry L. "Wittgenstein, Verbal Creativity, and the Expansion of Artistic Style." In S. Greve and J. Macha, eds., *Wittgenstein and the Creativity of Language.* London: Palgrave, 2015, 141–76.

Joyce, James. *Ulysses.* New York: Random House/Modern Library, (1914) 1961.

Malcolm, Norman. *Knowledge and Certainty: Essays and Lectures.* Upper Saddle River, NJ: Prentice Hall, 1963.

Murdoch, Iris. "Against Dryness: A Polemical Sketch." *Encounter* XVI (1961): 16–20.

Parker David. *The Self in Moral Space: Life Narrative and the Good.* Ithaca, NY: Cornell University Press, 2007.

Quigley, Megan. *Modernist Fiction and Vagueness: Philosophy, Form, and Language.* Cambridge, UK: Cambridge University Press, 2015.

Ryle, Gilbert. *Aspects of Mind.* Ed. Rene Meyer. Oxford: Blackwell, 1993.

Ryle, Gilbert. "Self-Knowledge." In Quassim Cassam, ed., *Self-Knowledge.* Oxford: Oxford University Press, 1994, 19–42.

Strawson, P. F. "The First Person—and Others." In Quassim Cassam, ed., *Self-Knowledge.* Oxford: Oxford University Press, 1994.

Wittgenstein, Ludwig. *The Blue and Brown Books.* Oxford: Blackwell, 1958.

Wittgenstein, Ludwig. *Philosophical Investigations.* Revised 4th edition. Ed. P. M. S. Hacker and Joachim Schulte. Trans. G. E. M. Anscombe, P. M. S. Hacker, and Joachim Schulte. Malden, MA: Wiley-Blackwell, 2009.

Chapter 3

Feeling *Ulysses*

An Address to the Cyclopean Reader

VICKI MAHAFFEY AND WENDY J. TRURAN

Leopold Bloom, the unlikely hero of *Ulysses*, proclaims in the "Circe" episode of *Ulysses* that he is an "[e]xperienced hand" able to "make a true black knot" (15: 2805–7). Though "true black knot" suggests a secure bond, like all knots it has the potential to be untied and re-knotted, offering a metaphor for Joyce's view of life as processual and uncertain. Bloom's hand synecdochically stands in for some of his best qualities, namely, his ability to weave together disparate strands (of thought, religion, politics, intimate feeling, and so on) to form a complicated, if contingent, whole. This knotting ability metaphorically illustrates Bloom's capacity to engage dynamically with the complexities of life; he must think and feel at the same time to alternately connect and unravel strands of experience.

As a part of the body, the hand also registers the impact, the touch, of the everyday. Readers learn in "Circe" that Bloom is ambidextrous, but according to his "doctor" Buck Mulligan, that ambidexterity is latent (15: 1780). Bloom's ability to be even-handed,

Joyce's Ulysses. Philip Kitcher, Oxford University Press (2020). © Oxford University Press.
DOI: 10.1093/oso/9780190842260.001.0001

or fair, is demonstrated throughout *Ulysses*; however, the fact that his talent is "latent" (or under-developed) also hints at one of the problems that *Ulysses* confronts: evenhandedness must be cultivated. It is easier to rely on one dominant hand than to discipline oneself to use both equally; similarly, it is easier to adopt a single perspective than to consider something from different angles. The danger of doing what seems easiest and most natural instead of accepting the discipline to be even-handed, to see from more than one perspective, and to supplement sight with input from the other senses is what we are calling (with nods to both Homer and Joyce) Cyclopean.

In our essay we consider the rewards of approaching the book as an affective text: one that moves us and that we move, one that we encounter with our living bodies. To "feel *Ulysses*," rather than merely cast one's eyes over it, is to engage the nexus of the senses together with the emotions in the act of reading, and the invitation to encounter a book this way can be uncomfortable. *Ulysses*, however, rewards readers who *feel* with, through, and about bodies— textual and their own.[1] This suggestion comes not only from over thirty-five years of experience teaching and writing about Joyce and modernism (Mahaffey) and from recent scholarship at the intersection of affect and modernist studies (Truran) but also from a

---

1. Readers tend to forget their own bodies (along with their own memories) in the act of imaginative engagement; *Ulysses* provides incentives to remember. Such bodily awareness on the part of the reader is stimulated when the material is erotic or frightening, which helps to explain why *Ulysses* is so scandalously assertive in its descriptions of sexuality (especially in "Nausicaa," "Circe," and "Penelope") and defecation (in "Calypso"). Bloom and Molly model the body's reactions to reading. When Bloom picks up the post in "Calypso" and sees a letter for "Mrs Marion Bloom" that he knows is from Blazes Boylan, "[h]is quickened heart slow slowed at once" (4: 244). Later, when he sees Boylan's straw hat, tan shoes, and "turnedup trousers" from a distance, "[h]is heart quopped softly" (8: 1168–9).

careful reading of Joyce's *own* pedagogical methods. Joyce's literature resists the Cyclopean reader's preference for closed (as opposed to close) readings. A *closed* reading arises from a desire to "see" and to "know" the text (and implicitly the world at large) in a primarily intellectual, and therefore disembodied, way. We offer, in place of a philosophical approach to Joyce, a *literary* approach to philosophy. Our main interlocutors emerge from feminist, queer, and literary studies and are contributing to the developing interdisciplinary field of affect theory.[2] However, these theorists, including Lauren Berlant, Sara Ahmed, and Eve Kosofsky Sedgwick, engage closely with philosophy, taking up questions of identity, subjectivity, phenomenology, and epistemology.[3] We trust, however, that our reading demonstrates the affordances of literary analysis in approaching Joyce and the question "How to live?" that is at the center of this collection.

2. Reading is a sensorial experience affected by forces of encounter, although readers don't always consciously experience it that way. Affect theory provides a useful way of reconceiving the reading self as porous, responsive, and part of an ever-unfolding process of being in relation with the world. Affects are forces of modification; to be affected is to be changed or moved in some way by the impact of an encounter with something, whether a subject, an object, an idea, or an emotion.

3. See Lauren Berlant, *Cruel Optimism* (Durham, NC: Duke University Press, 2011); Sara Ahmed, *The Promise of Happiness* (Durham, NC: Duke University Press, 2010), *Queer Phenomenology: Orientations, Objects, Others* (Durham, NC: Duke University Press, 2006), *The Cultural Politics of Emotion* (Routledge, 2004); Eve Kosofsky Sedgwick, *Touching Feeling: Affect, Pedagogy, Performativity* (Durham, NC: Duke University Press, 2003).

In the philosophical tradition, we align ourselves not with the empiricism and rationalism of seventeenth- and eighteenth-century European philosophy, but with the way the American transcendentalists (especially Emerson) took up the challenge of Goethe to value authentic experience--not abstractly, but as something that is shared with others and which points beyond itself. Both Nietzsche and William James are part of this lineage. See John Kaag and Martin Clancy. "Can Transcendence Be Taught?," *Chronicle of Higher Education*, October 7, 2016, https://www.chronicle.com/article/Can-Transcendence-Be-Taught-/237994 (accessed July 24, 2019).

In this essay, we challenge "scopic dominance" in approaches to reading *Ulysses*—an over-reliance upon the visual at the expense of other senses. We are interested in what happens when the distance between seer and seen is collapsed, and in the mechanisms that collapse it. We focus on the sense modalities of sight and touch as illustrative of Joyce's approach to senses, perception, and epistemological questions more broadly.[4] James Joyce was, as a writer, invested not in sensorial dominance but in "ambidexterity"—the encompassing capacity that his hero Leopold Bloom latently possesses. Throughout his later writing Joyce implicitly advocates for a sensual synesthesia. Although most people rely heavily on the sense of sight, he reminds readers (in "Cyclops" especially) that to perceive an object accurately, one needs to adopt more than one perspective, to use more than one "eye."[5] His semi-autobiographical character, Stephen, is more attuned to sound than sight. In "Proteus," he thinks, "Rhythm begins, you see. I hear" (3: 23). And earlier, in *A Portrait of the Artist as a Young Man*, he asks himself whether, being "weak of sight," he loved "the rhythmic rise and fall of words better than their associations of legend and color" (IV: 696–8). In *Finnegans Wake*, the sight-dominant Shaun asks the hearing-dominant Shem, "Do you hear what I'm seeing?" (193: 10) because Shem and Shaun are defined by their preference for sound and sight, respectively.[6] In contrast, women in both *Ulysses* and *Finnegans Wake* are most closely associated with touch or feeling. "First we feel. Then we fall" (627: 11), Anna Livia Plurabelle reflects about herself and her daughter near

---

4. For valuable discussions of touch and blindness that have informed our thinking, see Mark Paterson, *Seeing with the Hands: Blindness, Vision, and Touch after Descartes* (Edinburgh: Edinburgh University Press, 2016), as well as his earlier book, *The Senses of Touch: Haptics, Affects, and Technologies* (London: Bloomsbury, 2007).
5. See Kitcher on Joyce's perspectivism in chapter 6 of this volume.
6. This is partly a response to Wyndham Lewis' attack on Joyce's *Ulysses* in *Time and Western Man* (1927), in which Lewis opposed his own reliance on the visual to Joyce's (allegedly inferior) obsession with the aural.

the end of *Finnegans Wake*. Joyce seems to invest value not in any one sense, but in the ability to develop and deploy all five in the effort to demonstrate how the "glowing sensible world" and "an inner world of individual emotions" are never really separate, and both are, in fact, co-constituted by "a lucid supple periodic prose" (*Portrait*, IV: 699–703). In order to read *Ulysses* with maximum effect, a reader is challenged to do what no one character manages to achieve: to live fully and intensely with their "creatureliness," meaning to fully acknowledge and embrace "the immanence of human finitude." Stimulated by the sight and sound and touch of the words on the page, the reader must attune to their own body (including feelings, emotions, sensations, ideas, judgments, intuitions) while remembering the inevitable partiality of their attunement to the textual and corporeal body.

Firstly, applying a critical method important in *Ulysses*, we use Shakespeare to illustrate a paradoxical transition in Joyce from sighted "blindness" to the feeling that comes from unsighted touch. In the "Scylla and Charybdis" episode of *Ulysses*, Stephen recalls "Lir's loneliest daughter," Cordelia (9: 314).[7] The connection to Cordelia is significant as it points to the effects of the "enlightened vision" of the powerful (here Lear) on those who feel (Cordelia). Those who rely on the power afforded through scopic dominance cannot identify those who really care about them, but the play follows Lear and his double, Gloucester, as they lose the power and vision that blind them to compassion and even love, teaching them the beauty of audient touch, with

---

7. Although the allusion to Shakespeare's *King Lear* is routed through a line from the song "Silent, O Moyle" (about the Irish Poseidon figure, Manannán McLir), Stephen is identifying himself with the isolation of both Fionnuala and Cordelia (he has not been invited to submit poems to George Russell's anthology of younger poets).

its attendant closeness to others. In the fourth act of *King Lear,* a mad Lear, dressed in wildflowers, commands blind Gloucester, "Read thou this challenge." Gloucester replies, "What, with the case [sockets] of eyes?" Lear reminds him he can still see "how this world goes," to which Gloucester replies, "I see it feelingly" (Act IV, scene 6). His experience of loss has taught Gloucester to see, to read, differently, with his heart and ears (Lear advises him, "Look with thine ears"). Lear, too, once suffered from the ease with which he "read" the world. He lacked empathy and imagination, a lack that was masked and enabled by his kingly power, but his capacity for oversight is replaced by powerful feeling after he relinquishes his kingdom and has become vulnerable; only then is he open to being touched by others. It is through loss—of his kingdom and his daughters—that Lear is able to see (and feel) the truth about his family. The real lack, in *King Lear,* the kind that is most destructive, is not the inability to see, but rather an inability to feel, which most strongly afflicts the powerful, and those who rely on a single visual point of view. Sight, as in much feminist and psychoanalytic criticism, is closely associated with power or potency, but that power is often attended by "blind" callousness. It is only after Gloucester and Lear lose the potency associated with sight and oversight, respectively (remember the persistent metaphorical connection between eyeballs and testicles), that they find themselves able to "see feelingly." In Lear's case, the intensity of the newly discovered feelings associated with self-revelation drives him mad; he is, in the colloquial Irish sense, "touched"—his wits are disarrayed. To "see feelingly," in Gloucester's sense, is thus to reorient oneself to the set of forces and relations that enable encounters between text and reader, reader and world.

THE CYCLOPEAN READER AND
SCOPIC DOMINANCE

Ulysses is a text committed to representing and celebrating corporeality and thus invites readers to pay attention to all their senses as they read, but sight and sound often dominate critical discussions.[8] Sara Danius suggests that sound and vision are primary senses to modernist aesthetics, and that "sight and hearing define the sensory universe of *Ulysses*."[9] Martin Jay, in his history of visuality, emphasizes how deeply embedded the visual is in language and cultural and social practices, leading to what he calls the "ocularcentrism" of Western cultures and languages.[10] Yet a half-blind writer, James Joyce, designed a book that cannot be fully appreciated or understood with the eyes alone. Too great a reliance on vision makes readers into what Homer called "Cyclopes"—one-eyed giants who view other beings as little more than food for their own consumption. The problem with the Cyclopes, as we see in the "Cyclops" episode of *Ulysses*, is (to quote the Christian gospels) that they can see the mote in the other person's eye but not the beam in their own.[11] The Cyclopean barfly narrator in Joyce's episode betrays himself as lacking self-awareness in just this

---

8. Scholars have also begun to explore smell in Joyce, and two recent papers have taken up Teresa Brennan's idea of the transmission of affect and smell, see Teresa Brennan, *The Transmission of Affect* (Ithaca, NY: Cornell University Press, 2004); Anne Fogarty, "'The Odour of Ashpits and Old Weeds and Offal': The Transmission of Affects in *Dubliners*," in *James Joyce: The Recirculation of Realism*, ed. Franca Ruggieri and Enrico Terrinoni (Edizioni Q, 2014) and Laura Frost's "James Joyce and the Scent of Modernity," in *The Problem with Pleasure: Modernism and Its Discontents* (New York: Columbia University Press, 2013).

9. Sara Danius, *The Senses of Modernism: Technology, Perception, and Aesthetics.* (Ithaca, NY: Cornell University Press, 2002),152. The scholarship on the importance of vision and sound in Joyce's work is extensive and varied and cannot be exhaustively listed here. Recent work includes Derek Attridge, "Joyce's Noises," *Oral Tradition* 24, no. 2 (2009): 471–84.

10. Martin Jay, *Downcast Eyes: The Denigration of Vision in Twentieth-Century French Thought.* (Berkeley: University of California Press, 1993), 3.

11. Taken from Matthew 7:3–5, "And why beholdest thou the mote that is in thy brother's eye, but considerest not the beam that is in thine own eye?"

way when he complains about the chimney sweep that "near drove his gear into my eye" (12: 3). Not only does he lack self-awareness; he also sees without depth, which is something that is sacrificed when two eyes (the ability to maintain a bodymind open to more than one perspective) are replaced with one, such as a dogmatic commitment to a single ideology, such as Catholicism or Irish nationalism. The Cyclopes, children of the god Poseidon, illustrate the danger of an overreliance upon a mode of perception that lacks positional accuracy as well as self-reflexivity: the eye illuminates the limitations of everyone but the viewer herself, whose self-importance can become unconsciously engorged by that imbalance. In order to engage with objects (whether phenomenal or textual) more fully, one must learn to distrust the illusion of superior understanding offered by an overreliance upon uni-perspectival vision and to amplify data from the other senses: hearing, smell, taste, but especially touch.[12]

Touch is distinguished from other senses in the essential role it plays in animal life, as Jacques Derrida (drawing on Aristotle) explains: "Touch may well exist apart from other senses, but Aristotle stresses that without it, no other sense would exist . . . all animals possess this sense."[13] Touch is fundamental to our experience of the world and our awareness of our relationships both in it and to it. Mark Paterson summarizes the complexity of touch in relation to vision:

12. Touch is a sense that has been largely overlooked in relation to modernism. A notable exception to this is Abbie Garrington's *Haptic Modernism: Touch and the Tactile in Modernist Writing* (Edinburgh: Edinburgh University Press, 2013). Garrington's extensive exploration of the haptic in modernism does not, however, focus on the metaphorical link between touch and feeling, as we are attempting to do here.

13. Jacques Derrida, *On Touching—Jean-Luc Nancy*, (Stanford, CA: Stanford University Press, 2005), 24. Christopher P. Long, in his discussion of the status of touch in Aristotle's *De Anima*, points out that in Aristotle's hierarchy of the senses, "the tongue, organ of taste, is also, as flesh, the medium of touch." "On Touch and Life in the *De Anima*," in *Phenomenology and the Metaphysics of Sight*, ed. Antonio Cimino and Pavlos Kontos, (Lieden: Brill, 2015), 86.

[T]ouch, like vision, articulates an equally rich, complex world, a world of movement and exploration, of non-verbal social communication. It is a carnal world, with its pleasures of feeling and being felt, of tasting and touching the textures of flesh and food. And equally it is a profound world of philosophical verification, of the communication of presence and empathy with others, of the co-implication of body, flesh and world.[14]

In Joyce's depiction of the everyday lives of people, he makes manifest the sensations, unconscious drives, affective forces, and emotions that constitute the thinking-feeling realities of his characters. Implicit in Joyce's depiction of touch is the claim that emotions are necessary and central to sociality: central to communal living. Through his emotional and imaginative experiences throughout the day, Bloom articulates and enacts a model of sociality that he manifests through the emotional labor of care—demonstrated by Bloom's concern for Mina Purefoy and his care of Stephen. The reader is invited to contemplate or possibly adopt this care-ful sociality.

The self-protective and self-isolating effects of an ocularcentric system are magnified through the practice of a voyeuristic (or self-erasing) manner of reading—a physically and emotionally distanced engagement that permits the pleasure (and frustrations) of visual encounter without either party experiencing risk or the possibility of being changed.[15] This distance (between seer and seen) is what makes visuality, in Maren Tova Linett's judgment, "an inadequate mode for thinking and knowing."[16] The seeing self has an advantage due to the

14. Paterson, *The Senses of Touch*, 2.
15. Bloom's response to watching Gerty MacDowell in "Nausicaa" is pleasurable to the point of orgasm, but at the end of the voyeuristic episode the two are still detached from one another and unchanged by the fantasy encounter.
16. Maren Tova Linett, *Bodies of Modernism: Physical Disability in Transatlantic Modernist Literature* (Ann Arbor, MI: University of Michigan Press, 2017), 5. She also points out

self-protective safety of being able to see without necessarily being seen. No such protection is possible with touch, because to touch is also to *be* touched. Physical touch has an unavoidable reciprocity to it, and that physical connection has the potential to trigger an emotional bond (or, in the case of violence, rupture) that may develop and deepen over time. In *Ulysses*, we see two men whose focus on what they see around them diverts their attention from how they themselves contribute to the situations that hurt them. On this particular day, however, they are in the process of learning (in the case of Stephen) or recapturing (in the case of Bloom) greater mutuality of feeling by helping themselves recognize and take responsibility for their own inadequacies. Over the course of a day, these characters encounter and (imperfectly) recognize their own vulnerability through a series of virtual "contacts" with others, both living and dead. The vulnerability that afflicts them most acutely concerns their respective relations with a woman: Stephen's mother and Bloom's wife.

Richie Goulding and Bloom provide one example of how to read feelingly when they listen to Simon Dedalus perform "M'appari" in the "Sirens" episode. Simon has just sung the first line, "When first I saw that form endearing," the words of which are woven through the description to follow: "Braintipped, cheek touched with flame, they listened feeling that flow endearing flow over skin limbs human heart soul spine" (11: 668–9). Simon sings the next line, "*Sorrow from me seemed to depart*," and the narrator elaborates, "Through the hush of air a voice sang to them, low . . . touching their still ears with words, still hearts of their each his remembered lives. Good, good to hear: sorrow from them each seemed to from both depart when first they heard" (11: 674–8, italics in original). The song coming from the singer's body transmits a powerful affect, signaled

---

that one of the key questions for Woolf, and modernism more broadly, was "whether one can express in language what the body feels" (9).

by flushed cheeks and goosebumps in the listeners. The music acts as a medium that "touches" the listeners' hearts by awakening their own memories. Touch is not localized like hearing but is rather distributed across "skin limbs heart soul spine." With ears, hearts, and personal memories touched, they feel (individually and collectively) released from sorrow along with the singer. One unexpected effect of such heightened listening-feeling is that it momentarily dissolves the boundaries between individuals. Not only do the listeners meld together—"look, form, word charmed him Gould Lidwell, won Pat Bloom's heart" (11: 720), but character and performer and listener blend too: Simon (the singer) and Lionel (the character) and Bloom (the listener) become "Siopold" (11: 752): Simon, Lionel, Leopold. This temporary union reflects the nature of touch, a connection that muddles the distinction between inside and outside, subject and object, toucher and touched. All, like touch, are active and passive, forming something collective that goes beyond experience that is merely individual.

The writer most famous for exploring the linkage between perception and memory is, of course, Marcel Proust. In *Remembrance of Things Past,* the taste of a madeleine dipped in tea opens up a space-time wormhole of involuntary childhood memories.[17] *Ulysses* is built around a similar but also distinctively different moment linking sense-perception with memory: when Bloom sips a glass of burgundy in Davy Byrne's he experiences the taste as the "secret touch" of the "sun's heat," a touch "telling me memory." Joyce uses metaphors that accent the modality of touch—heat/coolness, softness, gentle

---

17. Sara Danius in *The Senses of Modernism* has an interesting reading of Proust that differentiates between "the human eye" and the "cinematic eye." She suggests that when Proust interacts with his beloved grandmother he sees her with the "human eye" and his vision is filtered through his love for her. In contrast, when Proust recalls seeing his grandmother without her knowing he is there, he sees her without sentiment or feeling, and thus she is shriven, old, and ugly; "the camera eye is a relentless conveyor of truth" (Danius 15).

pressure—which stresses how intimate and immediate the memory is to Bloom while at the same time conveying the sensuality of the moment to the reader. Bloom recalls in his imagination the beautiful daring of Molly's intimate touch: "Coolsoft with ointments her hand touched me, caressed: her eyes upon me did not turn away." The mutuality of their kiss—"she kissed me. I was kissed"—is reflected in the gaze uniting the young lovers. Their physical intimacy permits a direct regard that Bloom finds wonderful ("O wonder") and lifegiving (8: 897–918). The touch that binds Molly and Leopold is reciprocal to an unusual degree, which may help to explain why the memory recurs throughout the book as a powerful touchstone for both of them.

Unlike that of the narrator in Proust's novel, the memory of touching on the Hill of Howth is not a childhood memory, but an erotic and sexual milestone. It is stimulated by Bloom's taste of wine, but it is narratively framed by something Bloom sees and hears: two flies stuck on the pane, buzzing. Presumably they are stuck together, in an insect fuck with overtones of helplessness licensed by the rhyme with "stuck." The contrast between two people who are stuck together after sixteen years of marriage and two people who voluntarily and joyfully exchange different kinds of seed is a poignant one. The memory does not explicitly record an ejaculation of semen (or seed) from Bloom, but it does linger on an anticipation of that moment in which Molly is the inseminator, putting into Bloom's mouth "the seedcake, warm and chewed" (8: 907). One early magical moment of willing and reciprocal bodily gifts, in contrast with a chronic state of helpless proximity, is summed up when Bloom looks back at the two flies: "Me. And me now" (8: 917). The love between Molly and Leopold is characterized by both kinds of touch (mutual and passionate, habitual and inert), combining nostalgic ecstasy with humorous incongruity.

As the Hill of Howth episode demonstrates, touch has no privileged organ. Unlike the auditory system, whose primary organ is the ear, feeling involves entire bodies: "we touch using our skin, muscles, joints, and we can touch using nearly every surface along the whole body."[18] Joyce uses the notion of touch in multiple ways, drawing on a long philosophical tradition that begins with Aristotle. He signals the senses via affect, "cheek touched with flame" (11: 668); sex and desire, "give us a touch, Poldy" (6: 90–1); greeting and acknowledgment, "He touched to fair miss Kennedy a rim of his slanted straw" (11: 346); sentiment, "A fresh torrent of tears burst from their lachrymal ducts and the vast concourse of people, touched to the inmost core, broke into heartrending sobs" (12: 652–4); and even secret communication, "*her forefinger giving to his palm the passtouch of secret monitor*" (15: 2011–2, italics in original). To feel the text, to read feelingly, is not merely to think about touch, but also to be touched, to be "read"; to join *with* the text in an experience of mutual relation. "Mutual" is taken from the Latin *mutuus* meaning "done in exchange," and, significantly, *mutuus* is from the Aryan root *mei* meaning "to change, go, move." It is the reciprocity of reading and being read—touching and touched—that students often instinctively refuse, and that Bloom, at least, usefully models.[19] To *feel Ulysses* is to draw on a now obsolete meaning of mutuality, which is to be *responsive*, thus, to enter into a relationship with the text—to touch it and be moved or changed by it.

18. Matthew Fulkerson, "Touch," in *The Stanford Encyclopedia of Philosophy,* https://plato.stanford.edu/archives/spr2016/entries/touch n.p. There is an abundance of touch-specific language that captures different elements of how touch is registered. For example, "cutaneous" refers to a brush upon the skin; "haptic" is touch experienced through the somatic senses. Touch is also registered through movement and awareness of this movement (kinaesthesis) and through an awareness of bodily position (proprioception).

19. Joyce's exploration of the mutuality of touch does not necessarily mean equality or reciprocity of the same kind or intensity of feeling. Consensual and knowing touch might be empowering, but to be touched is not necessarily reciprocal or positive.

(UN)TOUCHABLE FEELINGS—STEPHEN

Stephen's development from *A Portrait of the Artist as a Young Man* to *Ulysses*, stimulated and haunted by grief and guilt, exemplifies a transition-in-progress from the intellectualized thinking and sexual feeling of the young to a greater awareness of the complex multi-modal affect that becomes possible, at least, with maturity. At the end of *Portrait*, Stephen's mother implicitly characterizes him as "heart-less," or unfeeling, when she says she prays he will discover what the heart is and what it feels. Stephen's perspective is somewhat differ-ent: he sees his "heartlessness" as a necessary armor that protects him from the squalor and dysfunction all around him. At the beginning of chapter 5, he is dominated by feelings of anger, loathing, and bitter-ness; he describes his heart as "bitten" by the voices he hears around him, and he comforts himself by summoning to his mind the words of writers. His only relief is searching "for the essence of beauty" amid their "spectral words" (V: 87–8). As he admits to himself when reciting verses to his friend Davin, "the verses and cadences of oth-ers . . . were the veils of his own longing and dejection" (V: 232–4). He distances himself from his feelings by channeling them through the words of others.

Stephen's seeming heartlessness is a performance of his desire to be untouchable—to be autonomous and unmoved. His cold intellect and his aloof bearing signal not just his pride but also his sensitivity—he is "touchy" in the colloquial sense of overly sensitive. In *Portrait*, he is deeply affected by his relationships, but he rarely shows his feel-ings, and others don't experience him as capable of caring for them. Stephen's friend McCann calls him "an antisocial being, wrapped up in [himself]" (V: 125). Davin calls him "a terrible man" who is "always alone" (V: 983–4). To be alive, McCann and Davin imply, is to be interpersonally connected to others, and therefore to be responsible for their physical and emotional well-being. The famous scene in which Cranly asks Stephen if he loves his mother (Stephen replies that he doesn't know what those words mean [V: 2,346–7, 2349] and Cranly rejoins, "Has your mother had a happy life?" [V: 2361]) shows Cranly trying to reposition Stephen imaginatively, to make him see his family life through his mother's eyes, colored by *her* suffering (to which Stephen is contributing), to feel with and for her. Cranly follows this up with an actual touch that "thrills" Stephen. But Stephen's need to escape the bonds of feeling, an escapism he confuses with freedom, is at this point greater than his compassion.

Although he protects himself against empathizing with others, Stephen is nonetheless acutely aware of other people's loveless-ness. He regards it as a spiritual deadening that renders their service merely servile, mortifying their will and preventing their souls from expanding toward light and beauty, which, for Stephen, is a higher form of love. When he encounters the dean of studies building a fire, he reflects upon the irony of the fact that the man himself has no spark: his eyes are "pale" and "loveless," and in them "burned no spark of Ignatius' enthusiasm" (the name Ignatius *means* "fiery" [V: 437]). Even the legendary learning of the Jesuits "had not fired his soul" (V:439–49). Instead, he used "the shifts and lore and cun-ning of the world . . . without joy in their handling or hatred of that in them that was evil" (V: 440; 442–3). Despite being a priest, a voca-tion devoted to love, the dean of studies is without feeling: "for all this silent service it seemed he loved not at all the master and little, if at all, the ends he served" (V: 444–6). He has become a mere tool, "like a staff in an old man's hand, to be left in a corner, to be leaned on in the road at nightfall or in stress of weather, to lie with a lady's nosegay on a garden seat, to be raised in menace" (V: 447–50). The instrumentality used to define the dean accents the one-sidedness of his relations. There is no mutuality linking the hand and the staff. The dean has forgotten, or perhaps never realized, that his role as teacher should put him in relation to others, not reduce him to a mere instrument. Stephen implies that if the dean loved his life—the "master" or "the ends he served"—then he would not be reduced to a useless, discarded, or dangerous instrument.

When the topic shifts from the "useful art" of lighting a fire to another object that gives light—a lamp—once again the priest's limitations become clear: he can think only of a real lamp, whereas Stephen is using the lamp as a metaphor for the writings of Aristotle and Aquinas, which cast a light that allows him to work on a theory of aesthetics. Stephen feels his mind checked "by the priest's face which seemed like an unlit lamp"—once again, the priest's lack of feeling, linked to a lack of imagination, means that he has no warmth or power to illuminate.[20] Stephen goes through several stages of response to this man: "a smart of dejection," a feeling of being disheartened by the priest's "firm dry tone," and finally "a desolating pity," which "began to fall like a dew upon his easily embittered heart for this faithful servingman of the knightly Loyola . . . one whom he could never call his ghostly father" (V: 584–9). We do not learn until *Ulysses* that the man that Stephen will ultimately recognize as his non-biological father is not a priest at all, but a half-Jew: Leopold Bloom. Stephen's recognition of both the dean's limitations and his dogged loyalty moves Stephen to a pity that touches and softens his parched heart.

The Stephen of *Portrait,* then, is caught between two positions: he is acutely aware of the deadening effects produced by lack of feeling, but he has refused to allow himself to feel for (or with) others in a (futile) effort to preserve his pride and his freedom. In

20. Philosophy has always been linked to imagination and creativity for Joyce, as his comment about Vico's *Scienza Nuova* reveals: "I don't believe in any science . . . but my imagination grows when I read Vico as it doesn't when I read Freud or Jung." Joyce cited in Richard Ellmann, *James Joyce,* 2nd edition (Oxford: Oxford University Press, 1982), 693.

For more on Joyce's use of Vico, see Donald Philip Verene, *James Joyce and the Philosophers at Finnegans Wake* (Evanston, IL: Northwestern University Press, 2016).

Ulysses, he offers a different reason, his fear of being subsumed by the
other's feelings. His anxiety underscores the dangers of empathy and
over-identification: the loss of any sense of difference. Pondering the
death of a recently drowned man, Stephen wonders whether he himself would attempt to save him, concluding that he would want to try
but not at the cost of his own existence: "I want his life still to be his,
mine to be mine. A drowning man. His human eyes scream to me out
of horror of his death. I . . . With him together down . . . I could not
save her. Waters: bitter death: lost" (3: 323–30). His thoughts move
from the drowning man to his dying mother, as he is faced with his
own impotence to forestall a fearful death. Similarly, in "Wandering
Rocks" he feels fear at the thought of trying to save Dilly from a
metaphorical drowning: "Save her. Agenbite. All against us. She will
drown me with her, eyes and hair. Lank coils of seaweed hair around
me, my heart, my soul. Salt green death. We" (10: 875–8). In contrast to Bloom's emotional ethics, Stephen avoids the obligation to
another's life by recognizing his own limitations. Rather than seeing
himself as Daedalus who has made wings with which to escape, here
Stephen sees himself as someone who might himself drown. Yet, as
Hypatia Vourloumis points out in her "Ten Theses on Touch," to
deny contact, in Stephen's case emotional closeness, is still to make
touch central even in its absence: "[A] strenuous intention towards
non-touching or dissenting imperative to not touch or be touched
can be just as much about touching otherwise."[21] Stephen would like
touch to be "otherwise," to be reciprocal and based on a mutual vitality, rather than one that might destroy both self and other: "[Y]ou
will not be the master of others or their slave" (3: 295–6).

By the time *Ulysses* begins (over a year after the end of *Portrait*),
Stephen is riddled by self-doubt and remorse of conscience

---

21. Hypatia Vourloumis, "Ten Theses on Touch, or, Writing Touch," *Women & Performance: A
Journal of Feminist Theory* 24, nos. 2–3 (2014): 232–38, 233.

("agenbite of inwit")[22] over his resistance to his mother's dying wishes. Still in mourning, he is haunted by nightmares of her corpse threatening him with death, "her eyes on me to strike me down" (1: 276). He fights her threat: "No, mother! Let me be and let me live" (1: 279). Three pages into the novel, we see Stephen on the top of the tower remembering his dream of his dead mother coming to him, reproachful, in her graveclothes, and the narrator tells us, "Pain, that was not yet the pain of love, fretted his heart" (1: 102). As we see in "Circe," it is only after she is dead that Stephen's mother can touch him, reaching toward his heart with the crab claws of cancer. Death here acts as a reminder of human limitation, limitations that are hidden by youth and able-bodied health. Stephen eventually learns to feel his mother's touch (which he hasn't done since he was a child who pondered over whether to kiss her), but the belatedness and posthumous nature of the hallucinatory contact make it horrific.

A TOUCH OF DEATH—BLOOM

Bloom too comes into contact with death, the limit that permanently severs all possibility of mutual relation as it removes the dead from the world of sensual touch. The possibility of the loss of flesh reinforces Bloom's commitment to corporeal relationships. In the "Hades" episode Bloom confronts death in multiple ways, as his attendance at the burial of his friend Paddy Dignam also evokes the memory of the passing of his young son, Rudy, years earlier. Whereas touch is usually mutual and conscious, Bloom ponders that the touch of death means the end of all awareness of touch. As his thoughts stray to Molly's tender ministrations during Rudy's

---

22. Stephen's phrase for remorse of conscience, "agenbite of inwit," stresses the connection between the "bite" in "agenbite" and the one in "remorse," which stems from *remorderer*, "to bite again."

laying out, Bloom also recalls the "touch"—slang for sex—that led to Rudy's conception. Molly had asked him, "Give us a touch, Poldy. God, I'm dying for it," and Bloom wistfully thinks, "How life begins" (6: 80–1). Sex, death, and touch are all knotted together for Bloom in the "Hades" episode, the end of life stirring him to embrace what remains more emphatically. Bloom ponders this impulse: "Love among the tombstones. Romeo. Spice of pleasure. In the midst of death we are in life. Both ends meet" (6: 758–9). He even imagines the dead being aroused by the scent of sex, "smell of grilled beefsteaks to the starving," tantalizing those who can no longer get a "touch" (6: 760–1). By facing death rather than seeking to escape it, Bloom is able to see the death in life but also its reverse, life-in-death. Like Odysseus returning to the world from Hades, Bloom turns his mind to Molly—to life and intimate touch: "Plenty to see and hear and feel yet. Feel live warm beings near you. Let them sleep in their maggoty beds. They are not going to get me this innings. Warm beds: warm fullblooded life" (6: 1003–5). For Bloom, Molly—his bed sharer, a female or "sacred lifegiver"—represents life (15: 4648–9). Bloom asserts his commitment to life in tactile terms—warmth, pressure of bodies, flesh upon flesh. He tends his marital bond through acts of intimate care and attention—preparing her breakfast, ordering her lotion, getting her books. Yet the "touch" she is "dying for" on June 16, 1904 is sexual and mutually pleasurable, something Bloom fails to offer.

In middle age, after sixteen years of marriage, the sexual desire of the Blooms has seemingly settled down into companionable intimacy that is no longer predicated on mutual sexual touch. Their sleeping arrangements, top-to-tail, indicate an awkward proximity that lacks romance and prevents the couple (literally) from seeing eye-to-eye: "living with him so cold never embracing me except sometimes when he's asleep the wrong end of me" (18: 1399–1400). Philosopher Kym Maclaren argues that "intercorporeal intimacy," which is not limited to sexual intimacy, "enables selfhood and makes possible the development of true *intersubjectivity*—a relation between two subjects who recognize each other's alterity." She explains, "[T]ouch, in any human situation, can help incarnate us, draw us into our bodies to realize our intertwinement with and differentiation from others. Touch can enliven anyone, move us to become ourselves anew."[23] Molly wants more than Bloom's tender ministrations, she wants to feel enfleshed and connected through sexual intimacy. Bloom, paradoxically and perhaps subconsciously, does satisfy her need for sexual intimacy but by using a proxy: Blazes Boylan. Bloom absents himself (and arranges for their daughter Milly's absence) so that Molly's adulterous assignation can take place.

Touch can be virtual and textual as well as physical; written letters touch the heart, Molly reminisces about Bloom's courtship: "writing every morning a letter sometimes twice a day I liked the way he made love then" (18: 327–8). Molly declares, "I wish somebody would write me a loveletter," which "fills up your whole day and life" (18: 734–5). The emotional filling up, she suggests, can change one's perspective on the world: "something to think about every moment and see it all round you like a new world" (18: 738–9). It was Bloom's ability to touch her emotionally through words and sensations that attracted her to him: "him and his mad crazy letters . . . that . . . had me always at myself 4 and 5 times a day sometimes" (1176–9).[24] His words touch her, and she touches herself, illustrating both the ambiguity of the medium of touch and the intimate connection

---

23. Kym Maclaren, "Touching Matters: Embodiments of Intimacy," *Emotion, Space and Society* 13 (2014): 95–102, at 96, 101, italics in original.

24. Martin Jay points out that unlike the other senses of there seems to be a close, if complicated, relationship between sight and language. He cites the work of Robert Rivlin and Karen Gravelle, who demonstrate that "the ability to visualize something internally is closely linked with the ability to describe it verbally. Verbal and written descriptions create highly specific mental images . . . The link between vision, visual memory, and verbalization can be quite startling" (*Downcast Eyes*, 8).

between toucher and touched. However, this mutuality has become unequal—Bloom's touching words have been redirected to his flirtatious correspondence with Martha Clifford. Bloom has "forgotten" how to touch Molly in a sexual or a literary way, and that lack of mutual touch (so beautifully exemplified on the Hill of Howth) has emotional consequences. Bloom and Molly have a companionable intimacy, as their conversation about Bloom's evening in "Ithaca" suggests, but Molly misses the sexual and epistolary intimacy of their younger years.

It is through the intimacy of blind touch (Bloom is asleep and the room is dark) that the possibility of future relations and corporeal communications is kept open. Bloom and Molly connect through the silent communion of touch: "Warm beds: warm fullblooded life" (6: 1003–5). In the dark, both sense one another, as their minds move through possible "readings" of their own situations (individual and joined) in "Ithaca" and "Penelope." In "Ithaca" Bloom's final gesture before sleep is to kiss Molly's bottom as a gesture of connection and possible reconciliation: "He kissed the plump mellow yellow smellow melons of her rump" (17: 2241). This is not the kiss of their courtship—the passionate exchanges of seed, both equally kisser and kissed—but it is a touch, flesh pressed to flesh, a gesture of affection given and received. In Molly's view such kisses do not satisfy her need for romance or reassure her of her continuing desirability because they are not expressive or pleasurable enough: "[H]e'd kiss anything unnatural where we haven't 1 atom of any kind of expression in us" (18: 1402–3). Yet the rump kiss repairs to some extent (for Bloom at least) the rupture of the affair. It is in the language of touch and the mutuality of the kiss that the hope for their future rests. Molly recollects the mutual kiss of their youth along with Bloom's words, "[H]e said I was a flower of the mountain," signifying his ability to see the wild beauty of her body clearly: "yes so we are flowers all a womans body yes that was one true thing he said in his life . . . that was why I liked him because I saw he understood or felt what a woman is" (18: 1576–9). During their courtship, when the text of Molly's body was unfamiliar, Bloom was nonetheless able to read her feelingly—"he . . . *felt* what a woman is"—which enabled a meaningful connection between them. Molly thinks of a kiss as more intense and personal than sex ("theres nothing like a kiss long and hot down to your soul"), especially sex that has become routine, ("just the ordinary do it and think no more about it"), (18: 105–6, 101–2). Sex can become thoughtless, but their first, viscerally intense kiss she can still recall sixteen years later: "[M]y God after that long kiss I near lost my breath" (18: 1575–6). It is through mutual, active touch that a deep, multivalent, and lasting understanding is produced.

FEELING IN THE DARK

Joyce considers another way to read the world when he introduces the Blind Stripling. Excellent work has been done on Joyce's treatment of blindness in *Ulysses*;[25] our contribution is to demonstrate how Joyce uses the disability of blindness (inability to see one's environment) to reveal a comparable disability to which everyone is subject: blindness to oneself. Moreover, Joyce looks to actual blindness not only to gain a better understanding of the problem of limited vision, but also for ways of compensating for it, by expanding the imagination and relying more heavily on touch. Joyce's multifaceted representation of blindness might be said to blend Paul de Man's notion of "blindness

25. For a non-exhaustive consideration of Joyce and blindness, see Andre Cormier, "'Our eyes demand their turn. Let them be seen!': The Transcendental Blind Stripling," *Joyce Studies Annual* (2008): 203–25. Disability studies scholars have produced fine work on literature and blindness more broadly: Georgina Kleege, "Dialogues with the Blind: Literary Depictions of Blindness and Visual Art," *Journal of Literary and Cultural Disability Studies* 4, no. 1 (2010): 1–15; J. M. Rodas, "On Blindness," *Journal of Literary and Cultural Disability Studies* 3, no. 2 (2009): 115–30; Naomi Schor, "Blindness as Metaphor," *differences: A Journal of Feminist Cultural Studies* 11, no. 2 (1999): 76–105.

and insight" with Linett's extension of his work in "blindness and intimacy."[26] The kind of heroism that Stephen and Bloom exhibit springs
not from any inherent superiority to others but from a capacity to
realize their limitations and their receptiveness to alternative avenues
of discovery. Their blindness is neither physical nor total; it is simply
one among many of their ordinary flaws. The fact that Bloom and
Stephen have been blind to the feelings of important women in their
lives does not make them admirable or despicable, but it has given
them an opportunity to learn to see their limitations (and the consequences for the women they love) more honestly.

When Bloom and Stephen imagine themselves as actually blind,
it models for readers the unexpected and even beautiful side benefits of accepting a limitation (like Lear), even an imagined one. So
in "Proteus," Stephen closes his eyes, commanding himself, "Shut
your eyes and see" (3: 9). He then thinks of the ashplant hanging
by his side, and tells himself, "Tap with it; they do" (3: 16). He does
this to better understand Aristotelian philosophy as well as to experience what actual blindness might feel like. In "Lestrygonians,"
Bloom engages in a less cerebral, more corporeal meditation that
begins with observations about the accomplishments of "dark men"
and ends with an experiment to see if he can see colors through
touch alone:

> Look at all the things they can learn to do. Read with their fingers.
> Tune pianos. Or we are surprised they have any brains. Why we
> think a deformed person or a hunchback clever if he says some-
> thing we might say. Of course the other senses are more . . . Dark
> men they call them.

26. Paul de Man, *Blindness and Insight: Essays in the Rhetoric of Contemporary Criticism*, 1983;
Linett, *Bodies of Modernism.* De Man's work seeks to identify the blind spots in criticism
that are both unseen by the writers and necessary for the insights they do have, whereas
Linett argues that blindness offers a particular intimacy.

Sense of smell must be stronger too. Smells on all sides, bunched together. Each street different smell. Each person too. Then the spring, the summer: smells. Tastes? They say you can't taste wines with your eyes shut or a cold in the head. Also smoke in the dark they say get no pleasure.

And with a woman, for instance. More shameless not seeing... Must be strange not to see her. Kind of a form in his mind's eye. The voice, temperatures: when he touches her with his fingers must almost see the lines, the curves. His hands on her hair, for instance. Say it was black, for instance. Good. We call it black. Then passing over her white skin. Different feel perhaps. Feeling of white. (8: 1115–31)

Bloom extends Stephen's exploration of the "ineluctability" of the visual and audible by focusing on the "lesser," more embodied and "animal" Aristotelian senses: smell, taste, and touch. Bloom's reflection on what "they say" reveals how ubiquitous ocularcentric thinking is if vision even impacts the sense of taste: "can't taste wines with your eyes shut." Bloom challenges those who presume blindness is akin to ignorance, "we are surprised that they have any brains," and reminds himself, "Better not do the condescending" (8: 1092). Despite his empathy, Bloom does lapse into a condescending commonplace— that the blind have compensatory "gifts" to make up for their deficit: "other senses are more."[27] As Linett points out, there is a long association of blindness with ignorance which relies "on the ableist assumption that knowledge comes through sight."[28] Bloom's musings, however, emphasize difference over deficit.

27. Bloom's emphasis on smell and touch in this passage challenges the usual view that sight and hearing are the most important of the "compensatory" senses. So blind people are often presumed especially auditory, and deaf people especially visual. Bloom imagines smell and touch as the improved senses, gesturing to a broader, and more visceral, conception of experience.

28. Linett, *Bodies of Modernism*, 56.

A theory of learning via touch emerges from Bloom's musings, a process that models feeling *Ulysses* for the reader. Initially Bloom's curiosity is piqued, and connection established, when he gently touches the Blind Stripling's elbow and takes "the limp seeing hand to guide it forward" (8: 1090–1). The phrase gestures to the translation of knowledge, in this case a "queer idea of Dublin," from sight to touch. It is the Stripling that accrues knowledge, not the sighted man, "[s]izing me up I daresay from my hand" (8: 1098). The Stripling thanks Bloom for his assistance crossing the road and confidently continues his journey: "The blind stripling tapped the curbstone and went on his way . . . feeling again" (8: 1104–5). It is in fact Bloom (not the Blind man) that is left to follow ("Mr Bloom walked behind the eyeless feet") and remain in ignorance, left—like many philosophers—to ponder the experience of the blind and its link to sighted experience (8: 1106). Bloom then tries to imagine seeing by touch: he slowly feels his hair above his ears, which he describes as "[f]ibres of fine fine straw" (8: 1136), and the "downy hair" of his right cheek. Deciding that his cheek isn't smooth enough, he ducks into a less well-traveled street: "Walking by Doran's publichouse he slid his hand between his waistcoat and trousers and, pulling aside his shirt gently, felt a slack fold of his belly. But I know it's whitey yellow. Want to try in the dark to see" (8: 1140–3).[29] Touch becomes a means of accumulating knowledge that rivals sight. Using it, Bloom imagines that he is able to differentiate between colors and to produce imaginative forms: "Kind of a form in the mind's eye." Communication (as well as knowledge accumulation) is achieved via smell and taste, but primarily via touch. Bloom's curiosity and willingness to learn from

29. Bloom is practicing what Eve Sedgwick, drawing on Renu Bora, would later call "textural perception." Sedgwick explains that "to perceive texture is always, immediately, and de facto to be immersed in a field of active narrative hypothesizing, testing, reunderstanding of how physical properties act and are acted upon over time" (*Touching Feeling*, 13). Bloom's curiosity leads him to physical experimentation in order to "see feelingly."

those with different abilities is an example of what Martin Jay calls ocular-*eccentricity* ("the antidote to privileging any one visual order or scopic regime").[30]

Bloom and Stephen are blind in one sense (to wife and mother, respectively, and to the fears in themselves that produced such insensitivity), despite the fact that they also know how to feel for others. When they think of or encounter a limitation (here a bodily disability), they slow down and feel even ordinary things through their other senses. This is also what happens when people become aware of the fragility or shortness of life: their perceptions of everyday life become more acute, and the emotional texture of their relationships is heightened through the use of imagination and identification.[31] Thus Joyce offers a model for readers that prompts them to slow down, pay attention to the quotidian, draw on *all* their senses, reflect on their emotional reactions, and use imagination and identification while retaining a respect for the independence of the Other.

Bloom's description of what it's like to be blind is eerily similar to a description of what it is like to read a book. Although readers of printed books (as opposed to ones in Braille) aren't physically blind, they don't necessarily "see" what is happening; imagination is selective and in that sense partly creative. Joyce treats Stephen's walk over Sandymount strand in "Proteus" as an exercise in "reading" the phenomenal world; sensory perceptions are regarded as "signs" (following the example of Jacob Boehme) to be observed more carefully in an effort to feel and read circumambient reality more fully. Stephen

---

30. Jay, *Downcast Eyes,* 591.
31. See Laura Carstensen et al., "Emotional Experience Improves with Age: Evidence Based on Over 10 Years of Experience Sampling," cited in Atul Gawande, *Being Mortal: Medicine and What Matters in the End* (New York: Metropolitan Books/Henry Holt, 2014). Their studies showed that feeling for others becomes more imperative when one faces the reality of one's limitations as a mortal human being. When the certainties of life have been shaken, people need greater emotional connection to those closest to them; especially strong is the "need for everyday comforts, for companionship, for help achieving [one's] modest aims" (100).

grapples with questions of how we know what we experience in the world, his mind wrestling with ontological and epistemological questions, just as Odysseus must "hang on" and "grip" the Old Man of the Sea to get his answers.[32] He closes his eyes to see what sensory delights are diminished or occluded by sight; the ears cannot be closed, but Stephen accents sound by thinking about time, sequence, and rhythm. Stephen thinks through an Aristotelian lens; Aristotle famously privileges the nobility of sight, due to its proximity to and ability to inform the intellect, over the "base" materiality of touch in his hierarchy of the senses.[33] Accordingly, Stephen first explores the modalities of vision and hearing as he "reads" the bay of Dublin, contemplating the detritus upon the beach—"seaspawn and seawrack . . . that rusty boot"—considering the proper sensible quality of what he sees ("snotgreen, bluesilver, rust: coloured signs" [3: 2–5]) and hears ("crackling wrack and shells" [3: 10]). The sensible world is rendered more vivid and tangible by the association of green with snot and the assonant and onomatopoetic language used to reproduce the sounds of crackling wrack.[34]

32. Homer, *Odyssey*, trans. Stanley Lombardo (Indianapolis, IN: Hackett, 2000), book 4, l. 446, p. 56.
33. In Aristotle's inquiry into the soul there are multiple hierarchies, including that of the soul over the body, and the senses are ranked: sight is superior to hearing, smelling, and finally touch (taste is a variant of touch). See *De Sensu et Sensibili* (Of Sense and the Sensible) and *De Anima* (Of the Soul), c. 350 BC. Aristotle condemns touch because it can lead to eroticism and distract from higher reasoning, though touch also offers the possibility for aesthetic pleasure distinct from bestial pleasures. Yet he also posits touch as the foundational sense of all sentient life, writing that for humans "touch is the best guarantor of what is." Cited in Pascal Massie, "Touching, Thinking, Being: The Sense of Touch in Aristotle's *De Anima* and Its Implications," *Minerva: An Internet Journal of Philosophy* 17 (2013): 74–101, at 88.
34. Removing the primary sense of sight is necessary for Stephen to fully explore the other senses, yet these senses also contribute to seeing: "[S]hut your eyes and see," he tells himself (3: 9). Blindly feeling his way along the beach, reassured by the sounds he hears, the modality of the audible, he asks, "Has all vanished since?" (3: 25). No idealist, Stephen laughs at himself and returns to his primary mode of touching the materiality of the world—sight—"*Basta*! I will see if I can see. See now. There all the time without you: and ever shall be, world without end" (3: 26, 27–9).

Stephen performs his own philosophical and aesthetic experiments, touching and reading the environment, wondering how Aristotle came to his conclusions. He then remembers that Aristotle adds "in bodies" (3: 2–4), and that Aristotle thought that humans rely on sense data for immediate knowledge of the world: "[H]e [Aristotle] was aware of them bodies before of them coloured. How? By knocking his sconce against them, sure" (3: 4–6). Aristotle's model of sense perception acknowledged that touch, despite being the sense he ranked lowest, was also the most fundamental, and shared by all living beings. The image of Aristotle "knocking his sconce" against bodies playfully gestures to the centrality of touch to perception (to knock against something is to have contact with it). Stephen's metaphors also become more haptic. As he contemplates the waves, he thinks, "The whitemaned seahorses, champing, brightwindbridled, the steeds of Mananaan" (3: 56–7). The whitemaned (visual) horses champ (audible, including the grinding of teeth against bridle); the ineffable touch of air is "brightwindbridled" and renders the wind tangible, allowing its fast rush to be felt. Joyce's language is textured and visceral and is especially evocative when read aloud, uniting Stephen's modalities into a tasted and tactile reality. Vourloumis calls this the "haptics of language—language as matter, as sonic, textural and bodily performance." She suggests that language can be "felt both cognitively and linguistically" and calls for readers—as Joyce implicitly does—"to think poetics then as touch and touch as poetry, for to do and make language is to know what it is to be touched by language and to touch language in return."[35] Stephen's experiments in "Proteus" show that touch is essential for the reader, that touch produces a deeper and more expansive form of curiosity, and the impressions generated by it reverberate from the senses to the emotions.

35. Vourloumis, "Ten Theses on Touch," 235.

REACHING OUT—TO THE READER

We have been arguing that too heavy a reliance on visual modes of apprehension limits the encounter between text and reader. If a reader has developed a habit of reading vicariously, through an imaginative over-identification with the characters that licenses an escape from the self, he or she may also be "blinded." Her vicarious experience may rely on the "camera eye" of the third-person omniscient narrator, supplemented by whatever she may see through the more limited vision of the protagonist. Joyce interferes with this more usual way of drawing readers into a fictional world by structuring his book more "dramatically."[36] Disoriented, the new reader of *Ulysses* finds herself at the top of a Martello tower, eavesdropping on a bizarre conversation between two men to whom she has not been introduced. She becomes a ghost who has been interpellated into another moment in time, set in a country she may not even know, watching a man who is shaving pretend to transform his bowl of lather into the body and blood of "Christine" while trading gibes with a sleepy and disgruntled roommate. She is literally "in the dark," because she isn't sure where she is and she has no idea where this is going. To stay in the fictional world, she must feel her way forward, without real guideposts or useful precedents from her experience of reading other novels. She feels the "touch" of Joyce's language, often strange ("Chrysostomos" [1]), as she gathers her impressions and struggles to read on.

---

36. It stages a dramatic encounter between the reader and an unfamiliar kind of book by constructing obstacles that make it difficult for a reader to "lose" herself while reading (a form of voyeurism): the narrators refuse to provide context to make the reader feel at home in the fictional world, and obstructions are multiple and unstable (e.g., narrative styles change with the time of day). These estranging techniques either alienate readers or else cause them to revert to vicarious emotional responses that are not their own.

In contrast, to be "touched" by the characters in *Ulysses* (printed letters that conjure imagined people but evoke real emotions), readers must remain themselves, aware of their changing reactions and questions, while at the same time being both curious and receptive. The linguistic force can then impact the body of the reader, leaving affective, emotional, and intellectual traces on the mind (both conscious and unconscious). The reader may then feel uncomfortable, unprepared, uncertain about what is happening. Those feelings have been very deliberately produced by the way the author has structured the novel's opening. In order to continue reading, the reader must sustain tolerance for an array of changing feelings unfamiliar to experienced readers, because they are *hers*, not those of a protagonist. If she can stay in this strange fictional unfolding—one eye on the text and the other on herself, seeing feelingly—some things will become clear to her, but many other things will remain elusive, seem gratuitous or excessive; nonetheless, the sensations will still feel new, even a century after *Ulysses* was published. This is the dynamism of reading *Ulysses* "feelingly," the forces of affect and of touching/being touched always producing new entanglements and insights. She will be encountering the unknown as herself, trying to keep her senses attuned to what is unfolding through the language moment by moment, hour by hour, through many dislocations, changes of style, and even changes of protagonist. She will be experiencing someone else's day, and feeling every moment of it, perhaps for the first time, through a mutual, dynamic, embodied relationship with language that still has the ghostly ability to touch her flesh, mind, and heart.

Feeling *Ulysses* is not a "method" in the sense of "a procedure designed to produce at will a certain result through the adoption of specific steps,"[37] but rather an open orientation toward reading that approaches Keatsian negative capability in its tolerance of not finding

37. De Man, *Blindness and Insight*, xxi.

immediate answers. It does not offer a final insight into the text, or even the reading subject, nor does it enable the reader to emerge from darkness into light or from blindness into vision. Instead, it serves to remind readers that reading is a process of unfolding, in which readers feel their way slowly (and repeatedly) within the co-constituted worlds of language, emotion, knowledge, and sensation. It asks the reader not only to see and hear, but also to touch the text and to be touched, and perhaps altered by it, in return.

BIBLIOGRAPHY

Ahmed, Sara. *The Cultural Politics of Emotion*. New York: Routledge: 2004.

Ahmed, Sara. *The Promise of Happiness*. Durham, NC: Duke University Press, 2010.

Attridge, Derek. "Joyce's Noises." *Oral Tradition* 24, no. 2 (2009): 471–84.

Berlant, Lauren. *Cruel Optimism*. Durham, NC: Duke University Press, 2011.

Brennan, Teresa. *The Transmission of Affect*. Ithaca, NY: Cornell University Press, 2004.

Carstensen, Laura et al. "Emotional Experience Improves with Age: Evidence Based on Over 10 Years of Experience Sampling." In Atul Gawande, ed., *Being Mortal: Medicine and What Matters in the End* (New York: Metropolitan Books/ Henry Holt, 2014).

Cormier, Andre. "'Our eyes demand their turn. Let them be seen!' The Transcendental Blind Stripling." *Joyce Studies Annual* (2008): 203–25.

Danius, Sara. *The Senses of Modernism: Technology, Perception, and Aesthetics*. Ithaca, NY: Cornell University Press, 2002.

de Man, Paul. *Blindness and Insight: Essays in the Rhetoric of Contemporary Criticism*. Minneapolis: University of Minnesota Press, 1983.

Derrida, Jacques, trans. Christine Irizarry. *On Touching—Jean-Luc Nancy*. Stanford, CA: Stanford University Press, 2005.

Ellmann, Richard. *James Joyce*. Revised ed. Oxford: Oxford University Press, 1982.

Fogarty, Anne. "'The Odour of Ashpits and Old Weeds and Offal': The Transmission of Affects in *Dubliners*." In Franca Ruggieri and Enrico Terrinoni, eds., *James Joyce: The Recirculation of Realism*. Italy: Edizioni Q, 2014.

Frost, Laura. *The Problem with Pleasure: Modernism and Its Discontents*. New York: Columbia University Press, 2013.

Fulkerson, Matthew. "Touch." In *The Stanford Encyclopedia of Philosophy*. https:// plato.stanford.edu/archives/spr2016/entries/touch.

Garrington, Abbie. *Haptic Modernism: Touch and the Tactile in Modernist Writing.* Edinburgh: Edinburgh University Press, 2013.

Homer. *Odyssey.* Trans. Stanley Lombardo. Indianapolis, IN: Hackett, 2000.

Jay, Martin. *Downcast Eyes: The Denigration of Vision in Twentieth-Century French Thought.* Berkeley: University of California Press, 1993.

Kaag, John and Martin Clancy. "Can Transcendence Be Taught?," *Chronicle of Higher Education,* Oct. 7, 2016. https://www.chronicle.com/article/Can-Transcendence-Be-Taught-/237994 (accessed July 24, 2019).

Kleege, Georgina. "Dialogues with the Blind: Literary Depictions of Blindness and Visual Art." *Journal of Literary and Cultural Disability Studies* 4, no. 1 (2010): 1–15.

Lewis, Wyndham. *Time and Western Man.* LondonL Chatto & Windus, 1927.

Linett, Maren Tova. *Bodies of Modernism: Physical Disability in Transatlantic Modernist Literature.* Ann Arbor, MI: University of Michigan Press, 2017.

Long, Christopher P. "On Touch and Life in the *De Anima.*" In Antonio Cimino and Pavlos Kontos, eds., *Phenomenology and the Metaphysics of Sight* (Leiden: Brill, 2015).

Maclaren, Kym. "Touching Matters: Embodiments of Intimacy." *Emotion, Space and Society* 13 (2014): 95–102

Massie, Pascal. "Touching, Thinking, Being: The Sense of Touch in Aristotle's *De Anima* and Its Implications." *Minerva: An Internet Journal of Philosophy* 17 (2013): 74–101.

Paterson, Mark. *Seeing with the Hands: Blindness, Vision, and Touch after Descartes.* Edinburgh: Edinburgh University Press, 2016.

Paterson, Mark. *The Senses of Touch: Haptics, Affects, and Technologies.* London: Bloomsbury Publishing, 2007.

Rodas, J. M. "On Blindness." *Journal of Literary and Cultural Disability Studies* 3, no. 2 (2009): 115–30.

Schor, Naomi. "Blindness as Metaphor." *differences: A Journal of Feminist Cultural Studies* 11, no. 2 (1999): 76–105.

Sedgwick, Eve Kosofsky. *Touching Feeling: Affect, Pedagogy, Performativity.* Durham, NC: Duke University Press, 2003.

Verene, Donald Philip. *James Joyce and the Philosophers at Finnegans Wake.* Evanston, IL: Northwestern University Press, 2016.

Vourloumis, Hypatia. "Ten Theses on Touch, or, Writing Touch." *Women & Performance: A Journal of Feminist Theory* 24, nos. 2–3 (2014): 232–38.

Chapter 4

Ulysses May Be a Legal Fiction

SAM SLOTE

According to a much-retold anecdote from Richard Ellmann's biography of Joyce, the BBC was preparing a radio documentary on Joyce and wanted to interview Richard Best, recently retired from the National Library of Ireland. Best was reluctant and asked why he would be of any relevance to a program on Joyce, to which the BBC interviewer pointed out that he was a character in *Ulysses*. To this, Best quite sensibly retorted, "I am not a character in fiction. I am a living being."[1] Ellmann presents this story as an illustration of the perils of interpreting and diagnosing verisimilitude in *Ulysses*. There is a character called Richard Best in the "Scylla and Charybdis" episode, who, like the Best of 1904, was the assistant director of the National Library. These two Bests share a name and a number of other attributes,[2] but, as per Best's outburst to the BBC reporter, they are somehow not the same. There is some difference between them, a difference that the Best approached by the BBC posits as

---

1. Richard Ellmann, *James Joyce,* revised edition (New York: Oxford University Press, 1982), 363–64.
2. For example, both Bests had translated Marie Henri d'Arbois de Jubainville's book *Le Cycle mythologique irlandais.*

Joyce's Ulysses. Philip Kitcher, Oxford University Press (2020). © Oxford University Press.
DOI: 10.1093/oso/9780190842260.001.0001

fundamental. What I would like to investigate is the character of this difference and its implications for one book called *Ulysses*.

Ulysses provides an interesting case study for this for several reasons: besides Best, Joyce incorporates a number of characters based (to varying extents) upon real people.[3] And beyond mere people, he also worked very hard to represent Dublin as accurately and meticulously as possible, thereby, in many ways, further blurring an easy division between fact and fiction. For example, in "Wandering Rocks," Joyce plotted each of the characters' movements in Dublin by using a stopwatch and a map and, as documented by Clive Hart, the coordination of all the timings works out perfectly on the actual cityscape.[4] In many ways, it seems as if *Ulysses* could somehow "fit into" the actual Dublin of 1904 with minimal disruption. Of course, Joyce strayed from adhering to perfect documentary facticity in several ways, sometimes deliberately, sometimes accidentally. For example, the Mirus bazaar opened on May 31, not on June 16, and while it was indeed opened by the Lord Lieutenant, he did not arrive in a lavish cavalcade through Dublin as is depicted in "Wandering Rocks."[5]

Ulysses presents itself *almost* as a work of fact and, in so doing, it invites the reader to question the nature of fiction. Philosophers have developed a vocabulary for trying to discuss and diagnose the ontology of fiction and fictional characters, as if fictitious entities could be subject to the logical operations applied to facts. The problem stems from the fact that "there are sentences in language that seem to commit one to fictional entities,"[6] that is, one can speak of fictional

---

3. Many of these are catalogued in Vivien Igoe's book *The Real People of Joyce's "Ulysses"* (Dublin: UCD Press, 2016).

4. Frank Budgen, *James Joyce and the Making of "Ulysses"* (New York: Oxford University Press, 1989), 124–25; Ian Gunn and Clive Hart, *James Joyce's Dublin* (London: Thames and Hudson, 2004), 58–59.

5. Robert M. Adams, *Surface and Symbol* (New York: Oxford University Press, 1962), 7.

6. Fred Kroon and Alberto Voltolini, "Fiction," in *Stanford Encyclopedia of Philosophy*, http://plato.stanford.edu/entries/fiction/ accessed July 1, 2016.

entities in ways that can apparently—but not always—make sense. On the one hand, fictional realists posit that there can be fictional entities, that is, entities can have, among other attributes, the condition of non-existence. Not existing is not necessarily an impediment for being. On the other hand, antirealists do not believe that fictional entities exist and that mere potentiality is no guarantee of being. And thus they propose that every sentence about a fictional entity need only be paraphrased in order to resolve or reconcile the fictionality of fiction into fact. For example, a realist would have no issues, *prima facie*, with the sentence "Leopold Bloom had a meal at Davy Byrne's." But an antirealist would understand this sentence as really meaning something like "In James Joyce's novel *Ulysses*, the character Leopold Bloom had a meal at Davy Byrne's."

This already, quickly leads to a problem. A slightly different statement, like "Leopold Bloom had a meal at McDonald's," is liable to be met with various objections—the first being, probably, the anachronism. However, it is not automatically evident if one can legitimately label this a false assertion. Certainly, this is a false assertion apropos the text of *Ulysses*, but even on this matter there could be some room for doubt since not all of Bloom's actions on June 16, 1904, are recorded in *Ulysses* (and, indeed, as I'll argue shortly, *Ulysses* represents much less than one might think). But, as a statement about a fictional entity, this claim is neither true nor false. That is, a statement about a fictional entity does not necessarily reside within an economy of verifiability.

Because of this lack of verifiability, fictional realism tends toward possible worlds theory: that there are multiple, even infinite possible worlds of which only one, ours presumably, is actual. But there are other possible worlds where, say, Bloom has a meal at Davy Byrne's or, in another, at McDonald's, or yet another where Captain Ahab seeks revenge against a great white snail. These would be the fictional worlds. While the statement "Leopold Bloom ate lunch at

McDonald's" is false within the world indicated in *Ulysses*, it could well be true in other fictional worlds. The suggestion of an infinite number of possible worlds can happen because within any single fictional construct (such as a novel) there are so many possible gaps (and thus permutations) left to fill. That is, possible worlds theory is a symptom of another problem within fiction, its incompleteness.

In reading fiction, one does not need to affiliate with either the realists or the antirealists. Possible worlds are not the only possibility for making sense of fiction. A more pragmatic approach and less epistemologically cumbersome perspective is also possible as long as one is willing to tolerate a little cognitive dissonance, that is, an ability to think within multiple, even discordant perspectives. In fact, some discord might even be the salient element of the nature of fiction. Judging the truth of a statement about a fiction is simply a matter of determining whether the fiction *endorses* that statement.[7] Endorsement can refer to either a statement within that work of fiction or outside it, as in a work of secondary criticism. I will start with external statements since these are easier, at least at first. The statement "Stephen Dedalus wears black clothes on June 16, 1904" can be considered true because, while never explicitly stated in the text, *Ulysses* contains more than enough information to endorse that claim: Stephen turns down Mulligan's offer of gray trousers because he is in mourning for his mother (1: 120–2) and twice he is mockingly called "parson" (14: 1451, 15: 65) and once "the drunken minister" (14: 1444–5).

In its general form, the endorsement theory functions like this: the text of *Ulysses* endorses this statement because the text provides various other statements as corroboration *and* there is nothing to undermine the endorsement. Thus, the statement "Stephen Dedalus wears

---

7. I am indebted to Philip Kitcher for suggesting this idea, which helped clarify a lot of issues for me.

black clothes" is endorsed by *Ulysses,* whereas the statement "Milly Bloom has a twin sister named Ermentrude" is (unambiguously) not endorsed by the text. Endorsement does not entail a strict falsifiability, merely compatibility. In practical terms, this means that the fiction has to be somewhat sequestered from what one would colloquially think of as the real world. I say "somewhat sequestered" because the degree would depend upon certain parameters internal to that fiction: one holds the fictionality of *Ulysses* to a separate degree than that of *Star Wars;* in the former the rules of physics as we understand them prevail,[8] in the latter, not quite so much. This is more than just a suspension of disbelief, which is why I use the term "cognitive dissonance." One can believe in the events of a narration while still also believing it all to be lies. Samuel Johnson famously noted that spectators in a theater "are always in their senses and know from the first act to the last that the stage is only a stage, and that the players are only players."[9] Disbelief is not, as such, suspended, but rather two (or more) different, possibly incompatible frames of belief are overlaid. Fiction thus occasions what Yuval Noah Harari calls a "dual reality,"[10] a state in which one acknowledges two discordant perspectives, such as the player and the play.

The first complication to the endorsement theory is that the text of *Ulysses* is not clearly defined. The first edition, published in Paris in 1922, was greatly flawed, and every subsequent iteration of the text, even ones which contain corrections to redress the flaws of the

---

8. Although one would have to make an allowance for the laws of physics as understood in the early twentieth century as there is a reference to the theory of an "omnipresent luminiferous diathermanous ether" (17: 263), which was widely accepted by physicists before the Einsteinian dispensation.

9. Samuel Johnson, "Preface to Shakespeare," in Frank Brady and W. K. Wimsatt, eds., *Selected Poetry and Prose* (Berkeley: University of California Press, 1977), 299–336, at 311.

10. Yuval Noah Harari, *Sapiens: A Brief History of Humankind* (London: Vintage, 2011), 36. Harari argues that this ability to hold discordant perspectives is the hallmark of the cognitive revolution that allowed *Homo sapiens* to prevail (27–44).

first edition, has introduced further flaws or otherwise contestable variants.[11] Thus, the phrase "the text of *Ulysses*" does not refer to a single, stable entity that enjoys universal consensus (even within this volume). This has some implications for the endorsement theory. To take an amusing example, a colleague of mine once told me that early in his career he had an article rejected because a reviewer objected to his discussion of a non-existent dot at the end of the "Ithaca" episode. In point of fact, "Ithaca" does end with a dot or point, in answer to the question "Where?" (17: 2331), but this is accidentally missing in many editions and individual printings because, occasionally, well-meaning typesetters believe it to be an errant mark and blot it out (for example, it is missing in all Shakespeare and Company printings from 1926 onward and from the 1936 Bodley Head). There can be different ways of interpreting the dot, it admits varying perspectives,[12] but these all assume that the dot is there on the page.[13] And, much to my colleague's dismay, the reviewer did not endorse his article because the reviewer's copy did not endorse the dot.

Following from the problem of defining what constitutes the text, there is the matter of what one could call the extended text of *Ulysses*, or its paratext. This would include the various preparatory drafts and manuscripts Joyce wrote, as well as perhaps explanatory comments made in letters and other paratextual matter. Such paratextual matter can help resolve at least some editorial problems. For example, the presence of the dot in "Ithaca" can be confirmed by looking at the proof pages where Joyce left instructions to the printer that the

---

11. I explain this in more detail in Sam Slote, *"Ulysses" in the Plural* (Dublin: National Library of Ireland, 2004).

12. See, for example, Austin Briggs, "The Fell Stop at the End of 'Ithaca': Thirteen Ways—and Then Some—of Looking at a Black Dot," *Joyce Studies Annual* 7 (1996): 125–44.

13. The thirty-first printing of the Vintage Books imprint of Random House printing of Gabler's edition does have the dot, but in the wrong place, flung on page 573, between lines 1030 and 1031.

point should be "bien visible."[14] Furthermore, Joyce's explanatory comments elucidate various passages of *Ulysses* and, indeed, some of these comments have become quasi-canonical, such as the two (non-identical) schemata that he prepared for his friends. Reading *Ulysses* can involve a thick palimpsest of variant texts and paratexts.

The degree of authority these paratexts exert can be contested and this creates a complication for the endorsement theory. For example, in "Ithaca," when Stephen takes his leave of Bloom, the sound Bloom hears is described as "[t]he double reverberation of retreating feet on the heavenborn earth, the double vibration of a jew's harp in the resonant lane" (17: 1243–4). Over the years, some critics have taken this statement at face value and claimed that Stephen has taken out a (previously unseen) Jew's Harp from his pocket and is playing it as he walks away.[15] However, this reading is contradicted by an entry on one of Joyce's "Ithaca" notesheets: "SD bootsoles on flags of hollow lane twanged a fourfold chord, scale of a jew's mouth harp."[16] This note is compatible with and endorsed by the line in "Ithaca" since what is being described is the *sound* Bloom hears: he is not necessarily hearing a Jew's Harp, but rather the sound of Stephen's boots on the lane, which is described as similar to a Jew's Harp. And so, the text on its own endorses both readings (the sound is from a Jew's Harp or from Stephen's boots), but when taken in conjunction with the paratextual note, only one reading is endorsed.

Beyond the Joycean paratext is the historical paratext, that is, matters of historical accuracy and pertinence. To return to Best, how

14. Michael Groden et al., eds., *The James Joyce Archive* (New York: Garland, 1978–79), 21: 140.
15. For example, Robert D. Newman, "Transformatio Coniunctionis: Alchemy in *Ulysses*," in Robert D. Newman and Weldon Thornton, eds., *Joyce's "Ulysses": The Larger Perspective* (Newark: University of Delaware Press, 1987), 168–86, at 180.
16. Phillip Herring, *Joyce's "Ulysses" Notesheets in the British Museum* (Charlottesville: University Press of Virginia, 1972), 455.

much do the biographical details concerning Best and other real-life people matter to *Ulysses*? Best's superior at the National Library, William Lyster, is called a Quaker in *Ulysses* (9: 1, *et passim*) when, according to the 1901 census, he was of the Church of Ireland.[17] Despite this, the *Dictionary of Irish Biography* erroneously claims he is "[o]f a quaker family."[18] Joyce's Dublin eclipses the Dublin that actually existed in a kind of groovy Borgesian twist. But, if the real-world Lyster was of the Church of Ireland, does that inevitably mean that the Lyster of *Ulysses* has to be such as well? While the historical paratext contradicts the text of *Ulysses*, there is nothing within *Ulysses* to hint at the possibility that Lyster might not be a Quaker. The Lyster of *Ulysses* is thus a Schrödinger's Quaker, he both is and is not a Quaker depending upon how one wants to construe *Ulysses* in relation to realms of external fact (realms which are, as the *Dictionary of Irish Biography* shows, not entirely infallible).

These examples all involve relatively minor passages within the text, but they show that the endorsement theory can admit multiple statements, that it can allow for multiple perspectives. That is, while some statements may be contested, they might still suggest interesting possibilities; although certainly some types of incorrect statements about *Ulysses* (such as "Bloom eats lunch at McDonald's" or "Bloom is based on my grandfather") really aren't that interesting at all. More than just a "dual reality," fiction occasions a multiple reality, that is, a multiplicity of perspectives apropos a fractious and ambiguous reality. Rather than instantiate other, possible worlds, the multiplicity of

17. Magee suggests that Joyce called Lyster a Quaker because he would wear a broad-rimmed black hat—like those associated with the Quakers—to cover his bald head. Patricia Hutchins, *James Joyce's World* (London: Methuen, 1957), 50–51.

18. David Murphy, "Lyster, William Thomas," in *Dictionary of Irish Biography*, https://dib.cambridge.org, accessed July 10, 2016. Murphy cites as a source *A Biographical Dictionary of Irish Quakers* (Dublin: Four Courts, 2008), although the second edition of this book makes no mention of Lyster at all. It is more than likely that the (spurious) connection between Lyster and the Quakers originates only with Joyce.

possible endorsements indicates that works of fiction are inevitably incomplete and it is up to the reader to fill in these gaps in ways that may (or may not) be compatible with and thus endorsed by that work. But such interpretive "gap-filling" will never, *pace* the fictional realists, completely eliminate levels of discordance. Even a work like *Ulysses*, which is not short, and which was very carefully written by a very controlling author, has its *gaps*, some deliberate, some accidental, others inevitable. No representation can account for every detail. Indeed, as "Ithaca" makes vivid, the more that is explained, the more there will always need to be explained. And so, the reader plays or negotiates toward some completion, filling in some gaps, working with or against the narrative medium. But these gaps are not homogeneous in character. The stylistic and perspectival multiplicities and peculiarities of *Ulysses* require that the protocols for endorsement must be adaptable to specific contextual circumstances, and thus be variable. The "truth" in fiction is *negotiable*. This helps suggest a difference between truth and fiction (and fictitious truth). A text is not sufficient grounds for endorsement since it needs the cooperation of its readers. Conversely, one can never read just the text itself, one is always bringing oneself to the proceedings—one's knowledge, one's sensibilities, one's ignorance, one's *perspective*. Thus, one is, as the *Ulysses* Best says in "Scylla and Charybdis," quoting Mallarmé, "*reading the book of himself*" (9: 115) when filling in the gaps of narrative.

To take an example of incompleteness, when Bloom enters the living room in "Ithaca" he bumps his head because the furniture had been moved unexpectedly. As is typical with the Ithacan narrative voice—which shares some of the mendacity of the narrative voice of "Wandering Rocks"—we are given the semblance of a lot of detail about the impact, the injury, and about the translocation of the furniture, but nothing about *who* exactly moved the furniture. In a very interesting and symptomatic article called "Molly's Masterstroke," Hugh Kenner takes this specific lacuna as a clue to a larger lacuna within the book, namely, what exactly happened during Molly and Boylan's tryst. As he writes, "But Joyce was no priest of the Eternal Imagination for nothing, and as the priest's liturgies reflect and inflect the operations of the Church Invisible, Joyce was always pleased to have the foreground operation he dwelt on backed up by unseen happenings we can extrapolate."[19] And *extrapolate* is exactly what Kenner does, and with gusto. And in the background of this extrapolation, authorizing the interpretation, lies Kenner's assumption of an omnipotent Joyce setting the scene in the living room for the furniture to be moved. Since Bloom has been gone all day, the furniture could have been moved only by either Molly or Boylan and Kenner claims it must have been Boylan because the extent of rearrangement would have been too much for Molly. For Kenner, this leads to another question: *why*:

> Here documentation lapses, leaving us, though with that irrefutable shifted furniture: that ponderous walnut sideboard, that piano . . . [Molly] is an inexperienced adulterer. Her bonds with her husband have been long in the weaving. The moment to betray him is at hand, the moment to step outside her role as faithful Penelope . . . For Molly, it is easy to assume, this was suddenly too much . . . Like Emma Bovary, like Eveline, she has recourse to literary models . . . Already she is in a pornographic novel, playing the conquered woman. She will modulate that role with the help of one of pornography's simplest postulates, that sexual and muscular vigor are manifestations of the same energy. Drain him, therefore, with exercise. She will postpone, perhaps evade, the physical moment: certainly reduce it . . . She will wear Boylan down moving furniture, heavy furniture.

19. Hugh Kenner, "Molly's Masterstroke," *James Joyce Quarterly* 10, no. 1 (Fall 1972): 19–28, at 19–20.

And so, it seems we are to imagine Blazes Boylan, redfaced, putting his shoulder to the sideboard, tugging at the piano, lifting and carrying the sofa and the majolicatopped table, relocating the heavy chair, the light chair.[20]

Despite the fanciful prose, there is nothing implausible about Kenner's supposition, or, rather, interlinked network of multiple suppositions. He has taken a prompt from the text—the absence of detail about how the furniture was moved—and filled it in in such a way as to fill in another detail, Molly's purported ambivalence about her affair. Kenner is also reading this supposition through his reading of other texts: like Emma Bovary, like Eveline, like Molly, *he* has recourse to literary models.

Just as Kenner's masterstroke was occasioned by a textual lacuna, Kenner's own little narrative, his own fiction about Molly's ambivalence, is itself not without a lacuna or two. This does not necessarily disprove or invalidate his claims, but on one of the "Penelope" notesheets Joyce wrote, "Molly will change furniture."[21] There are all sorts of reasons why this paratextual note need not contravene Kenner, but it does complicate his claim that the translocation of the furniture has to be beyond Molly's abilities. What is significantly more problematic for Kenner is that the text is actually less clear on the matter of the translocation than it might seem. As is common throughout "Ithaca," the text only *simulates* comprehensiveness, just as a writer such as Joyce can only simulate omnipotence. What's crucial for this to work is that the reader is (consciously or unconsciously) complicit in this simulation of comprehensiveness. A reader—like Kenner in this example—falls into the trap of believing *Ulysses* to be complete

20. Ibid., 26.
21. Herring, *Joyce's "Ulysses" Notesheets*, 280.

even when it is, of course, incomplete. Indeed, this is how the movement of the furniture is described:

> A sofa upholstered in prune plush had been translocated from opposite the door to the ingleside near the compactly furled Union Jack (an alteration which he had frequently intended to execute): the blue and white checker inlaid majolicatopped table had been placed opposite the door in the place vacated by the prune plush sofa: the walnut sideboard (a projecting angle of which had momentarily arrested his ingress) had been moved from its position beside the door to a more advantageous but more perilous position in front of the door: two chairs had been moved from right and left of the ingleside to the position originally occupied by the blue and white checker inlaid majolica-topped table. (17: 1281–90)

This certainly seems comprehensive and thorough, but it isn't. As Ian Gunn and Clive Hart note, "The reader is told the original and final positions of the sofa and sideboard, but only the original position of the two chairs and the final positions of the table and piano."[22] This is certainly less fanciful and perhaps less *fun* than Kenner's reading, but it is the one that happens to pay attention to what is actually in the text in front of us. We are simply not given enough information to determine the disposition of the furniture in the living room both before and after the rearrangement. The text thus does not endorse Kenner's masterstroke. A work of fiction like *Ulysses* both invites *and* disbars interpretive leaps and further fictions such as Kenner's and even such as Gunn and Hart's. Gaps such as this thus fail to endorse Joyce's own claim in a letter to Frank Budgen that in "Ithaca" "the

22. Gunn and Hart, *James Joyce's Dublin,* 72.

reader will know everything and know it in the boldest and coldest way."[23] Neither reader nor writer can know everything.

The various approaches to fiction within logic treat statements concerning fictional objects as exact syllogisms, but fictional entities fit into syllogistic formulae only awkwardly. This is because the author (even one such as Joyce) cannot do all the "work" that is required for the fictional apparatus to function. The input of its readers will be required as to how many allowances can be made: some readers might not bristle at the statement that Bloom ate at McDonald's, whereas others would. But of the readers who would disagree with the McDonald's business, many of them would be perfectly happy with Kenner's masterstroke or the anachronism involving the Mirus bazaar. Reading fiction thus requires a degree of tolerance for ambiguity and incompleteness.

Joycean exegesis is matched in ingenuity and ambition by the subset of Sherlock Holmes fandom obsessed with what is called the "Great Game," which is the application of Holmesian ratiocination to redress the various lacunae and inconsistencies within the Holmes canon. Holmes is commonly used as a generic example of a fictional entity in philosophical accounts of fictional realism, yet, as far as I know, the Great Game has not been mooted in such discussions, even though it offers some interesting, complicating relevance.[24] Dorothy Sayers, one of the earliest practitioners of the Great Game, explains:

The game of applying the methods of the "Higher Criticism" to the Sherlock Holmes canon was begun, many years ago, by Ronald Knox, with the aim of showing that, by those methods,

23. James Joyce, *Letters*, vol. 1, ed. Stuart Gilbert (New York: Viking, 1957), 160.
24. See, for example, Saul Kripke, *Naming and Necessity*, revised edition (London: Blackwell, 1980), 157–58.

one could disintegrate a modern classic as speciously as a certain school of critics have endeavoured to disintegrate the Bible. Since then, the thing has become a hobby among a select set of jesters here and in America. The rule of the game is that it must be played as solemnly as a county cricket match at Lord's; the slightest touch of extravagance or burlesque ruins the atmosphere.[25]

Conan Doyle famously did not care much for his creation and his stories are laced with inconsistencies and errors. Part of the conceit of the Great Game is to feign being a dogmatic proponent of the endorsement theory. The practitioners assume that the texts as written are unambiguously and unequivocally accurate and that any apparent mistake is merely an invitation for deductive reasoning. That is, any and every statement in the texts must be able to endorse any other statement and that any apparent failure of endorsement is merely a gap that can be supplemented by deductive reasoning. One particularly shrewd piece of interpretation involves Watson's name. In the story "The Man with the Twisted Lip," Watson's wife, Mary, calls him "James,"[26] yet in every other story where his first name is given, it's John. We are told elsewhere that Watson's middle initial is H., although Conan Doyle neglects to elaborate what it stands for. Sayers' masterstroke is to claim that the H. stands for *Hamish* and thus Mary has a little nickname for her husband, the Anglicized form of this name.[27] Alternative theories to explain the inconsistency of Watson's first name are certainly possible (and have been proposed), showing that endorsement need not be exclusive, but rather admits of multiple perspectives. This is perhaps not that different from Joycean interpretation, or, indeed, any interpretative act of filling in the gaps.

25. Dorothy L. Sayers, *Unpopular Opinions* (London: Victor Gollancz, 1946), 7.
26. Arthur Conan Doyle, *The Adventures of Sherlock Holmes* (London: George Newnes, 1892), 129.
27. Sayers, *Unpopular Opinions*, 148–51.

Conan Doyle, of course, didn't care much for his Holmes and thus never really bothered about any mistakes he might have made, while Joyce did care about his. But this did not stop Joyce from making mistakes. In "Scylla and Charybdis" Stephen haughtily proclaims, "A man of genius makes no mistakes. His errors are volitional and are the portals of discovery" (9: 228–9). This is a particularly shrewd line on Joyce's part since it absolves him, as the author—and a *soi disant* man of genius—of making any mistakes. Since a man of genius makes no mistakes, anything that *seems* like a mistake in *Ulysses* must actually be something ingenious that can be discerned only by a suitably astute reader. So, because of this line, Joyce shunts the responsibility for error from the author to the reader by saying, in effect, there are no mistakes in this text, just artistic brilliance that may or may not be properly apprehended. It is almost as if, in this line, Joyce is endorsing a great game of his own.

Error and the apprehension—or misapprehension—of error are thus fundamentally enmeshed within Joyce's aesthetics and are entwined with Joyce's attempts toward an exacting verisimilitude. On November 2, 1921, Joyce wrote his aunt Josephine to ask if "an ordinary person [could] climb over the railings of no 7 Eccles Street."[28] It is not known what, or even if, Aunt Josephine replied to this question about the railings of 7 Eccles Street. In 1909 Joyce had seen his friend J. F. Byrne, then resident at that address, execute such a maneuver, but Byrne was of an athletic build and Joyce needed to know if someone less fit could also do it in order to determine the wording for the passage in "Ithaca" when Bloom, lacking the key to his front door, jumps over the railings of his house to get to the unlocked kitchen door below (17: 84–9).[29] Since his aunt Josephine never replied to this question, Joyce gave Bloom a stature

28. Joyce, *Letters,*, 175.
29. See also J. F. Byrne, *Silent Years* (New York: Farrar, Straus and Young, 1953), 157.

equivalent to Byrne's in order to make this feat plausible within the realm of factual Dublin.

However, this desire to be factually accurate led Joyce into error elsewhere. Bloom's height and weight follow from Byrne: five foot nine (17: 86–7) with a weight of eleven stone and four pounds at his most recent measurement on May 12, that year's Ascension Day (17: 91–2). Elsewhere in "Ithaca" we are told that his chest measures 29½ inches after two months' exercise under Sandow's regime, as opposed to a mere 28 inches before (17: 1818). Unfortunately, for a man of Bloom's height and weight, a chest measurement of 40 to 42 inches would be expected by most tailors. So, the information about Bloom's height and weight does not endorse the information about Bloom's chest.

Just as Joyce had his reasons for giving Bloom his height and weight, he also had his reasons for giving Bloom those incongruous chest measurements—even if those reasons work against Bloom's measurements. Kenner pointed out that Eugen Sandow's book *Strength and How to Obtain It*, which Bloom owns (17: 1397), includes in the back a selection of testimonials from satisfied customers. The very first one of these, from a Mr. Thomas Fox of Limehouse, includes the exact same measurements as are given to Bloom. So Bloom has the height and weight of a Byrne and the chest, biceps, and forearms of a Fox. However, just a few pages before Fox's chest measurements are given, he notes in his effusive letter to Sandow that he is only five foot in height and weighs just seven stone: the proverbial 98-pound weakling.[30]

Although Kenner has laid out a possible, if not probable, scenario for Joyce having made a simple mistake by inadvertently mixing the

---

30. Eugene Sandow, *Strength and How to Obtain It* (London, 1897), 40–41, 37–28, cited in Hugh Kenner, "*Ulysses*," revised edition (Baltimore, MD: Johns Hopkins University Press, 1987), 164–5.

measurements of two individuals of unequal physique, he proposes that we read Bloom's incongruous measurements as deliberately chosen by Joyce as an affect of free indirect discourse: "Not all men know their own chest measurements nor even what a plausible one would be, as witness the fact that Bloom's twenty-eight-inch chest was forty years [*sic*] striking anyone as unlikely."[31] Since the supplied chest measurement does not represent an anatomically correct individual, it instead indicates Bloom's own fallible self-knowledge. In this way, even mistakes can be massaged to fall under the dispensation of the legal fiction of authorial omnipotence. The text is incomplete at this point of correlating Bloom's height and weight with his chest size because the inconsistency is not explained within the text. Precisely because the text is incomplete various hypotheses can be proposed to redress this lacuna. The individual hypotheses are neither true nor false, but rather more or less plausible or more or less aesthetically pleasing.

There is also another possibility amid these possibilities: perhaps *Ulysses* is set in a world where Bloom's measurements as given in text are well within a normal range. I do not think that there's anything in the text of *Ulysses* that would contradict such a proposition and thus it could actually be endorsed. This is why possible worlds theory is so tempting to use when accounting for fiction: a fictional world is but one possibility, albeit a possibility that lacks a predicate of actuality. And each possible world yields multiple possible interpretive states, such as a possible world in which Bloom's measurements are normal or another possible world where Garryowen breaks into 7 Eccles Street and rearranges the furniture. Likewise, of all the possible worlds with a consulting detective named Sherlock Holmes, some have a John Watson, others a James Watson, and others still a John Hamish Watson. A further alternative is that the incongruity in

31. Ibid., 165.

Bloom's measurements need be read only at face value: it does not *need* additional explanation or interpretation. Although, certainly, *Ulysses*'s readers—just as Holmes's readers—can try to devise such ingenious explanations. But this brings us back to the incompleteness of representation, the vacuum into which readers' ingenuities pour.

The example of Bloom's mismatched measurements could be read as an instance of Joyce neglecting to perfectly correlate one passage with another, thereby creating an accidental inconsistency. While Joyce was a very careful and controlling author, he is not infallible. Inconsistencies in *Ulysses* are not as common as with the Holmesian corpus, but they are still non-negligible. This creates another complication for the endorsement theory since this means that not everything in the text will tie together. For example, in "Calypso," Bloom remembers the first time he met Molly was at Luke Doyle's house in Dolphin's Barn where there was a game of charades (4: 345), while in "Sirens" he thinks that he first met her at Mat Dillon's house in Terenure (11: 725). Going through the drafts of these passages— and others that relate to the Blooms' courtship—Luca Crispi has proven that the inconsistency is not Bloom's confusion but rather Joyce's failure to correlate elements of Bloom's backstory: "The textual history of these scenes indicates that it was James Joyce himself who was imprecise about these facts in the novel, and this narrative inconsistency will always be a part of the novel."[32] Thus, Bloom's history contains non-endorsing statements. This creates the possibility for another dimension in which there is no single stable entity that one could call "the text of *Ulysses*": because *Ulysses* was composed over an extended period and was the product of numerous revisions, not all of which were perfectly and consistently implemented, it will inevitably include elements that fail to be mutually endorsing.

---

32. Luca Crispi, *Joyce's Creative Process and the Construction of Charatcters in "Ulysses"* (Oxford: Oxford University Press, 2015), 140; see also 140–7.

Rather than resort to possible worlds to account for all these inconsistencies between *Ulysses* and the world, or, indeed, within *Ulysses*
itself, endorsement theory takes a narrower approach: that these are
disjunctions within perspectives instead of being portals to other,
non-actual full-fledged worlds. Endorsement theory allows for
incompleteness and disjunction and thereby tolerates ambiguity and
imperfection.

With its hallucinatory phantasmagoria and baroque theatrical
contrivances, "Circe" provides an excellent testing ground for thinking through disjunctions of fiction. According to Arthur Power, Joyce
once remarked that in "Circe," "I approached reality closer in my opin-
ion than anywhere else in the book, except perhaps for moments in
the last chapter. Sensation is our object, heightened even to the point
of hallucination."[33] The key word in Joyce's claim is *approached*: like
Ulysses "Circe" is but an approach toward and approximation of an
asymptotic reality. Within "Circe" Bloom is subjected to all sorts
of hallucinations that stand apart from the rest of the action within
Bella Cohen's brothel and their environs. For example, the so-called
Messianic scene—in which Bloom is elevated to the giddy heights
of, successively (but not necessarily in order of importance), "Lord
mayor of Dublin" (15: 1365), "future chief magistrate" (15: 1372),
"alderman sir Leo Bloom's" (15: 1383), "Leopold the First," King of
Ireland (15: 1472), successor to Parnell (15: 1514), "the man that
got away James Stephens" (15: 1532), and so on until he is the new
Messiah (15: 1852)—occurs as an interruption to Zoe's comment,
"Go on. Make a stump speech out of it" (15: 1353); "Talk away till
you're black in the face" (15: 1958). It is as if the text—or perhaps
more precisely the *Arranger*[34]—takes the first part of Zoe's statement

33. Arthur Power, *Conversations with James Joyce* (Dublin: Lilliput, 1999), 86.
34. David Hayman defines the Arranger as a "significant, felt absence in the text, an unstated
but inescapable source of control" in *"Ulysses": The Mechanics of Meaning*, revised edition

quite literally and the Messianic scene begins with Bloom, "*in work-man's corduroy overalls*" (15: 1355), making a stump speech about the evils of tobacco, which, in turn, begins his improbably rapid political rise and then fall, at which point we return, eventually, to Zoe's inter-rupted comment. The Messianic scene can thus be construed as a fic-tion (Bloom's political rise) performed upon another fiction (Bloom and Stephen at the brothel). It is not even necessarily the case that Bloom is experiencing an instantaneous hallucination, rather the sequence is a textual operation extrapolated upon him by some nar-rational medium that reveals aspects of his personality and charac-ter that might otherwise remain hidden. If there is an Arranger, then Bloom is *arranged*.

If the Messianic scene begins as a tangential aside that follows from Zoe's comment "Make a stump speech out of it," it then con-tinues by an internal logic of one thing leading to another, or text proliferating text, as Bloom's "stump speech" leads to cheers and his elevation to Lord Mayor of Dublin. During his ascendency, he retains various characteristic traits and quirks, such as his imper-fect mastery of various facts: "Sir Walter Ralegh brought from the new world that potato and that weed [tobacco] . . . That is to say he brought the poison a hundred years before another person whose name I forget brought the food" (15: 1356–60). Initially, Bloom claims Ralegh brought both tobacco and the potato to Europe, before correcting himself to state that the potato was a separate discovery, the specific details of which elude him.[35] Even within a hallucination, Bloom remains somewhat scatterbrained, which is to say that Bloom

---

(Madison: University of Wisconsin Press, 1982), 123). See also Philip Kitcher's essay in this volume for a discussion of the Arranger.

35. "Hieronymus Cardan, a monk, is supposed to have been the first to introduce [the potato] from Peru into Spain, from which country it passed into Italy and thence into Belgium" (*Encyclopedia Britannica*, 11th edition, s.v. "potato").

remains Bloom.[36] Likewise, Mulligan, Madden, Crotthers, Costello, and Dixon all appear and testify to Bloom's sexual delinquency; as Dixon states, "Professor Bloom is a finished example of the new womanly man . . . He is about to have a baby" (15: 1798–1810), at which point Bloom gives birth to octuplets. While the birthing does not, as such, "happen" within one tranche of the novel's action, it can be taken to indicate any number of aspects about Bloom's personality, from his empathy to his various little sexual perversions.

One function of the hallucinations in "Circe" is to provide an exaggerated, even burlesque representation of otherwise submerged aspects of Bloom's personality. For example, the Blooms' former maid, Mary Driscoll, appears as if a witness in a trial to testify that Bloom had sexually abused her: "He surprised me in the rere of the premises, Your honour, when the missus was out shopping one morning with a request for a safety pin" (15: 885–6). Bloom protests, "She counterassaulted" (15: 890), a point that is corroborated by Molly's recollection that the attraction between Bloom and Driscoll seemed to have been mutual (18: 55–6). And so, while Driscoll's enstaged courtroom allegation is exaggerated and distorted, it is not exactly false. In a manner of speaking, this hallucination is a legal fiction that reveals Bloom's sexual guilt, that is, a transposition of guilt onto a fictionalized court of law.

---

36. Since I am a pedant, I must comment upon the spelling "Ralegh" and its implications for this passage. *Ralegh* was one of the various spellings the man himself used for his own name. "The spelling Raleigh, which posterity has preferred, happens to be one he is not known to have ever employed." William Stebbing, *Sir Walter Ralegh* (Oxford: Clarendon Press, 1891), 31. Joyce unambiguously wrote "Ralegh" here, but a typesetter changed this to "Raleigh" on a late page proof (Groden et al., *James Joyce Archive*, 26: 124), which is how this name appeared in all editions previous to Gabler's. Elsewhere in *Ulysses*, in "Scylla and Charybdis," Joyce used the form "Raleigh" (9: 628). And so this crux rests on two axes: an axis of variation across published editions and an axis of Joyce's (apparent) inconsistency across his text. Furthermore, in at least the Gabler edition, in a passage where Bloom is characteristically addled, his speech is transcribed in such a way as to accord with an unconventional albeit historically accurate spelling.

The Messianic scene and at least most of the other hallucinatory scenes in "Circe" show that the double consciousness model is endorsed by *Ulysses*, that is, one reads the Messianic scene while still believing Bloom to be sitting in a brothel, awkwardly flirting with Zoe. There are of course numerous scenes within "Circe" that are ambiguous in terms of being within the naturalistic setting or, somehow, apart from it. For example, Stephen's hallucination of his mother definitely occurs within the naturalistic setting of the brothel since his behavior creates several consequences that are remarked upon, such as the damage done to the lamp. Conversely, Stephen and Bloom's joint vision of Shakespeare in a mirror (15: 3821–9) is also likely an event within the naturalistic setting (Bloom and Stephen each see their own reflection in the mirror), but is relayed in such a way as to emphasize a surreal quality.

The hallucinatory intrusions (or quasi-intrusions) are metafictional moments within the text that allow for different sets of perspectives upon Bloom and Stephen, perspectives that would not ordinarily be within the formal repertoire of a work of supposedly naturalistic fiction. This would be the way, I think, in which we could evaluate Joyce's claim to having "approached reality closer" in "Circe," that these new perspectives of Bloom and Stephen reveal aspects that would otherwise remain obscure. For example, "Circe" closes with Bloom's vision of his dead son, Rudy, near Stephen's prostrate body. Unlike Stephen's vision of his mother, it is not exactly clear if this vision belongs within the naturalistic setting or if it is another "operation" performed upon Bloom as in the Messianic scene. The vision has no overt impact on the start of the next episode, "Eumaeus," when Bloom helps Stephen get up from the ground. The vision does not necessarily add much to a reader's knowledge of Bloom as such since it has been clear through most of *Ulysses* that Bloom is still emotionally fragile in the wake of Rudy's death, some ten years earlier. But, the tenor of the vision is both fascinating and deeply affecting.

This is a passage that I did not think too much about until after my son was born, and now I can't read it without crying.

> (*Silent, thoughtful, alert he stands on guard, his fingers at his lips in the attitude of secret master. Against the dark wall a figure appears slowly, a fairy boy of eleven, a changeling, kidnapped, dressed in an Eton suit with glass shoes and a little bronze helmet, holding a book in his hand. He reads from right to left inaudibly, smiling, kissing the page.*)
>
> BLOOM
> (*wonderstruck, calls inaudibly*) Rudy!
>
> RUDY
> (*gazes, unseeing, into Bloom's eyes and goes on reading, kissing, smiling. He has a delicate mauve face. On his suit he has diamond and ruby buttons. In his free left hand he holds a slim ivory cane with a violet bowknot. A white lambkin peeps out of his waistcoat pocket.*)
> (15: 4955–67)

Rudy's appearance here is overdetermined. It includes elements from Bloom's memories, such as the "white lambkin," the "fair corselet of lamb's wool" (14: 269) that Rudy was buried with, as well as elements from how Bloom imagined he might have grown up had he lived, such as being dressed in an Eton suit (6: 75–6) and reading Hebrew, like Bloom's grandfather (7: 206). But there is more to Rudy's attire than memories of his brief life and Bloom's preterite hope for the future he and his son never had. The revenant is a *changeling,* a sham decoy, with a grotesque mauve face, and attire cobbled together from fairy tales (Cinderella), nursery rhymes (Little Bo-Peep), children's stories (Lord Fauntleroy), and Greek mythology (Hermes). Bloom can imagine Rudy only as a fiction, as being cobbled together out of various fictions. Thus, a kind of fictionalization is directly thematized within this passage in which Bloom calls to a vision that does not reply. Bloom's grief is fictitious, many times over. Marilyn French precisely gets at the affective aspect of this passage: "For noble Leopold Bloom can find a purpose to his life only in a fairy-tale/nursery rhyme symbol—a fact that is at once ludicrous, pathetic, outrageous, comic, and true to human experience."[37] Before this passage, we know that Bloom is still sad over his son's death, but now we see some figurations of that sadness, some fragmentary manifestations of Bloom's imperfect strategies for coping with the deepest of griefs. Of course, these might not be *Bloom's* own coping strategies, but metaphoric displacements, that is, fictions of grief that are used as proxy representations of Bloom's grieving. He may be deluded, he may be partially deluding himself, but in so doing, he can live on.

Reading fiction is an exercise in juggling multiple, discordant perspectives—the dual or multiple layers of fissured facts and fictions. On one level, Bloom sees an uncanny apparition of his dead son, grown but unreachable; on another, this apparition is merely a textual contrivance of the Arranger, applied to indicate Bloom's stages of grief. On yet another level, none of this happened, and this is all a product of Joyce's writing. All these perspectives—and more—are valid and would all come into play in acts of reading *Ulysses*. Conversely, no one of these perspectives tells us all that can be told.

Because the world is incomplete and always just slightly beyond our understanding, we invent fictions to explain our world to us, fictions that are themselves, in turn, inevitably incomplete and beyond human ken. Fictions that are particularly well-crafted—such as *Ulysses*—allow us some knowledge and insight, not just despite, but *because* of their incompleteness. *Ulysses*, by merging the real with the fictitious, along with the blurring of facts and fictions, shows just how porous and pervasive and evasive categories of fiction can be. Rather than treat fiction as either something pernicious from which

37. Marilyn French, *The Book as World* (New York: Paragon, 1993), 206.

we must be carefully inoculated or, conversely, as something that can be comfortably subordinated to reality (in the manner of the fictional realists), fiction is already intricately intertwined with reality. The discordant, partial perspectives of fiction afford both delusion and insight.

BIBLIOGRAPHY

Adams, Robert M. *Surface and Symbol*. New York: Oxford University Press, 1962.

A Biographical Dictionary of Irish Quakers. Dublin: Four Courts, 2008.

Briggs, Austin. "The Fell Stop at the End of 'Ithaca': Thirteen Ways—and Then Some—of Looking at a Black Dot." *Joyce Studies Annual* 7 (1996): 125–44.

Budgen, Frank. *James Joyce and the Making of "Ulysses."* New York: Oxford University Press, 1989.

Byrne, J. F. *Silent Years*. New York: Farrar, Straus and Young, 1953.

Conan Doyle, Arthur. *The Adventures of Sherlock Holmes*. London: George Newnes, 1892.

Crispi, Luca, *Joyce's Creative Process and the Construction of Charatcters in "Ulysses."* Oxford: Oxford University Press, 2015.

Ellmann, Richard. *James Joyce*. Revised edition. New York: Oxford University Press, 1982.

French, Marilyn. *The Book as World*. New York: Paragon, 1993.

Groden, Michael, et al., eds. *The James Joyce Archive*. New York: Garland, 1978–79.

Gunn, Ian, and Clive Hart. *James Joyce's Dublin*. London: Thames and Hudson, 2004.

Harari, Yuval Noah. *Sapiens: A Brief History of Humankind*. London: Vintage, 2011.

Hayman, David. *"Ulysses": The Mechanics of Meaning*. Revised edition. Madison: University of Wisconsin Press, 1982.

Herring, Phillip. *Joyce's "Ulysses" Notesheets in the British Museum*. Charlottesville: University Press of Virginia, 1972.

Hutchins, Patricia. *James Joyce's World*. London: Methuen, 1957.

Igoe, Vivien. *The Real People of Joyce's "Ulysses."* Dublin: UCD Press, 2016.

Johnson, Samuel. "Preface to Shakespeare." In Frank Brady and W. K. Wimsatt, eds., *Selected Poetry and Prose*. Berkeley: University of California Press, 1977, 299–336.

Joyce, James. *Letters*. Volume 1. Ed. Stuart Gilbert. New York: Viking, 1957.

Kenner, Hugh. "Molly's Masterstroke." *James Joyce Quarterly* 10, no. 1 (Fall 1972): 19–28.

Kenner, Hugh. "*Ulysses.*" Revised edition. Baltimore, MD: Johns Hopkins University Press, 1987.

Kripke, Saul. *Naming and Necessity*. Revised edition. London: Blackwell, 1980.

Kroon, Fred, and Alberto Voltolini. "Fiction." In *Stanford Encyclopedia of Philosophy*. http://plato.stanford.edu/entries/fiction/. Accessed July 1, 2016.

Newman, Robert D. "Transformatio Coniunctionis: Alchemy in *Ulysses*." In Robert D. Newman and Weldon Thornton, eds., *Joyce's "Ulysses": The Larger Perspective*. Newark: University of Delaware Press, 1987, 168–86.

Murphy, David. "Lyster, William Thomas." In *Dictionary of Irish Biography*. https://dib.cambridge.org. Accessed July 10, 2016.

Power, Arthur. *Conversations with James Joyce*. Dublin: Lilliput, 1999.

Sandow, Eugene. *Strength and How to Obtain It*. London, 1897.

Sayers, Dorothy L. *Unpopular Opinions*. London: Victor Gollancz, 1946.

Slote, Sam. *"Ulysses" in the Plural*. Dublin: National Library of Ireland, 2004.

Stebbing, William. *Sir Walter Ralegh*. Oxford: Clarendon Press, 1891.

Chapter 5

Doing Dublin in Different Voices

DAVID HILLS

VOICES IN A TEXT

Mr Bloom walked unheeded along his grove by saddened angels, crosses, broken pillars, family vaults, stone hopes praying with upcast eyes, old Ireland's hearts and hands. More sensible to spend the money on some charity for the living. Pray for the repose of the soul of. Does anybody really? Plant him and have done with him. Like down a coalshoot. Then lump them together to save time. All souls' day. Twentyseventh I'll be at his grave. Ten shillings for the gardener. He keeps it free of weeds. Old man himself. Bent down double with his shears clipping. Near death's door. Who passed away. Who departed this life. As if they did it of their own accord. Got the shove, all of them. Who kicked the bucket. More interesting if they told you what they were. So and So, wheelwright. I travelled for cork lino. I paid five shillings in the pound. Or a woman's with her saucepan. I cooked good Irish stew . . .

I've been helped along wonderfully and rescued from many missteps by patient comments from Philip Kitcher and an anonymous reviewer for Oxford University Press.

Joyce's Ulysses. Philip Kitcher, Oxford University Press (2020). © Oxford University Press.
DOI: 10.1093/oso/9780190842260.001.0001

Besides how could you remember everybody? Eyes, walk, voice. Well, the voice, yes: gramophone. Have a gramophone in every grave or keep it in the house. After dinner on a Sunday. Put on poor old greatgrandfather. Kraahraark! Hellohellohello amawfullyglad kraark awfullygladaseeagain hellohello amawf krpthsth. Remind you of the voice like the photograph reminds you of the face. Otherwise you couldn't remember the face after fifteen years, say. (6: 928–48, 962–7)

Joyce and his three great protagonists—Stephen, Bloom, Molly—share certain striking opinions about the dead and their voices.

The repose of the dead takes care of itself without our prayers: they are at rest already, beyond our power to add or detract. The dead are gone, out of reach, in that nothing we do now can gratify or punish them, give them pain or give them pleasure, in any way. It would have been better and more honest to have saved the sweater in which we buried poor Rudy and given it to some needy living child. It would be better and more honest, going forward, to stop visiting poor Father's grave on the anniversary of his suicide, hoping to tell him things we haven't yet told him or to hear from him things as yet unheard. As Christ himself preached, let the dead bury the dead. Easier preached than practiced, of course. The two men in this story who profess to consider mourning an empty sham are dressed in mourning themselves: Bloom, out of respect for social appearances; Stephen, out of contempt for them.

The least distinctive and distinguishing thing about the dead is their being dead, their having died, a matter in which most of them displayed no initiative whatsoever. Got the shove, all of them. Better to dwell on their distinctive deeds and accomplishments, things about them we can rightly admire and actively emulate in their admitted absence, remembering all the while that the dead themselves have no stake in how we fare when we follow and try to surpass the examples they set for us. The best way to privately remember and publicly commemorate the dead is by emulating their distinctive accomplishments, large and small: their mighty deeds, their little ways, their good Irish stew.

What the dead leave behind that most vividly embodies and preserves their power as examples is our memory of their voices. The quickest and most reliable way to make a dead loved one freshly available to our emulative powers is to recall the distinctive lilt of her voice or a distinctive turn of phrase to which she was addicted.

At this point Bloom's progressive entrepreneurial imagination, his urge to devise and implement rational social reforms involving lucrative business opportunities for Bloom himself, lures him out on a limb of his own. Perhaps the most up-to-date way to preserve and renew our auditory memories of the dead is to equip every graveside or dining room with a suitable set of gramophone recordings, produced in advance for this very purpose. That way the dead can speak to us directly, renewing our memories of them and the power of their example, whenever we see fit . . .

To which Bloom's internalized other, born of the mockery that regularly greets his earnest efforts at piecemeal social engineering, promptly reacts with a refuting raspberry: "Kraahraark! Hellohellohello amawfullyglad kraark awfullygladaseeagain hellohello amawf krpthsth."

In this challenging sentence—good luck reading it aloud!—we hear the scratchy honk of primitive first-generation gramophones. We hear Bloom himself, since this derisive squawk is part of Bloom's interior monologue, part of what he says to himself as he walks unheeded along his grove. And we hear the distinctive deflationary voice of the scoffers with whom Bloom's imagination is condemned to struggle, day in and day out. Listened to in this last spirit, the line is a snatch of *virtual backtalk,* served up to Bloom by Bloom's internalized audience.

We hear more than one voice, speaking to more than one effect, in the same words. What we don't hear in the text, what we can't hope to hear there, given principles on which Joyce and his protagonists are in hearty agreement, are the dead's own voices.

PARALLAX

Shift your perspective on a static array of physical objects and your view of it changes in familiar ways. Previously occluded objects and features of objects come into view while previously visible ones slip from sight. Objects and features that dominated your view at first dwindle into mere details, while new ones loom up and come to dominate in their place. Objects that adjoined one another may become visually estranged, while ones that were far apart become visual neighbors. The closer a particular object is to us, the easier it is to modify its role in our view by shifting from side to side; the further away it is, the harder it is to do this. Disparities between distinct views of the same array of objects constitute an important indication of how far away each of them is, an important "depth cue." Such is *parallax*. The concept is used, but not explained, in *The Story of the Heavens* by the Irish astronomer Robert Ball, one of numerous volumes of popular geography and popular science that grace the library of Leopold Bloom (17: 1373). Bloom puzzles over the word *parallax* repeatedly during his day, much as he puzzles over its more famous companion, *metempsychosis*.

The concept of parallax, if not the word, fascinates Stephen as well. A Thomistic Aristotelian in most philosophical matters, Stephen briefly flirts with Berkeley's *New Theory of Vision*, on which visible things are collections of visual ideas and visual ideas are a conventional language God employs to converse with us about urgent matters of tactile fact— the pleasures and pains we'd be in for, were we to exercise our wills in various ways. For Berkeley, visual height and visual breadth are things we can genuinely see, but *depth*, distance away from us, is something invisible we swiftly, effortlessly infer or think out by interpreting two-dimensional visual signs. "Proteus":

> Who watches me here? Who ever anywhere will read these written words? Signs on a white field. Somewhere to someone in your flutiest voice. The good bishop of Cloyne took the veil of the temple out of his shovel hat: veil of space with colored emblems hatched on a field. Hold hard. Colored on a flat: yes, that's right. Flat I see, then think distance, near, far, flat I see, east, back. Ah, see now! Falls back suddenly, frozen in stereoscope. Click does the trick. (3: 414–20)

In the John Smibert portrait of 1730 (National Portrait Gallery, London), Berkeley wears a soft black shovel hat of old-fashioned academic regalia, the spitting image of Stephen's own "Hamlet hat." So the role of Berkeley is a natural one for nearsighted Stephen to try on for size. *Flat I see, then think distance.*

We make deliberate explicit use of parallax when we calculate a nearby star's distance using changes in its position against a background of more distant "fixed stars" over the course of half a year. The diameter of the earth's orbit serves as the baseline over which we shift our point of view on the star and its background. We make unconscious implicit use of parallax in ordinary binocular depth perception, exploiting the shorter baseline that separates our two eyes.

Parallax differs from other familiar depth cues (interposition, shadow, atmospheric perspective, and the like) in that it depends on disparities between distinct equally good views. If we firmly and permanently commit ourselves to a single point of view on things, then no matter how carefully we occupy it and how assiduously we exploit it, this particular cue will be unavailable to us.

This so-called measure of distance is really a measure of closeness. For the *greater* an object's parallax (given a particular shift from side to side, a particular baseline), the *closer* it is to the spectator. This suggests a new and initially counterintuitive way of thinking about social or psychological closeness, intimacy. We often suppose that the more intimate we are with particular people or things, the more stable and steady our impression of them is as a result. What if this has things backward? What if the more intimate we are with particular things, the more volatile our sense of them tends to become? Alexander Nehamas says we never stop asking ourselves what it is we see in our friends and loved ones: their value and interest for us is always still to be confirmed and still to be continued.[1] The one man in her life Molly can't make up her mind about in the pages of "Penelope," the one who cuts a radically different figure each time he comes up in her thoughts, is her estranged husband Poldy. Perhaps this is a hopeful sign, for him and for their marriage.

There are two main ways the storytelling of *Ulysses* invites us to derive depth from disparity, to see (and hear) flat, then think distance. Both were of interest to Hugh Kenner, who viewed the book as a sustained assault on the monocular narrative objectivity pursued by the likes of Flaubert and Henry James. It is not for nothing that *Ulysses* tangles with and defeats a Cyclops.

The first is Joyce's *aesthetic of delay,* his way of letting diverse aspects of a single event or circumstance swim into view at widely separated points in the text as they figure in the thoughts and remembrances of different characters at different times:

> Two different versions at least, that is Joyce's normal way; and the uncanny sense of reality that grows in readers of *Ulysses* page

---

1. Alexander Nehamas, *Only a Promise of Happiness: The Place of Beauty in a World of Art* (Princeton, NJ: Princeton University Press, 2007), 53–63.

after page is fostered by the neatness with which versions of the same event, versions different in wording and often in constituent facts—separated, moreover, by tens or hundreds of pages—reliably render one another substantial.[2]

Conceive of this as *long baseline parallax*. Over hundreds of pages the book gradually constructs a connected picture of the evening at Mat Dillon's when Bloom and Molly first met, Molly the winner and Bloom runner-up in a game of musical chairs, an evening when Stephen was present as well, an evening that appears to have given lilacs and the shade cast by lilac bushes a permanent place in Bloom's conception of the good life. Also, perhaps, the evening Bloom beat John Henry Menton in a game of bowls, causing the ladies to laugh at Menton, inadvertently ruining Menton's hopes of pursuing Molly himself, and seeding an angry grudge against Bloom on Menton's part that persists to this day. One of the pleasures of rereading *Ulysses* is to watch such accumulations of flat, individually insignificant, widely scattered details "fall back suddenly" and take on the frozen depth of Wordsworthian spots of time.

A second way to get us to see flat, then think distance, call it *short baseline parallax*, multiplies points of view on a fictional event or circumstance within the confines of a single passage by multiplying the distinct voices we hear in the text and the distinct ways they make themselves heard.

Such effects usually require us to recognize a character's distinctive vocabulary, diction, and habits of thought in the words on the page, but they needn't do so. Here is an early bit of business between Stephen and Buck Mulligan from "Telemachus"; Stephen's soft black Hamlet hat happens to figure in it:

2. Hugh Kenner, *Ulysses*, rev. ed. (Baltimore, MD: Johns Hopkins University Press, 1987), 75.

He [Mulligan] emptied his pockets on to the table.

—There's your snotrag, he said.

And putting on his stiff collar and rebellious tie he spoke to them, chiding them, and to his dangling watchchain. His hands plunged and rummaged in his trunk while he called for a clean handkerchief. *God, we'll simply have to dress the character. I want puce gloves and green boots. Contradiction. Do I contradict myself? Very well then, I contradict myself. Mercurial Malachi.* A limp black missile flew out of his talking hands.

—And there's your Latin quarter hat, he said. (1: 511–9)

Now the one getting dressed and calling out for things, the one reasonably suspected of a Wildean yen for puce gloves and green boots, is Buck Mulligan. But the words I've italicized aren't Mulligan's own words, spoken out loud by Mulligan himself. At this point Mulligan is engaged in a whimsical conversation with his collar, tie, and watchchain, chiding them for various kinds of misconduct— a conversation we readers aren't privy to. If the narrative switched from describing Mulligan's nonverbal doings to quoting Mulligan's spoken words at "God, we'll simply have to dress the character," we would get a new line and a dash to mark this fact. We get nothing of the sort. So the italicized words come from Stephen's interior monologue. More specifically, they are words put in Mulligan's mouth by Stephen's unspoken thoughts: it is Stephen who imagines Mulligan likening himself to Oscar Wilde and Walt Whitman, Stephen who imagines Mulligan praising himself as "Mercurial Malachi." The speech Stephen imagines for Mulligan replaces or drowns out Mulligan's actual speech in the book's account of this brief exchange.

No dash, hence no real quoted speech, hence interior monologue instead. The only appropriate owner for interior monologue to this particular effect at this particular point is Stephen. The thoughts and words are wholly in character for Mulligan, but Mulligan's mind is occupied elsewhere with noisy and ingenious (unreported) chatter about rebellious accessories and clean handkerchiefs. The signals are swift, small, and easy to miss, but clear enough when carefully thought through.

The sense in which Stephen puts these words in Mulligan's mouth is rather special. They occur to him as a rueful running commentary on what Mulligan is actually saying and doing—as words Stephen himself *could* say, *aping* Mulligan, in a piece of backtalk designed to disparage Mulligan's actual antics. But having composed this fitting bit of backtalk, Stephen keeps it to himself. As so often in his dealings with Mulligan, he bites his tongue. Another bit of virtual backtalk, then, like dismissive squawk we encountered in "Hades." But while that backtalk was addressed *to* the thinker himself (Bloom) by internalized others, this backtalk is addressed *by* the thinker himself (Stephen) to actual others—or would be, if Stephen didn't bite his tongue and keep his backtalk to himself.

BAUDELAIRE'S MODERNISM: GHOSTS

The medley of disparate voices audible in the text of *Ulysses*—high and low, cultured and uncultured, careful and reckless, contemporary and antique—made a deep impression on Pound and Eliot when they read the book in manuscript. It prompted a turn in their own work from Browning-style dramatic monologues ("Hugh Selwyn Mauberly," "Prufrock") to dramatically fraught medleys like "The Waste Land" and the final form of the early *Cantos*. In this new work, voices from the historical or literary past and contemporary voices engage each other to mutually supportive or mutually critical effect.

It is as if we were reading the transcript of a sometimes solemn, some-times ill-tempered séance.

By the time they read *Ulysses*, Pound and Eliot were already struggling with a set of cultural and poetic problems inherited from Baudelaire. A helpful account of those problems, due to Walter Benjamin, runs as follows.[3]

Conditions of life in modern urban cosmopolitan societies are new and unprecedented in ways that profoundly diminish the author-ity the lives and actions of our ancestors can exercise over our own lives and actions, going forward. Conditions of work no longer leave room for the slow elaboration of edifying tales to break the boredom of routine tasks. And while we can still benefit from the experience of our ancestors, we can no longer make something of ourselves by apprenticing ourselves to them, reenacting their successes and com-ing to terms with their failures in ways that commemorate and emu-late at the same time. Older generations no longer have much to teach us on these special, imaginatively intimate terms.

The sustained receptive relation to particular others that emula-tion requires is harder and harder to achieve anyway. Modern urban work and modern urban leisure are increasingly anonymous, leav-ing less and less room for sustained pedagogical, familial, or erotic attachment. And the rapid, irregular, inorganic rhythms imposed on modern work by the machine and on modern leisure by the urban crowd put us on a critical, defensive footing in relation to our own experience—braced to deflect or absorb unforeseen shocks, and bored when the shocks we anticipate fail to materialize.

Baudelaire's *Les Fleurs du Mal* represents poetry's first sustained effort to come to terms with these changes. When the book looks

---

3. Walter Benjamin, "On Some Motifs in Baudelaire," in Howard Eiland and Michael W. Jennings, eds., *Walter Benjamin, Selected Writings, Vol 4, 1938–1940* (Cambridge, MA: Harvard University Press, 2003), 313–55.

backward in a recollective spirit, what it recalls is a generalized, mythologized youth in a historically and geographically indefinite kingdom by the sea—languid, sunny, perfumed, full of murmuring voices, but shadowed by inarticulate grievances and longings and bathed in a permanent helpless nostalgia. As if the only available past was the poet's own infancy and childhood, and the only terms on which they remained available to him were mythical ones, scrubbed free of dated identifying personal particulars. (See "L'invitation du Voyage" or "La vie antérieure.") When the book looks outward, it alternately deplores and celebrates the nineteenth-century city: its turbulence, its anonymity, its vice and crime, its extremes of wealth and poverty, glamour and squalor. Above all it celebrates the urban crowd, the idle reflective male wanderers, flâneurs, who make themselves at home in it, and the sudden, unforeseen, poignant encounters between strangers it facilitates.

In Passing (À une passante)

The traffic roared around me, deafening!
Tall, slender, in mourning—noble grief—
a woman passed, and with a jeweled hand
gathered up her black embroidered hem;

stately yet lithe, as if a statue walked ...
and trembling like a fool, I drank from eyes
as ashen as the clouds before a gale
the grace that beckons and the joy that kills.

Lightning ... then darkness! Lovely fugitive
whose glance has brought me back to life! But where
is life? Not this side of eternity?

Elsewhere! Too far, too late, or never at all!
Of me you know nothing, I nothing of you—
you whom I might have loved and who knew that too![4]

Benjamin comments:

> The crowd is nowhere named in either word or phrase, but all the action hinges on it, as the progress of a sailboat depends on the wind . . . The delight of the urban poet is love—not at first sight, but at last sight. It is an eternal farewell, which coincides in the poem with the moment of enchantment . . . The sonnet deploys the figure of shock, indeed of catastrophe. But the nature of the poet's emotions has been affected as well. What makes his body contract in a tremor . . . is not the rapture of a man whose every fiber is suffused with eros; rather, it is like the sexual shock that can beset a lonely man. [These verses] reveal the stigmata that life in a metropolis inflict upon love . . . a love which only a city dweller experiences . . . and which one might not infrequently characterize as being spared, rather than denied, fulfillment.[5]

Pound and Eliot share Baudelaire's sense of an impending crisis but find his response to that crisis poetically and culturally disappointing. Poetically disappointing, since the two sides of a single crisis receive expression in two separate sets of poems, neither of which gives direct voice to the cultural heritage whose imaginative availability has come under threat. Culturally disappointing, since the poems sound defeatist—as if a disorienting and demoralizing breach

---

4. Charles Baudelaire, *Les Fleurs du Mal*, trans. Richard Howard (Boston, MA: David R. Godine, 1985), 97–8, 275–6.
5. Benjamin, "On Some Motifs in Baudelaire," 323–4.

between past and present were bound to deepen and could never be healed.

The remedy Pound and Eliot propose, under the influence of what they take to be Joyce's example, is a poetic visit to the underworld, modeled on the one Odysseus makes in the *Odyssey* and its counterparts in the *Aeneid* and *Divine Comedy*. The dead are to get various things they need or want from us in exchange for various things we need or want from them, and various kinds of justice are to be meted out. Real benefits are to be exchanged, real condemnations issued, real reprieves sought despite all the irony, all the disappointment, all the diminished expectations. As Pound put it in his call on the dead Walt Whitman, "[L]et there be commerce between us!" The dramatic medleys of living and dead voices in "The Waste Land" and the *Cantos* are designed to re-open diplomatic relations among the living, the dead, and the divine under new and demanding conditions.

Joyce and his characters have no use for this vision and no patience with it. In this they resemble Beckett and his characters: "All the dead voices. They make a noise like wings. Like leaves . . . To have lived is not enough for them. They have to talk about it."[6] This may represent a deep difference between the Irish and American wings of literary modernism in English.

Unlike the inhabitants of Baudelaire's Paris or Eliot's London, Stephen and Bloom still find apprenticing themselves to the dead in a spirit of commemorative emulation a wholly appropriate, wholly feasible way to live, at least in principle. Lots of roles get tried on for size—auditioned for, if you will.

Stephen Dedalus plays the dissolute Bard, and also Hamlet ("my Hamlet hat," he remarks in self-appreciation). Leopold

6. Samuel Beckett, *Waiting for Godot* (New York: Grove Press, 2011), Act 2, 69.

Bloom plays, not willingly, the cuckold of classic farce, and toys with playing Mozart's Stone Guest, nemesis of the facile Don. Stephen does not know he is Telemachus, and Bloom does not know he is Ulysses.[7]

But if Stephen is Telemachus and Bloom is Ulysses, this isn't because their adventures add up to a parodic reenactment of the *Odyssey*—they don't. It's because the *Odyssey* is so prominent a part of their shared cultural heritage that they can emulate its key figures without realizing that they are doing so. And their performances in these unconsciously assumed roles are more sustained, heartfelt, and life-enhancing than their performances in more deliberately assumed roles of which they are fully aware. It is the characters of the *Odyssey* that live again in *Ulysses,* not the actions and incidents. And the way they live again is as objects to emulate, roles to assume.

USING HISTORY

An early essay of Nietzsche's, "On the Uses and Disadvantages of History for Life," provides some helpful distinctions.[8]

The past is a rich source of evidence and precedent when it comes to judging what might prove fruitful or unfruitful, safe or dangerous, going forward. This way of putting "history" in the service of "life" is as available to other animals as it is to us, since they remember and act on what they remember as effectively as we do. Other ways of making history serve life are distinctively human, since they call on distinctively human capacities to imagine and evaluate. Each of them

---

7. Hugh Kenner, *Joyce's Voices* (Berkeley: University of California Press, 1978), 40.
8. Friedrich Nietzsche, *Untimely Meditations,* 2nd edn., ed. Daniel Breazeale, trans. R. J. Hollingdale (Cambridge: Cambridge University Press, 1997) , 57–124.

comes with its own risks, its own "disadvantages," since imaginative engagement with the past easily veers off in enfeebling or demoralizing directions, sapping the life it was intended to serve. Nietzsche distinguishes three distinctively human ways of making history serve life, associated with three distinct modes of historical inquiry.

In *monumental* history, someone who can realistically aspire to power and creative action in an established line of human endeavor scours the historical record for conspicuous prior successes in his chosen line, successes that reassure him about the coherence and feasibility of his own ambitions, successes he can attempt to emulate and surpass. He enters on an imaginary apprenticeship to his predecessors, an apprenticeship that matures (when all goes well) into an imaginary competition between equals. Monumental history tends to yield a picture of the past structured like an alpine landscape—a few clearly etched peaks, rising mysteriously out of valleys cloaked in mist. Why understand what you don't intend to emulate?[9]

In *antiquarian* history, someone short on power and confidence, living in a time of stasis or decline, consoles himself and exalts himself by imaginatively identifying with his community and its past, a past whose distinctive glories he preserves and reveres. He makes himself a custodian of his community's past and conceives his own value in terms of his relation to *it* and *its* value, which he attempts to sum up in his own consciousness. Antiquarian history tends to yield a picture of the past focused tightly on one's own community and ancestry; it is fearful of and hostile to "everything new and evolving."[10]

In *critical history*, someone who aspires to renew or renovate pushes himself and his followers toward a vaguely envisioned, vaguely desired future using energies derived from an active repudiation

9. Ibid., 67–8.
10. Ibid., 72–4.

of some particular part of the past. Critical history tends to yield a picture of the past in the form of a reasoned indictment of some selected portion of it.[11] Yet the critical historian exists in the here and now thanks only to the very past he sees fit to condemn, inviting the inference that if the past in question shouldn't have been then, *he* shouldn't be *now*. This demoralizing conclusion can be avoided only if the historian imagines for himself another possible origin, one he can affirm in ways he can't affirm his actual origin, and commits himself, going forward, to equipping himself with a "second nature" wholly in accord with this other origin.

One must learn to manage one's historical inquiries and appetites by playing different modes of history off against one another. The rest of Nietzsche's essay explores how this might go in practice.

The thought that one can avoid self-condemnation only by giving oneself new origins is something Nietzsche associates with critical history and with his own practice as an historical writer. It obviously has a powerful appeal for Stephen Dedalus. But my own interest in Nietzsche's discussion takes me in two other directions.

On the one hand, it suggests a way to think about the social landscape Joyce's two wanderers must negotiate in the course of the otherwise unremarkable day they tentatively, temporarily join forces. The senses of the past on which which characters in *Ulysses* act may be superficial, moth-eaten, and myth-ridden by the standards of disciplined historical scholarship. Yet they suffer from these senses and attempt to derive nourishment and comfort from them along recognizable Nietzschean lines. The newspapermen and assorted idlers who haunt the offices of the *Weekly Freeman* and regale each other with favorite snatches of Irish political oratory, the aesthetes and partisans of Irish cultural revival who argue together in the National Library—these are antiquarian historians, of a sort. The Citizen and

11. Ibid., 75–6.

his cronies with their intricate historical resentments and program-
matic bigotries, the medicals with their reflexive reductive mockery
of everything their fellow citizens deem venerable or sacred—these
are critical historians, of a sort. Bloom and Stephen are aspiring
monumentalists, endeavoring to resolve personal crises and make
something of themselves by finding and emulating appropriate past
models while defeating or deflecting hostile takeovers of their doings
by squads of antiquarians and critics they encounter along their way.
By these means they hope to escape Dublin without actually leaving it.

On the other hand it suggests a way to understand the difference
between the uses of dead language we get in Pound and Eliot and
those we get in Joyce. Antiquarian historians must view themselves
as engaged in mutually beneficial commerce with the dead. Critical
historians must regard the dead as alive enough even now to remain
in their jurisdiction, with something to lose from their adverse judgments. Only monumental historians, emulators, can contentedly
regard the dead as truly gone and truly out of reach.

In "The Oxen of the Sun," Bloom asks after one Dr. O'Hare who
used to work at the Maternity Hospital, to be told by Nurse Callan
that he died an untimely death from stomach cancer ("bellycrab")
three years earlier. What ensues *in the story* is a weary, polite, conventional exchange of condolences and reflections on the human lot.
So sad to hear. To be taken so young! God's will, I suppose. Ashes to
ashes. Puts one in mind of one's own end. Etc. We aren't privy to the
exact words used by Bloom and Nurse Callan, since what ensues *in
the text* is a philological fireworks display, purporting to reveal the
origins of this small talk in grander and more fully considered utterances from past stages in the history of ethics, the history of religion,
the history of English diction and syntax.

Therefore, everyman, look to that last end that is thy death and
the dust that gripeth on every man that is born of woman for as

he came naked forth from his mother's womb so naked shall he
wend him at the last for to go as he came. (14: 107–10)

Nobody in the story produces or consumes this antique language. Its
only speaker is Joyce; its only hearers, the readers of *Ulysses*. It is as if
the chapter threw open the doors of a vast costume shop, organized
on loosely historical lines, containing a multitude of past moral out-
looks presented in their original idioms. We readers are free to flip
through the racks and try on whatever appeals to us. And when we
do try something on, the result is the revival of a role, not the resurrection of a person. No ghosts.

LOVE AT LAST SIGHT IN PARIS AND DUBLIN

In "Lotus Eaters," Bloom has just left the post office with a letter from
his clandestine pen pal, Martha Clifford, when he runs into C. P.
McCoy. McCoy notices that Bloom is in mourning; Bloom explains
that he's on his way to Paddy Dignam's funeral. Bloom wants to end
the exchange quickly so he can read Martha's letter, but he soon finds
himself with a different and more pressing reason to ditch McCoy:

> Mr Bloom gazed across the road at the outsider drawn up before
> the door of the Grosvenor. The porter hoisted the valise up
> on the well. She stood still, waiting, while the man, husband,
> brother, like her, searched his pockets for change. Stylish kind
> of coat with that roll collar, warm for a day like this, looks like
> blanketcloth. Careless stand of her with her hands in those patch
> pockets. Like that haughty creature at the polo match. Women
> all for caste till you touch the spot. Handsome is and handsome
> does. Reserved about to yield. The honourable Mrs and Brutus is
> an honourable man. Possess her once take the starch out of her.

—I was with Bob Doran, he's on one of his periodical bends, and what do you call him Bantam Lyons. Just down there in Conway's we were.

Doran Lyons in Conway's. She raised a gloved hand to her hair. In came Hoppy. Having a wet. Drawing back his head and gazing far from beneath his veiled eyelids he saw the bright fawn skin shine in the glare, the braided drums. Clearly I can see today. Moisture about gives long sight perhaps. Talking of one thing or another. Lady's hand. Which side will she get up?

—And he said: Sad thing about our poor friend Paddy! What Paddy? I said. Poor little Paddy Dignam, he said.

Off to the country: Broadstone probably. High brown boots with laces dangling. Wellturned foot. What is he foostering over that change for? Sees me looking. Eye out for other fellow always. Good fallback. Two strings to her bow.

—Why? I said. What's wrong with him? I said.

Proud: rich: silk stockings.

—Yes, Mr Bloom said.

He moved a little to the side of M'Coy's talking head. Getting up in a minute.

—What's wrong with him? He said. He's dead, he said. And, faith, he filled up. Is it Paddy Dignam? I said. I couldn't believe it when I heard it. I was with him no later than Friday last or Thursday was it in the Arch. Yes, he said. He's gone. He died on Monday, poor fellow. Watch! Watch! Silk flash rich stockings white. Watch!

A heavy tramcar honking its gong slewed between.

Lost it. Curse your noisy pugnose. Feels locked out of it. Paradise and the peri. Always happening like that. The very moment. Girl in Eustace street hallway Monday was it settling her garter. Her friend covering the display of esprit de corps. Well, what are you gaping at?

—Yes, yes, Mr Bloom said after a dull sigh. Another gone.

—One of the best, M'Coy said.

The tram passed. They drove off towards the Loop Line bridge, her rich gloved hand on the steel grip. Flicker, flicker: the laceflare of her hat in the sun: flicker, flick.

—Wife well, I suppose? M'Coy's changed voice said.
(5: 98–141)

I find it hard not to read this as a sendup of Baudelaire's vision of love at last sight in "À une passante." Once again two strangers, a rootlessly wandering man and a stately, striking, visibly prosperous woman, find themselves staring at each other on terms set by the urban bustle surrounding them, terms which assure in advance that their encounter won't be the start of anything lasting or consequential. Once again the man's vision of the woman organizes itself around a glimpse of gathered hem and exposed ankle as she abruptly steps forward and upward. Yet in Bloom's case this glimpse is merely imagined, since the noisy pug nose of the tram gets in the way at the crucial moment. And if we take "Eye out for the other fellow always. Good fallback. Two strings to her bow" to mean Bloom's interest in the sight of this woman is reciprocated, welcomed, or actively tolerated, we'd have only Bloom's word for this.

Neither of the parties to this meeting is unaccompanied, alone in the crowd, the way Baudelaire's parties had to be. The woman with the valise is shadowed by "the man, husband, brother, like her," who is busy paying the porter, while Bloom himself is shadowed all too stubbornly by McCoy. It's hard to be alone in Dublin.

In Baudelaire's vignette it is the woman who is dressed in mourning, hence singled out as solitary and bereft; in Joyce's it is the man. And although Bloom has cause for thoughtful sadness on this particular day, that cause has nothing to do with his outfit, which is something of a false flag. How close were Bloom and Paddy Dignam anyway? Bloom's mourning dress comes in handy for his more sustained, less frustrating encounter with Gerty McDowell later on: it makes her ascribe him the right kind of sadness for all the wrong reasons.

Speaking of Gerty, her encounter with Bloom wouldn't be possible unless each took the other for a complete stranger, yet their strangerhood is in fact anything but complete. When they spot each other on Sandymount strand, Bloom has just escaped the Citizen and the loquacious mutt Garryowen, and in "Nausicaa" itself we hear about a "photograph of grandpapa Giltrap's lovely dog Garryowen that almost talked it was so human," a photograph which is to grace the drawing room of Gerty's future home (13: 232). Just *one* degree of separation, then, between these total strangers! It is hard to find any resident of this fictional Dublin who isn't well known to the principals in some connection or other. I personally count only two real strangers in the entire book. One is the mysterious Man in the Macintosh at Dignam's funeral; the other this well-to-do woman with the valise, quite possibly a mere visitor to Dublin, quite possibly not even Irish. So much for urban anonymity. Dublin is a small world, and if you hope to lose yourself in its crowds, good luck with that.

"Reserved about to yield." "Possess her once take the starch out of her." "Eye out for the other fellow always. Good fallback." The bits of Bloom's interior monologue that frame this encounter are predatory, misogynistic, and smug along all-too-familiar lines—lines which prove to be profoundly out of character for Bloom himself. It is as if he momentarily assumed the role of Blazes Boylan, tried it on for size, and quickly discovered how poorly it suited him. Benjamin's comments on Baudelaire remain strikingly apt nonetheless: "no rapture here, just the sexual shock of a lonely man," "a love that is spared fulfillment rather than denied it."

I don't want to pull a long face at a designedly comic scene. Part of what's funny here is the way the same words from Bloom—"Yes,

yes. [sigh] Another gone."—take on one sense in his dialogue with McCoy, another in Bloom's interior monologue. Replying to McCoy as he does and must, Bloom may have the uneasy feeling that he's uttering an unintended double entendre in extremely bad taste. McCoy's follow-up—"One of the best"—*likewise* takes on both a public sense relating to Dignam and a private sense relating to the woman with the valise, a sense over which McCoy has no control and of which he may at first be entirely unaware. Dublin is a place where it's hard to mean simply what one intends to mean, what one had it in mind to mean in the first place.

McCoy may not remain unaware of these equivocations. He shortly asks "in a changed voice," "Wife well?" In Hitchcock's *Rear Window,* the housebound photographer Jeff (James Stewart) engages in a long campaign to persuade his friend Doyle from the local police force (Wendell Corey) that something extremely suspicious has been going on in one of the apartments across the courtyard. At one point Jeff catches Doyle staring out the rear window, smiling to himself, and straightening his tie at the sight of "Miss Torso," a dancer who lives in another of those apartments and often rehearses at home. Jeff's response is to round on Doyle and pointedly ask, "How's your wife?" "Fine, just fine," is the stammered reply.

ON TALKING BACK AND BITING ONE'S TONGUE

Philosophers in traditions spawned by Grice tend to regard the import of utterances and actions as settled by and confined to what their producers inferably intended them to mean in advance. They thereby set to one side instances of *brainstorming,* where speakers and agents elicit the aid of audiences in working out what their words and deeds are best taken to mean after the fact. They also set to one side the successful or unsuccessful, friendly or unfriendly takeover bids involved in *backtalk*—repartee, retort, banter, comeback, call it what you will. Backtalk consists of prompt, often witty efforts to revise or even reverse the original intended import of an utterance or action, the import it otherwise tends to retain going forward. The merry war between Beatrice and Benedick in *Much Ado about Nothing* is full of such stuff. The sense that effective backtalk can leave the targeted utterance or action meaning something it wasn't intended to mean, something it will continue to mean as a result of the backtalker's intervention, comes through more powerfully when the target is a noncombatant, someone who refuses to respond in kind:

> MESSENGER: He [Benedick] hath done good service, lady, in these wars.
> BEATRICE: You had musty victual, and he hath holp to eat it. He is a very valiant trencherman; he hath an excellent stomach.
> MESSENGER: And a good soldier too, lady.
> BEATRICE: And a good soldier to a lady, but what is he to a lord?
> MESSENGER: A lord to a lord, a man to a man, stuffed with all honorable virtues.
> BEATRICE: It is so indeed. He is no less than a stuffed man, but for the stuffing—well, we are all mortal. (1. 1. 45–56)

Ulysses has an undeserved reputation in some quarters for mocking its own characters, but it contains plenty of mockers, virtuosi of mean-spirited backtalk, and their wars are for the most part anything but merry:

> So in comes Martin asking where was Bloom.
> —Where is he? says Lenehan. Defrauding widows and orphans.

> —Isn't that a fact, says John Wyse, what I was telling the citizen about Bloom and the Sinn Fein?
> —That's so, says Martin. Or so they allege.
> —Who made those allegations? says Alf.
> —I, says Joe. I'm the alligator.
> —And after all, says John Wyse, why can't a jew love his country like the next fellow?
> —Why not? says J.J., when he's quite sure which country it is. (12: 1621–30)

Real backtalk is common enough, in literature and in life. Commoner still, I suspect, is *virtual* backtalk. There are retorts that occur to us only to be deliberately suppressed: we bite our tongues, as Stephen does in his early encounter with Mulligan. And there are retorts that occur to us too late for us to use them effectively: *l'esprit de l'escalier, Treppenwitz,* "staircase wit" (the term derives from Diderot's "Paradox of the Actor"). Withheld and untimely witticisms are a constant reminder of the extent to which the import of what we say or do is subject to friendly or unfriendly modification at the hands of others, especially those with credible claims to knowing us well. *Ulysses* makes this feature of our mental lives legible and audible in a new way.

FLAUBERT'S MODERNISM: FREE INDIRECT STYLE

In *Ulysses* Joyce wants the competing senses of things associated with different characters to jostle and contest one another within the confines of individual scenes, and he wants characters' senses of things to enjoy unencumbered access to the characters' own voices. One resource for these purposes is *interior monologue,* with its power to sustain virtual backtalk, virtual double entendre, and the like. Another is what Kenner dubbed *the Uncle Charles Principle*; it lets us hear a character's voice and be privy to what she might make of a particular thing or person when she herself is otherwise occupied. To understand writing produced in accord with this principle, *Uncle Charles Style* (UCS), we need to reflect on something older and more familiar, *free indirect style*.[12]

(FIS) He looked over at his wife. *Yes, she was tiresomely unhappy again, almost sick. What the hell should he say?*

In free indirect style, a literary narrative suddenly and temporarily switches gears. Up to now, the text has specified objective events that are supposed to occur and objective circumstances that are supposed to obtain at the current point in the story's development. Henceforth, until it shifts gears yet again, it will specify some particular character's perceptions and thoughts at the current point in the story's development. And it will do so by simply giving the content of those perceptions and thoughts. Free indirect style dispenses with the explicit references to a perceiving, thinking subject and explicit resort to content-hungry psychological verbs we find in *regular indirect discourse*:

(ID) He looked over at his wife. She *looked* so unhappy, *he thought*, almost sick. *He wondered* what to say.

When a character figures in the content of his own perceptions and thoughts, he'll be referred to in a manner already established by the background narrative, most often third-person pronouns: "What

---

12. The next three examples are adapted from James Wood, *How Fiction Works*, 10th Anniversary edn. (New York: Farrar, Straus, and Giroux, 2018), 6–7.

the hell should *he* say?" When timebound events and circumstances figure in the content of those perceptions and thoughts, they'll be expressed in a manner already established by the background narrative, most often the past tense: "She *was* tiresomely unhappy again." In these respects, free indirect style resembles regular indirect discourse.

A third familiar means of specifying a character's thoughts and perceptions, *direct discourse,* gives us what the character is supposed to say to himself, in more or less the character's own words:

> (DD) He looked over at his wife. "She looks so unhappy," he thought, "almost sick." "What should I say?" he asked himself.

Like direct discourse and unlike standard indirect discourse, free indirect style has access to the spatiotemporal perspective of its character at the time of the specified perceptions and thoughts, via a wide variety of deictic locutions other than person and tense. This is true regardless of whether the background narrative has done anything to give that perspective special significance:

> He took the paved path up to the front door and drew a deep breath.
>
> (FIS) If he didn't open *this* damn door *right now,* he'd regret it *tomorrow.*
>
> (ID) He thought to himself that if he didn't *immediately* open the door *in front of him,* he'd regret it *the next day.*
>
> (DD) "If I don't open *this* damn door *right now,* I'll regret it *tomorrow,*" he thought to himself.

Yet while direct discourse makes as if to quote and indirect discourse makes as if to paraphrase, free indirect style immerses us in the perceptions and thoughts it specifies. It encourages us to imagine perceptions, thoughts, and the objective events and circumstances with which they are concerned from the perspective of its presiding character with a directness and urgency that neither of its established rivals can match.

Free indirect style is like indirect discourse and unlike direct discourse in various other respects. Direct discourse can avail itself of a character's preferred ways of putting things without embracing or endorsing them—all it has to do is quote. Indirect discourse of either sort does its best to conform with norms of verbal and expressive decorum already established in the background narrative. If a character's own ways of putting things differ dramatically from those favored by the background narrative, her thoughts and perceptions may undergo drastic paraphrase to bring them in line with ways of putting things already in force. This needn't silence the character's distinctive voice, but it does tend to muffle it. On the other hand, free indirect style can employ ways of putting things that are available to the background narrative but out of reach for the character whose thoughts and perceptions are being specified. It can give words to otherwise inarticulate perceptions and hankerings. Flaubert makes spectacular use of this resource in *Madame Bovary.*

"And yet I love him!" she said to herself. It didn't matter! *She was not happy and never had been . . . Every smile hid a yawn of boredom, every joy a malediction, every pleasure its own disgust, and the sweetest kisses left on your lips no more than a vain longing for a more sublime pleasure.*[13]

If the character whose head we enter is complacently clueless about matters made clear in the background narrative, switches to

13. Gustave Flaubert, *Madame Bovary*, trans. Lydia Davis, reprint edn. (London: Penguin Classics, 2011), III, vi, 242.

and from free indirect style stick out like sore thumbs and we get authorial irony at the character's expense. In other cases there is no sharp break with either the background narrative's established ways of putting things or our own working sense of what can plausibly happen in the story; the switch to free indirect style is signaled by diction or syntax that conspicuously accords with a particular character's established routine habits of thought—e.g., a particular husband's penchant for declaring things *tiresome*. In such cases we often feel that the text continues to speak for its story while coming to speak for its character as well. "Thanks to free indirect style, we see things through the character's eyes but also through the author's eyes and language. We inhabit omniscience and partiality at once."[14] If a character seems reliable enough, and a story is concerned for the most part with what happens within his or her ken, the exact locations of switches into and out of free indirect style may not matter very much.

Follow the urban flâneur as he wanders into poetry and you encounter Baudelaire, Pound, and Eliot. Follow him into prose fiction and you encounter Frédéric Moreau, Flaubert, and a monocular, monaural storytelling strategy that Flaubert and his admirer Henry James did much to perfect and popularize.[15]

The narrative sticks to telling a single story in a forthright, orderly manner. It doesn't moralize or editorialize. It abstains from the generalizing essayistic asides we find in George Eliot, Proust, Mann, or Musil. It eschews flashback, flash forward, and the digressive nestings of stories within stories we find in the *Arabian Nights, Wuthering Heights*—or Homer's *Odyssey,* for that matter.

14. Wood, *How Fiction Works,* 10.
15. For a sympathetic summary account, see Wood, *How Fiction Works,* 37–57. For skepticism about its workability if adhered to at all strictly, see Wayne Booth, *The Rhetoric of Fiction,* 2nd edn. (Chicago: University of Chicago Press, 1983), 3–165.

The narrative is impersonal third personal in a pretty strong sense. Its sentences aren't to be attributed to a fictional character, named or unnamed, who recounts events and circumstances he or she personally witnessed or heard about after the fact. It strives to be consistent, neutral, and careful in how it puts things, avoiding individualizing verbal tics and changes of tone that might suggest changes in mood on the part of an otherwise self-effacing speaker. It strives not to sound spoken at all. It confines itself to stipulating what's supposed to occur or obtain at successive points in the tale it spins out. Such narratives are often called omniscient. Omnipotent is more like it, since what the sentences of the text say, goes; what the sentences *decree* to be part of the story *is* part of the story.

Resolutely objective in these respects, Flaubertian narrative is resolutely subjective in others. Apart from introductory passages serving to situate its story in time and space, it breaks into discrete scenes and confines what it specifies to occur or obtain within any particular scene to events and circumstances in the purview of some particular presiding focal character. It makes free use throughout the scene of deictic devices keyed to that character's spatiotemporal perspective. It thereby invites us to see everything through her eyes and hear everything through her ears for the duration of that particular scene. We aren't called on to imagine that everything we see, she sees, or that everything she hears, we hear. The narrative can and regularly will include details the focal character misses or misconstrues. Nevertheless, the purview of the focal character serves to organize and limit our access to a teeming world of unfamiliar and unprecedented events and circumstances, evolving at many different rates in response to many different causes. It keeps the world at bay.

Flaubertian narrative's favored device for specifying the thoughts and perceptions of its characters is free indirect style. But it restricts its employment of this device within a given scene to the thoughts and perceptions of that scene's presiding focal character. Since the character's spatiotemporal perspective is active throughout the scene, switches into and out of free indirect style may be quite hard to locate. A sense may develop that the focal character is perceiving his world in our name with a fairly high degree of reliability.

Flaubertian narrative is well-suited to modernity as Benjamin understood it: an era when emulative apprenticeship is dying, work and leisure alike take the form of unplanned and uncontrollable collisions, all that is solid melts into air, and each of us must find our own way among strangers.

Flaubert's Frédéric is the forerunner of what would later be called the flâneur—the loafer, usually a young man, who walks the streets with no great urgency, seeing, looking, reflecting. We know the type from Baudelaire, [and] from the all-seeing narrator of Rilke's *Notebooks of Malte Laurids Brigge* . . . This figure . . . is the author's porous scout, helplessly inundated with impressions. He goes out into the world like Noah's dove, to bring a report back.[16]

Joyce learned a great deal from Flaubert's methods but his love of polyphony and parallax inspired him to make significant alterations. *Ulysses* lacks the pronounced, steady, carefully maintained verbal decorum we've come to expect of impersonal third-person narrative. It relaxes Flaubert's ban on stories within stories. In episodes like "Wandering Rocks" and "Sirens," Joyce plays hob with Flaubertian

16. Wood, *How Fiction Works*, 45–6.

scene structure, refusing to confine the overt content of his narrative to the purviews of presiding characters and employing frames of reference whose relation to the characters is not at all straightforward.

Last but not least, where Flaubert might drop without explicit notice into free indirect style, a verbally unlabeled form of *indirect discourse*, Joyce drops without explicit notice into *interior monologue*, a verbally and typographically unlabeled form of *direct* discourse in which the subject of various thoughts and perceptions is referred to in the *first* person, the time at which she thinks these thoughts and has these perceptions is expressed in the *present* tense, and they are served up in words bearing the distinctive lilt and tang of the subject's own voice, prevailing verbal etiquette be damned.

Free indirect style doesn't disappear in *Ulysses*, but it tends to get repurposed. Its most sustained and spectacular appearance comes near the start of "Wandering Rocks" (10: 18ff.), where we get a free indirect rendering of Father Conmee's side of a conversation with Mrs. Sheehy, a rendering that is conspicuously uninformative about either party's unspoken thoughts. What looks like Flaubertian free indirect style can turn out to be something else entirely. Take this justly famous bit from "Nestor":

—History, Stephen said, is a nightmare from which I am trying to awake.

From the playfield the boys raised a shout. A whirring whistle: goal. What if a nightmare gave you a back kick?

—The ways of the Creator are not our ways, Mr Deasy said. All human history moves toward one great goal, the manifestation of God.

Stephen jerked his head toward the window, saying:

—That is God.

Hooray! Ay! Whee!

—What? Mr Deasy asked.

—A shout in the street, Stephen answered, shrugging his shoulders. (2: 378–86)

The italicized language might pass for a specification in free indirect style of what Stephen takes himself to hear (a shout, a whistle), together with a question these heard sounds prompt Stephen to ask (about the blows nightmares have the power to deliver). But the frontloaded prepositional phrase "From the playfield" is one of a long sequence of such phrases scattered through the chapter, all of them concerned with arranged sounds or shapes or postures:

... *from* the lumberroom came the rattle of sticks and clamour of their boots and tongues. (121)

On his cheek, dull and bloodless, a soft stain of ink lay, date-shaped, recent, and damp as a snail's bed. (127)

And so on (16, 70, 155, 163, 166, 201, 364), until at the very end of the chapter:

On his wise shoulders *through* the checkerwork of leaves the sun flung spangles, dancing coins. (449)

This last example makes the status of the earlier ones clear in retrospect. They represent thoughts of Stephen's, worded as he words them for his own benefit in thinking them to himself while searching for his own voice as a writer. No paraphrase here, hence no free indirect style. The habit of frontloading prepositional phrases is a phase Stephen is going through, and the gorgeousness of the final example is his gorgeousness. What looks locally like free indirect style is really interior monologue.

UNCLE CHARLES STYLE

Stephen Dedalus has a Granduncle Charles who squandered a fortune in Cork. When we meet him in *Portrait,* he's become an errand boy for his nephew Simon, Stephen's father. He's an important source of the family lore and political gossip Stephen eagerly soaks up in preparation for an as yet indefinite role in the adult life of his community.

Uncle Charles smoked such black twist that at last his nephew suggested to him to enjoy his morning smoke in a little outhouse at the end of the garden.

—Very good, Simon. All serene, Simon, said the old man tranquilly. Anywhere you like. The outhouse will do me nicely: it will be more salubrious.

—Damn me, said Mr Dedalus frankly, if I know how you can smoke such villainous awful tobacco. It's like gunpowder, by God.

—It's very nice, Simon, replied the old man. Very cool and mollifying.

Every morning, therefore, uncle Charles repaired to his outhouse but not before he had creased and brushed scrupulously his black hair and brushed and put on his tall hat. While he smoked the brim of his tall hat and the bowl of his pipe were just visible beyond the jams of the outhouse door. His arbour, as he called the reeking outhouse which he shared with the cat and the garden tools, served him also as a soundingbox, and every morning he hummed contentedly one of his favourite songs: *O, twine me a bower* or *Blue eyes and golden hair* or *The Groves of Blarney* while the grey and blue coils of smoke rose slowly from his pipe and vanished in the pure air. (II: 1–22)

"Serene," "salubrious," "mollifying," "do me nicely." These Latinate words and phrases express a soothing and amiable inaccuracy characteristic of Uncle Charles, just as an excitable, mildly profane, Anglo-Saxon bluntness is characteristic of his nephew Simon. And the text continues to express Charles's distinctive sensibility by means of words that are distinctively his after it stops quoting him. This is partly a matter of diction ("repair" in place of "go off," the then euphemistic "outhouse" and "arbour" instead of "shed" or "shack" or "privy") and partly a matter of syntax ("brushed scrupulously" instead of "scrupulously brushed"). We can readily imagine Charles saying, under suitable prompting, "I make it a practice to *brush scrupulously* before leaving the house, however briefly, for whatever purpose."

Kenner comments:

A speck of [Charles's] characterizing vocabulary attends our sense of him . . . This is apparently something new in fiction, the normally neutral narrative vocabulary pervaded by a little cloud of idioms which a character might use if he were managing the narrative.[17]

Zola defined art as a corner of creation seen through a temperament ("Salon of 1866"). Here the temperament in question is Uncle Charles's, and the fact that we are seeing creation through his temperament is signaled by characteristically Charlesian turns of phrase and thought. Yet like the background narrative from which it emerges, the paragraph refers to Charles himself in the third person, as "he" or "uncle Charles," and it specifies circumstances and events in which he is supposed to be caught up by expressing them in the past tense. In these respects, the passage behaves like free indirect style.

17. Hugh Kenner, *Joyce's Voices* (Berkeley: University of California Press, 1978), 17.

James Wood concludes that what we have here is precisely that—
an orthodox instance of good old Flaubertian free indirect style. After
all, free indirect style often signals its presence by turns of phrase or
thought we're prepared to treat as typical of an already salient character. "*Tiresomely* unhappy," "*What the hell* should I say?" "Mystifyingly,
[Kenner] calls this 'something new in fiction.' Yet we know it isn't.
The Uncle Charles principle is just an instance of free indirect style.
Joyce is a master of it." And before long Wood is citing Leopold
Bloom as another in a long line of flâneurs.[18]

Kenner exposes himself to Wood's objection by failing to specify
the distinctive storytelling function of his little clouds of idiom. Once
we make that function explicit, the objection collapses: free indirect
style and UCS are profoundly different, and UCS is profoundly new.
There are several ways to see this.

The paragraph breaks sharply with background verbal decorum: "repaired" and "outhouse" in a narrative that otherwise shuns
euphemism, "brushed scrupulously" in a narrative otherwise fas-
tidiously orthodox in its placement of modifiers. When free indirect
style is pulled in opposite directions by verbal decorum and a character's own voice, verbal decorum carries the day. Flaubert doesn't feel
duty-bound to sound like Emma when expressing Emma's thoughts.
He feels duty-bound to sound like Flaubert.

The purview to which the narrative restricts itself in describing
Charles's doings and the point of view from which we are invited to
imagine them don't belong to Charles himself. Our point of view is
from outside the privy, off to one side of its open door, hence well
away from Charles. All that can be seen of him from here is the protruding brim of his hat and the protruding bowl of his pipe. And the
passage offers a poignant detail—coils of multicolored smoke wind-
ing up out of the privy's *reek* into the *purity* of the outside air—to

18. Wood, *How Fiction Works*, 16, 29.

which dead-nosed Charles is spectacularly insensitive. We aren't invited to see Charles through Charles's own eyes, let alone smell the privy and its environs through his chronically insensitive nose. We see a corner of the world through Charles's temperament but not from his perspective. Free indirect style adopts its character's perspective and confines itself to his purview as a matter of course.

A second sensibility contributes to our passage's diction and syntax. The comparison of the privy's walls to the soundingbox of a stringed instrument or phonograph and the choice of the preciously nonstandard "soundingbox" over standard alternatives like "soundbox" or "sounding board" come from another sensibility, another voice. The same goes for the ostentatious chiasmus produced when "creased and brushed" is followed by "brushed and put on." This second sensibility belongs to Stephen, whose adolescent love affair with chiasmus is more continuously on display in chapter 4 of *Portrait*. The sensibility being epitomized in the italicized sentence is that of Uncle Charles, the authorial scout controlling our access to this sensibility is Stephen, and the sentence combines both their voices, as if they had collaborated in its composition.

Last but not least, the italicized sentence isn't in the right line of work to be free indirect style. For it doesn't serve to specify what Charles actually perceives and thinks when making his regular sojourns to the privy. On such occasions his thoughts would normally be elsewhere, on his (purportedly) cool and salubrious smokes and the (genuine) sweetness of his singing voice. What the passage calls on us to imagine as part of the story to which it contributes, what it serves to make fictional, is *counterfactual* in character. It concerns how Charles would or well might describe these sojourns when reflecting on them later from without. Invited to retrospectively summarize these sojourns (with a little help from a sympathetic grandnephew) Charles might produce of approve something along these general lines. So regarded, the passage constitutes a virtual retrospective self-portrait of Uncle Charles, painted with a little help from Stephen and depicting its subject from without, as is usual with self-portraits.

Why should readers of *Portrait* care how Uncle Charles *would* look to himself in this sort of hindsight? Here Nietzsche's ideas about history and its uses may come in handy. We should care about this because Stephen cares about it, and Stephen cares about it because he sees Charles as part of a tradition, part national, part familial, in which he is attempting to locate himself. "Self-Portrait of Uncle Charles" is to be a key exhibit in a Virtual Civic Museum curated by Stephen Daedalus, an exercise in antiquarian history on Stephen's part.

Turn now to "The Boarding House" in *Dubliners*. The story opens with brief general descriptions of Mrs. Mooney's establishment; her estranged and violent husband; her "hard case" son, Jack; and her nineteen-year-old daughter, Polly, who helps with the housework and helps the place appeal to its mostly single, mostly young male clientele. Mrs. Mooney sees a flirtation develop between Polly and one of the lodgers, a Mr. Doran, but does nothing to acknowledge it until it reaches a point where Polly's confessions and Doran's expected confirmations put her in a position to demand "reparation."

Once these introductions are out of the way, the story takes on a clearly marked scene structure, with an initial segment focused on Mrs. Mooney, a middle segment focused on Doran, and a final segment focused on Polly. Events and circumstances in a given segment are specified using the spatiotemporal perspective of its presiding focal character, and free indirect style makes us privy to that character's thoughts and perceptions from time to time.

Early in Mrs. Mooney's segment we get this striking sentence:

> The belfry of George's church sent out constant peals and worshippers, singly or in groups, *traversed* the little circus

before the church, *revealing their purpose by their self-contained demeanor* no less than by the little volumes in their gloved hands. (81–5)

The point of view from which we are to imagine all this is Mrs. Mooney's, looking out on the gathering worshippers through the windows of her boarding house's breakfast room; it is to her that the open area presents itself as a "little circus" in which the worshippers perform.

There are two collaborations under way here between parties who must conceal their roles from each other and from themselves. There is the short-term collaboration within the boarding house between Mrs. Mooney and Polly in landing Doran as son-in-law and husband, respectively. And there is the long-term collaboration in Dublin as a whole between houses of ill repute (like the boarding house) and custodians of good repute (like the worshippers) in constructing the reusable social trap Mrs. Mooney and Polly are about to spring, a trap which will imprison Polly just as surely as it imprisons Doran. Mrs. Mooney couldn't coerce her daughter and her lodger without the worshippers' help. Yet neither she nor they can afford to be aware of this fact, morally speaking, so neither she nor they *are* aware of it. She isn't thinking about the worshippers although they're certainly within her purview, and they certainly aren't thinking about her, so the sentiments expressed here aren't anyone's free indirect style. The sentence in which the worshippers get described from Mrs. Mooney's perspective is a vocal duet for Mrs. Mooney and the worshippers, much as our earlier sentence was a duet for Stephen and Uncle Charles. Mrs. Mooney provides the general perspective and the word "circus." The worshippers' routine ways of thinking and talking provide the intricate subordinations, the grandiose "traversed," and the self-satisfied talk of "revealed purpose" and "self-contained demeanor."

What the passage adds to the content of the story is once again counterfactual in nature: were the worshippers to reflect on the larger social scheme of things and their place in it, their role as dignified embodiments of sound community standards concerning love and marriage and the like, in relation to situations like that in the boarding house, from an external perspective resembling Mrs. Mooney's, this is the sort of description they would or might well give. The passage is another instance of Uncle Charles Style.

What use does the story have for such counterfactual fictional content? Here again Nietzsche can help. As the story has it, upholding public standards of virtue requires would-be upholders to be seen and heard in their capacity as embodiments of virtue. And enforcing these standards involves an unseemly collaboration with people who are anything but embodiments of virtue themselves. So in ascribing to themselves a "*self-contained* demeanor," the worshippers would display a complacent cluelessness about how upholding community standards really works. So this second resort to UCS is a savage piece of irony. It perspicuously maps a system of social control and social hypocrisy, with an eye to exposing it and condemning it. It is an exercise in critical history on Joyce's part.

Suppose that tucked away in the body of an otherwise impersonal third-person narration, a description of particular events and circumstances is marked out from its surroundings by the distinctive diction, syntax, and expressive or stylistic priorities of the special *sensibility* or *sense of things* associated with some particular person or kind of person, while the possessors of that sensibility are otherwise occupied.

When this happens, what we are called on to imagine is that the events and circumstances in question are such that a possessor of this sensibility would or might well approve the content and form of this description, if she were present then and there and focally engaged with those events or circumstances from the currently signaled spatiotemporal perspective (if any). What such a passage directly adds to the content of the fiction at this particular point in its development is profoundly *counterfactual* in nature. It concerns not how things *are* experienced and reacted to (in the fiction) but how they *would be* experienced and reacted to under fictionally unrealized conditions. Such is Uncle Charles Style (UCS).

Examples of UCS from *Portrait* and *Dubliners* tend to involve a curious vocal duet between the character or characters whose sensibility is being explored (Uncle Charles, the worshippers) and a perspective-providing scout character (Stephen, Mrs. Mooney). In *Ulysses* this complication tends to disappear, since the book is less reliant on Flaubertian scouts. Examples of UCS from *Ulysses* tend to be solo efforts on the part of a character's own distinctive voice.

1. "Hades":

> *The priest took a stick with a knob at the end of it out of the boy's bucket and shook it over the coffin. Then he walked back to the other end and shook it again. Then he came back and put it back in the bucket.* As you were before you rested. It's all written down: he has to do it. (6: 614–7)

The italicized part of this description is shaped—I can't very well say *informed*—by Bloom's ignorance of and freethinking indifference to Roman Catholic ritual. Yet it goes into a degree of external physical detail about interactions between priest and boy and stick and bucket that outrun what Bloom is plausibly thought to notice at the time. So it is Bloomian UCS, serving to signal how quickly Bloom can find himself out of his depth (religiously and socially) among those he knows as well as he knows anyone. Bloomian interior monologue kicks in (to memorably judgmental effect) only in the last two sentences.

2. "Wandering Rocks," Boylan orders up a fruit basket:

> The blond girl in Thornton's *bedded the wicker basket with rustling*
> *fibre.* Blazes Boylan handed her the bottle swathed in pink tissue
> paper and a small jar.
> —Put these in first, will you? he said.
> —Yes sir, the blond girl said, and the fruit on top.
> —That'll do. Game ball, Blazes Boylan said.
> *She bestowed fat pears neatly, head by tail, and among them ripe*
> *shamefaced peaches.*
> *Blazes Boylan walked here and there in new tan shoes about the*
> *fruitsmelling shop, lifting fruits, young juicy crinkled and plump red*
> *tomatoes, sniffing smells . . .*
> —Send it at once, will you? he said. It's for an invalid.
> (10: 227)

Boylan's sensibility is busily eroticizing the fruits and their placement, but Boylan himself is too busy putting the make on the salesgirl to notice at the time. This passage doesn't specify Boylan's occurrent thought and perception while ordering up the basket, as interior monologue or free indirect style would do in their different ways. Instead it is UCS, specifying what Boylan is permanently prepared to make of such spectacles. This may color our reflections much later on, when Bloom encounters the ruins of the fruit basket at 7 Eccles Street in the wee small hours (17: 304).

3. "Aeolus":

GENTLEMEN OF THE PRESS

Grossbooted draymen rolled barrels dullthudding out of Prince's
stores and bumped them up on the brewery float. On the brewery

float bumped dullthudding barrels rolled by grossbooted draymen out of Prince's stores.

—There it is, Red Murray said. Alexander Keyes.

—Just cut it out, will you? Mr Bloom said, and I'll take it round to the *Telegraph* office. (7: 20–7)

This follows a multiparagraph establishing sequence at the start of "Aeolus." We are about to enter the newspaper office to follow Bloom's attempts to negotiate an ad for Alexander Keyes. If the passage has a spatial point of view at all, it isn't that of an identifiable character who's aware of the barrels as they thump.[19]

Kenner treats this as a point where a perverse disembodied narrator "[clamps] his teeth on the bit"[20] and offers a formulation as indifferent to the workings of Bloom's mind and our own interest in following Bloom's adventures "as are whatever Newtonian equations can describe the momentum of dullthudding barrels."[21] A bit later he attributes the formulation to "a disembodied facility with words."

I don't think we need narrators, perverse or otherwise, to account for this formulation. What we have here is a piece of UCS, specifying the impression the draymen and their bumping barrels would or might well make on a generic editorial sensibility, routinely engaged in the weighing of syntactic alternatives, were a possessor of it to be appropriately aware of the barrels and the resulting din. This sensibility is anything but disembodied; the newspaper office we are about to enter teems with instances of it. It is simply unexercised, since none of those twitchy wielders of red pencils are in earshot of the dullthudding barrels. The impression the barrels would make or

---

19. Arguably each sentence has its own: the first sentence looks up at the brewery float from a perspective among the draymen; the second looks down at the draymen from a perspective located on the float.

20. Kenner, *Joyce's Voices*, 74.

21. Ibid., 63.

might well make on them is of narrative interest nonetheless, since it exhibits a standing system of rhetorical obsessions and preoccupations, certitudes and uncertainties, that anyone who sets foot in a Dublin newspaper office must somehow cope with.

4. "Sirens."

This last specimen renews our concerns with virtual repartee and long baseline parallax. It really begins back in "Scylla and Charybdis." Stephen has just asked his audience what "poor Penelope," Anne Hathaway, was up to "behind the diamond panes" in Stratford while Shakespeare was off in London for twenty years or so. We then get a snatch of interior monologue in which Stephen imagines Shakespeare imagining Anne's unfaithfulness:

> Do and do. Thing done. In a rosery of Fetter lane of Gerard, herbalist, he walks, greyedauburn. An azured harebell like her veins. Lids of Juno's eyes, violets. He walks. One life is all. One body. Do. But do. Afar, in a reek of lust and squalor, hands are laid on whiteness. (9: 651–4)[22]

Stephen's imagined Shakespeare consoles himself about imagined Anne's imagined infidelity along lines like these: I have had only one life to live, could be in only one place at a time, have had only one body to inhabit as I saw fit, acting as I thought best—which is just

22. John Gerard was an herbalist, gardener to Elizabeth's secretary of state, maker of a rose garden in London's Fetter Lane, and member of a theater company that competed with Shakespeare's. The colored memorial bust of Shakespeare in Stratford's Holy Trinity Church originally gave him hazel eyes and auburn hair. The azured harebell is the drooping flower, pale purple like a vein, with which Cymbeline's sons proposed to mourn Fidele (4. 2. 220–3). And in *The Winter's Tale* Perdita speaks of dim violets as "Sweeter than the lids of Juno's eyes" (4. 4. 118–22).

what I've done. If I've done that, and I have, there's no use crying over spilled marriages. (The abundance of pale purple in this passage may have us thinking of Molly Bloom even at the time.)

Sixty-four pages later, toward the end of "Sirens," Leopold Bloom's interior monologue goes as follows: "Too poetical that about the sad. Music did that. Music hath charms. Shakespeare said. Quotations every day in the year. To be or not to be. Wisdom while you wait" (11: 904–6). "Wisdom while you wait" provides a nice cue for Bloom to pause briefly in his own thoughts, in hopes some pertinent bit of Shakespearean wisdom will occur to him on the spot. (No such luck, I take it.) Then we get an extraordinary interpolation: "*In Gerard's rosery of Fetter lane he walks, greyedauburn. One life is all. One body. Do. But do*" (905–6). After which Bloom's monologue resumes: "Done anyhow. Postal order, stamp. Postoffice lower down. Walk now. Enough. Barney Kiernan's I promised to meet them" (909–10). "Done anyhow" refers to Bloom's just completed letter to Martha, which he is determined to mail as is, despite fresh misgivings about what he's said and how he's said it. This is a direct continuation of a train of thought that broke off after "Wisdom while you wait."

The language between "Wisdom while you wait" and "Done anyhow" is in some sense Stephen's, since it derives from what Stephen said to himself in the library back in "Scylla and Charybdis." But Stephen isn't on hand now, Bloom wasn't on hand when Stephen said these things to himself, and Bloom wouldn't have been privy to them if he had been, since Stephen never spoke them aloud. Not just the thought but the diction is vintage Stephen. So it is Stephen's UCS, deployed so as to signal what Stephen would or might well make of Bloom's plight, were he to know about it and were the two of them on terms that encouraged pensive commiseration.

Redeployed in this manner, Stephen's sentence would suggest that Bloom and imagined Shakespeare are in parallel fixes, to be thought through and coped with in parallel ways. Stephen might attempt to console Bloom in much the way Stephen's imagined Shakespeare attempted to console himself. You've got just one life, and one body in which to live it. Make the best of things from the side that's within your control, and the worst that befalls you at the hands of others, even your wife, can be no real cause for regret. *Do. But do.*

Imagined to follow such an effort to console, Bloom's "Done anyhow" would take on fresh import as a bit of backtalk, a polite but firm refusal to be consoled on the proposed lines, an expression of Bloom's determination to persist in his sadness. Whatever I do, whatever I did, *I'm done* (anyhow). What's sketched here is a merely possible conversational exchange, a merely possible episode in a merely possible future friendship.

WANDERING ROCKS

I've examined how UCS and various forms of virtual conversation function in *Ulysses* as sources of short baseline parallax. But what interest do these devices have in the story Joyce is out to tell, and how might they confer a desirable and revealing sense of depth? Why so many careful sketches of *merely virtual* verbal encounters between fictional speakers, *merely hypothetical* perceptual encounters between fictional characters and fictional situations?

Backtalk is a deliberate, witty way of retroactively changing or enriching the import of utterances and actions. But momentous reconstruals can be wholly unwitting and wholly witless. Think of the tip on the Gold Cup race Bloom inadvertently offers when he takes himself to be declaring himself done with his newspaper; the taunt he inadvertently issues to John Henry Menton when he takes himself to be helpfully pointing out a dent in Menton's hat; the insulting invitation Stephen inadvertently issues to Cissy Caffrey in Nighttown, and the matched threats to Crown and Church he issues moments later.

Our risk of receiving unwelcome reconstruals and our opportunities to receive welcome ones go up sharply when two conditions are met:

(a) Those around us are sufficiently gregarious and sufficiently aware of us and our doings to make our business their business.

(b) Our words and deeds lack a fully determinate original import because our production of them was less than fully intentional. So we won't have said or done anything in particular until a social process of brainstorming runs its course.

Both conditions are met by the narrated action of *Ulysses*.

When it comes to the first condition, we should notice that Joyce's Dublin is a place where it's hard to be alone in a crowd, hard to be anonymous—a place where the old continue to advise the young and the past is alive and kicking, a place where everybody has edifying or corrupting stories to tell, a place where everybody minds (and continually reshapes) everybody else's business. The welcome and unwelcome shocks Dublin delivers its citizens don't come from unforeseen and unprecedented encounters with strangers; they come from welcome and unwelcome construals at the hands of friends and neighbors and fellow citizens. Bloom and Stephen aren't flâneurs; they're peripatetic exiles from their usual homes and haunts, moving in crowds that are full of all-too-familiar faces.

When it comes to the second condition, we should note some salient differences between *Ulysses* and the story it retells or at least revisits. The *Odyssey* divides into episodes, each of which involves decisive action culminating in significant and irreversible change, even if some episodes leave their hero as far from home as ever. In *Ulysses* the episode isn't a unit of action at all. Decisive and irreversible change, let alone action, is in short supply. What happens on Bloomsday, after all? Paddy Dignam is laid to rest; Bloom works some shady accountancy magic with Dignam's insurance policy; the viceregal cortège winds its way through the city; a dark horse named Throwaway wins the Gold Cup; Molly Bloom and Blazes Boylan go through with their planned tryst; Mina Purefoy finally gives birth to her ninth child. Much of this is a matter of what merely happens rather than what's actively and deliberately done, and very little of it is directly narrated for our benefit. Parts of it we hear about indirectly from various characters; other parts we slowly infer with the help of long baseline parallax.

What *is* narrated consists for the most part in random thoughts and half-considered speeches and gestures—a drift of half-chosen, half-reflexive reactions to one's immediate physical and social surroundings, reactions for which the involved parties would (and should) take only so much responsibility. Most of them come and go quickly without explicit notice, their lasting significance confined to minute changes in a character's memories and habits. Some of them constitute overtures or invitations that other characters may or may not take up—it's too soon to tell. A few of them get pounced on by onlookers or overhearers who give them a momentousness out of all proportion to the motives that elicited them in the first place. Much of our own agency is like this, however little we hear about it in other people's novels.

Last but not least, all three of the book's protagonists—peripatetic Stephen and Bloom and stay-at-home Molly—are Nietzschean emulators, monumental historians, people whose imaginative appropriation of the past takes the form of hopeful competitive imitation of past models whose nature and value they understand only imperfectly so far. Such agents depend on hermeneutic contributions from others to round out the import of what they do or say. This makes them especially open to welcome construals and especially vulnerable to unwelcome ones.

Facts about Dublin as a place, facts about Stephen, Bloom, and Molly as agents, and Joyce's deep fascination with the half-considered, reactive side of human agency conspire to give special salience and special urgency to *what others are prepared to make of what we do or say.* And this is just what virtual conversation and Uncle Charles Style serve to express and explore. In a city like Dublin, what a socially active, socially available sensibility would make or might well make of a salient event or circumstance is a hermeneutic accident waiting to happen, a wandering rock, if you will, a decisive feature of the urban landscape.

The unreal cities of mainstream post-Baudelairean modernism—London, Paris, etc.—pose one set of challenges to human agents out to make something of themselves. Dublin poses a very different set. It affords standing opportunities and standing dangers to wandering monumentalists like Bloom and Stephen and stay-at-home monumentalists like Molly, out to protect themselves from unwelcome construals, avail themselves of welcome ones, and make of themselves something worth affirming in retrospect. No wonder *Ulysses* is eager to keep track of such things, and to teach us how to keep track of them ourselves.

BIBLIOGRAPHY

Baudelaire, Charles. *Les Fleurs du Mal*, trans. Richard Howard. Boston, MA: David R. Godine, 1985.

Beckett, Samuel. *Waiting for Godot.* New York: Grove Press, 2011.

Benjamin, Walter. "On Some Motifs in Baudelaire." In Howard Eiland and Michael W. Jennings, eds., *Walter Benjamin, Selected Writings, Vol 4, 1938–1940.* Cambridge, MA: Harvard University Press, 2003, 313–55.

Booth, Wayne. *The Rhetoric of Fiction*, 2nd edn. Chicago: University of Chicago Press, 1983.

Flaubert, Gustave. *Madame Bovary*, trans. Lydia Davis, reprint edn. London: Penguin Classics, 2011.

Kenner, Hugh. *Joyce's Voices*. Berkeley: University of California Press, 1978.

Kenner, Hugh. *Ulysses*, rev. ed. (Baltimore, MD: Johns Hopkins University Press, 1987).

Nehamas, Alexander. *Only a Promise of Happiness: The Place of Beauty in a World of Art*. Princeton, NJ: Princeton University Press, 2007.

Nietzsche, Friedrich. *Untimely Meditations*, 2nd edn., ed. Daniel Breazeale, trans. R. J. Hollingdale. Cambridge: Cambridge University Press, 1997.

Wood, James. *How Fiction Works*, 10th Anniversary edn. New York: Farrar, Straus, and Giroux, 2018.

Chapter 6

Something Rich and Strange

Joyce's Perspectivism

PHILIP KITCHER

> Those are pearls that were his eyes.
> Nothing of him that doth fade
> But that suffers a sea-change
> Into something rich and strange.

On Sandymount strand, fragments of *The Tempest* intertwine with lines from *Lycidas* and echo in the musings of Stephen Dedalus. Yet the metamorphosis of a corpse Stephen envisages has little "rich" or "strange" about it. The waterlogged body is "sopping in foul brine," with minnows nibbling in its groin. The images might stand for *Ulysses* itself. In Joyce's hands, Shakespeare's wondrous transmutation gives way to a squalid death and its "urinous offal," just as Homer's heroic wanderings become mundane peregrinations through a subservient

I am indebted to Richard Eldridge, David Hills, and Martha Nussbaum for some extremely perceptive and constructive comments on an earlier draft. An anonymous referee for Oxford University Press has also helped me to improve the final version.

Joyce's Ulysses. Philip Kitcher, Oxford University Press (2020). © Oxford University Press.
DOI: 10.1093/oso/9780190842260.001.0001

city. *Ulysses*, one might think, as high-minded early critics often did, debases the epic into the commonplace, the noble into the sordid.[1]

Joyce's achievement in his two last novels consists in showing how the comparison works differently, elevating the everyday rather than debasing the exceptional. The apparently quotidian displays itself as "something rich and strange." If literature, at its deepest and most transformative, has the ability to reshape the experiences of readers, to provide them with concepts and suggestions they have never previously recognized, the depiction of a Dublin day, June 16, 1904, can rank with almost any novel in enlarging and enriching understandings. *Ulysses* exposes unsuspected depths, revealing the extraordinary within the ordinary.

In doing so, it should change our moral vision. The disclosures of *Ulysses* do not consist in unwrapping mysteries. Rather they bring home the complexity of what is normally taken for granted, freeing readers from the simplifications embodied in the moral maxims by which we habitually steer. Idealizations give way to a fuller portrait of who we are and how we think and act. Dreams of perfection come to appear naïve. Lives that are blotched and flawed stand forth as recognizably valuable. Virtues are found in unsuspected settings. What had previously seemed disgraceful or squalid is understood and forgiven. Readerly sympathy extends, and, as it does, the centrality of mutual sympathy to the moral life becomes evident.

How is this accomplished? How does Leopold Bloom, advertising canvasser, take on heroic dimensions, and thereby challenge and extend our conceptions of humanity and of the possibilities of

---

1. This seems to have been one prominent strand in Virginia Woolf's complex reaction to *Ulysses*. In his admirably sensitive account of Woolf's project in *Mrs. Dalloway*, Edward Mendelson focuses Woolf's dissatisfaction with Joyce: *The Things That Matter* (New York: Anchor Books, 2007), 200–201. For all the brilliance of Mendelson's chapters on Woolf in this book, his endorsement of her reaction to *Ulysses* and his account of Bloom seem to me profoundly mistaken.

value in our lives? The richness and the strangeness discovered in the superficially dull, defeated, limited, and squalid arise from seeing Joyce's characters and their milieu from the right angle. Or, more exactly, from *many* angles. At the center of the novel's art is Joyce's perspectivism.

* * *

A perspective, as I shall use the term, is a way of organizing the world of experience. It demarcates objects through understanding different experiences as encounters with the same thing. It groups objects as relevantly similar to one another, as making up a type or species or kind. It picks out processes with beginnings and endings, it makes particular causal relations salient, it sets standards for normal functioning, and it treats selected outcomes as valuable or worthwhile. We live our lives within perspectives, and the world—or worlds—we experience are structured by them.

Of course, the freedom of perceiving or thinking subjects is limited. Something beyond the subject pushes back, blocking many attempts at construction. The world in which we live, the world-of-experience, bears the imprint of our organization: it contains pendulums and cricket matches, islands whose boundaries are drawn differently for different purposes, biological species demarcated to fit various projects of bringing order to experience. Yet we can also think of the world-in-itself, the world as all that exists independently of us and of our thought. Our efforts at ordering are constrained by what it will permit.

Some philosophers believe in a privileged prior organization of the world-in-itself.[2] In their view, the world-in-itself is maximally demanding. For the perspectivist, however, the apt choices are not

---

2. This "ultra realism" is forthrightly espoused by Michael Devitt and Richard Boyd (among others). It is tacitly adopted by many more who think of nature as divided up into kinds. In *The Advancement of Science* (New York: Oxford University Press, 1993), I slipped into ultra

reduced to a single option. There are many possibilities for building worlds of experience. In a famous chapter in his *Principles of
Psychology*, William James made the point eloquently:

> The mind, in short, works on the data it *receives* very much as a
> sculptor works on his block of stone. In a sense the statue stood
> there from eternity. But there were a thousand different ones
> beside it, and the sculptor alone is to thank for having extricated
> this one from the rest. Just so the world of each of us, howso-
> ever different our several views of it may be, all lay embedded
> in the primordial chaos of sensations, which gave the mere *mat-
> ter* to the thought of all of us indifferently . . . Other sculptors,
> other statues from the same stone! Other minds, other worlds
> from the same monotonous and inexpressive chaos! My world
> is but one in a million alike embedded, alike real to those who
> may abstract them. How different must be the worlds in the con-
> sciousness of ant, cuttle-fish, or crab![3]

James' concluding sentence suggests that the variation in worlds is
traceable to biological differences—alternative physiologies or sensory capacities. In a species capable of conscious reflection, however, perspectives can proliferate. James' fellow pragmatist, John
Dewey, extended the point, proposing that "things exist *as* objects
for us only as they have been previously determined as outcomes

---

realism. My retreats from it are charted in *Science, Truth, and Democracy* (Oxford: Oxford
University Press, 2001), especially chapters 3–5; *Preludes to Pragmatism* (Oxford: Oxford
University Press, 2012), especially chapter 5); and "Putnam's Happy Ending? Pragmatism
and the Realism Debates," *Graduate Faculty of Philosophy Journal* 38, no. 2 (2018): 431–42.
Similar views are also offered by Nelson Goodman in his important (but much misunder-
stood) *Ways of Worldmaking* (Indianapolis, IN: Hackett, 1978).

3. William James, *The Principles of Psychology*, volume I (Cambridge, MA: Harvard University
Press, 1981), 277. See also James's later discussion in his *Pragmatism* (Cambridge,
MA: Harvard University Press, 1975), especially Lecture VII.

of inquiries."[4] For people who come late in the history of human culture and inquiry

> experience is already overlaid and saturated with the products of the reflection of past generations and by-gone ages. It is filled with interpretations, classifications, due to sophisticated thought, which have become incorporated into what seems to be fresh naïve empirical material.[5]

Advances come when people find new ways to reconstruct the worlds they have inherited. Writers who disrupt old prejudices and point to new possibilities can pave the way. Dewey's conclusion should not surprise his readers: "[T]he arts, those of converse and the literary arts which are the enhanced continuation of social converse, have been the means by which goods have been brought home to human perception."[6]

Novels can change the world. For they can initiate processes of reflection in which readers are led to redraw boundaries and change older forms of salience—and the reconstructions give rise to actions in which all is changed utterly (and, with luck, new beauty is born). The novelist issues invitations to see alien things as alike or to sever old ties of kinship. Charles Dickens and Harriet Beecher Stowe and George Orwell achieve this in straightforward ways, by confronting readers with a single perspective, one powerful enough to move events and institutions in new directions. Joyce, I suggest, proceeds differently. By offering multiple perspectives, ultimately in dizzying variety, he challenges common conceptions, familiar features of our

---

4. John Dewey, *Logic,* volume 12 of *The Later Works* (Carbondale: University of Southern Illinois Press, 1991), 122.

5. John Dewey, *Experience and Nature,* volume 1 of *The Later Works* (Carbondale: University of Southern Illinois Press, 1981), 40.

6. Ibid., 322.

everyday world, at great depth and on many fronts. If we are never finished with *Ulysses* or with *Finnegans Wake*, it isn't because some parts of the "crossmess parzell" (FW 619: 5)[7] remain unsolved. Rather, there are always new opportunities for rethinking the structures of the familiar world.

* * *

One kind of Joycean perspectivism is thoroughly familiar, and well understood. Apparent on the first page of *Ulysses*, it was already present, as Hugh Kenner long ago taught us, in *A Portrait of the Artist as a Young Man*.[8] A distinctive word reveals the world a particular character inhabits. Stephen's Uncle Charles "repairs" to the privy. The flash of light from Buck Mulligan's golden tooth provokes Stephen to a one-word characterization: "Chrysostomos" (1: 26).[9] The Buck is an ancient rhetorician, perhaps a sophist, or, in his burlesque of the mass, maybe a perverted patriarch of the church. Joyce is a skilled pedagogue, teaching his readers by small steps. The Greek word for "golden-tongued" loudly signals a switch of perspective. We are instantly transported into Stephen's world.

Famously, *Ulysses* provides longer and more intimate visits to the worlds of its central characters. Joyce freely admitted that he was not the originator of the interior monologue, crediting a French predecessor, Édouard Dujardin. Perhaps the acknowledgment served to highlight his own achievement, since the monologues of *Les lauriers sont coupés* are stiff and stilted, far from the pregnant fragments assigned to Bloom and Stephen.[10] The Austrian Arthur Schnitzler,

---

7. I shall refer to *Finnegans Wake* by giving page and line numbers. Both the Faber edition (London, 1939) and the Viking edition (New York, 1939) offer the same pagination.
8. Hugh Kenner, *Joyce's Voices* (Berkeley: University of California Press, 1978), chapter 2, especially 16–17.
9. I refer to *Ulysses* by citing chapter and line number from the Gabler edition (New York: Vintage, 1986).
10. *Les lauriers sont coupés* (Paris: Flammarion, 2001).

whose *Leutnant Gustl* appeared in 1900, might have posed a more potent threat to Joyce's originality.[11] Yet even Gustl's fearful musings fail to capture the range and texture of inner speech. Famously Joyce pooh-poohed Freud's boast to have fathomed the unconscious, maintaining that the phenomena of *conscious* thought were still largely misunderstood and inadequately described.[12]

The reaction to Freud points toward one way in which interior monologue brings something new and significant to fiction. For it scotches any temptation readers might have had to conceive their inner speech as a coherent sequence of clear declarative sentences.[13] We become aware of the incompleteness of our thoughts, of sudden changes in direction, of vague moods and tendencies lurking behind them. Successful evocation of a fictional character's inner life thus has the potential to provide greater intimacy, to enable us to *feel* the lurching transitions, the gropings for clarity, and thus to understand more deeply and completely what it is like to view the world from another point of view. Inner monologue has the power to extend our sympathies in previously unavailable ways.

So, in *Ulysses*, I have a sense of greater intimacy with three characters—Stephen, Bloom, and (eventually) Molly—than I have ever felt with any other fictional figures.[14] Stephen comes first, as the primer through which we learn to read. The opening chapter eases readers into his consciousness. Short passages revealing Stephen's

---

11. Arthur Schnitzler, *Leutnant Gustl,* in *Meistererzählungen* (Berlin: Fischer, 2003), 51–84).

12. Garry Hagberg's contribution to this volume provides strong support for Joyce's boast.

13. Hence the rationale for viewing Joyce, and neither Dujardin nor Schnitzler, as the inventor of something significantly new. Brilliant though the depiction of Gustl's anxieties is, it doesn't bring readers to feel the tremors behind the thoughts expressed in the sentences he utters to himself.

14. I offer this as a personal reaction, not as a judgment bound to be widely shared. In doing so, I don't want to dismiss the accomplishments of other writers—George Eliot, Henry James, Flaubert, Thomas Mann, Proust, Dostoyevsky, and Tolstoy—in giving us entry to the lives and thoughts of their characters.

perspective are juxtaposed with more extensive and more straight-forward ("external") narration. "Nestor" elongates the periods dur-ing which the world is one structured by Stephen's idiosyncratic associations and his quirky erudition. Dialogue and external narra-tion are frequent enough still to provide guiderails for beginners. So far, however, interior monologue occurs only in short, relatively coherent sequences, with the identification produced not going sig-nificantly further than that conveyed by more conventional narrative technique. Only in the third section, "Proteus," does the would-be Joycean reader face a first serious test. The walk along Sandymount strand plunges us into Stephen's consciousness and into Stephen's world. For some readers, the discomfort of the plunge causes them to close the book. Possibly forever.

A methodological proposal: Much can be learned about Joyce's enterprise in *Ulysses*—about his aims, his achievement, and the tech-niques employed—by focusing on the points at which readers expe-rience the greatest challenges with this (famously "difficult") book. In teaching *Ulysses*, I have identified four main places in the novel at which students are tempted to give up. "Proteus," "Sirens," "Oxen of the Sun," and "Circe" generate bafflement deep enough to prompt even ambitious undergraduates to confess their confusion. Some of those who continue reading converge on a final verdict. They con-demn the difficulties as unnecessary. Joyce is seen as the obnoxious schoolboy who ostentatiously flaunts his cleverness. If the accusers learn of his famous claim to have "put in so many enigmas and puz-zles that it will keep the professors busy for centuries, arguing over what I meant," they see it as confirming their judgment—and per-haps enjoy a frisson of *Schadenfreude* in thinking that, in the end, their teacher is no better off than they are.

The common feature of the four chapters consists in their upping the ante with respect to narrative technique. Or, as I shall propose, in their being moments at which Joyce extends his perspectivism, and puts it to new uses. I hope to answer the common condemnation. Understanding the full scope of Joyce's perspectivism is the key to recognizing the literary and philosophical point of passages often dismissed as exercises in mere cleverness. With that key, we can find the richness within the strangeness.

In the following sections I shall try to show how Joyce's extension of his narrative techniques bring us into intimate connections with his central figures. In particular, in line with my methodological proposal, I shall focus on three of the four "problematic places."[15] These, I claim, are not gratuitous displays of cleverness. Rather, they expand our sympathies in ways we would not have anticipated. As a result, Joyce provokes the kind of restructuring of the world of experience Dewey saw as contributing to moral progress.

* * *

"Proteus" opens with allusions to Jakob Boehme, Aristotle, Dante, Bishop Berkeley, and Samuel Johnson, all familiar to Stephen, and so readily summoned up in the fragmentary phrases that succeed one another in his consciousness. Yet the wealth of references is not, in itself, the principal obstacle to understanding. Stephen's disjointed inner monologues in previous chapters were similarly permeated by erudite allusions. But the environment in which he moved and much of the past he recalled were accessible to the reader independently of his own vocabulary for characterizing them. In "Proteus" the guiderails are almost entirely gone. Only occasionally does Stephen's consciousness provide easy access to his Dublin surroundings: two women come "down the steps from Leahy's terrace" (3: 29); a dog ambles "about a bank of dwindling sand, trotting, sniffing on all sides" (3: 332–3). In these passages, parts of the surroundings briefly

---

15. The exception is "Circe," about which I shall say only a little. To deal with its complexities would require far greater space than I have here. In future work, I hope to have the chance to do it justice.

come into view. They are clearer in the case of the dog, whose mundane doings do not inspire Stephen to construct any elaborate web of intellectual connections—indeed his fear of dogs breaks through his abstract reflections.

Stephen's world, his individual reconstruction, is easily connected to the world in which Joyce's readers feel at home. Guided by our everyday conceptions and by the descriptions "Proteus" supplies, we can organize Stephen's environment at a gross level: sand, shingle, grass, seaweed, rocks, water, human figures, and so forth. Unlike Stephen, however, we don't connect the mundane elements in a web of arcane allusions. Ordinarily, we observe. Perceptual details matter to us. Stephen, by contrast, begins by reflecting on observation. He is less interested in what lies before him than in the relation of his perceptual experience to a world beyond that experience. Consequently, his musings are largely unconstrained. Nothing much pushes back against them. Stephen is less concerned with the seawrack and the rusty boot than in recognizing the "meanings" of objects arrayed in space and time—in learning to "read" the "signatures" embodied in the appearances. He remains the myopic[16] schoolboy to whom Joyce's previous novel introduced us. The world is a text to be studied, with the aid of those who have previously devoted their lives to

---

16. Stephen's reluctance to observe, and his predilection for intellectualizing his experience, may be intensified if, as a later chapter suggests, he has broken his glasses (15: 3628–9). There are ambiguities here. When Stephen says "Broke them yesterday," that would allow for two possibilities: first, that the glasses have been non-functional all day on June 16, having been broken on June 15; second, that Stephen, believing (or realizing) that he has remained in Nighttown after midnight, accurately identifies the breakage as occurring on June 16, at some time after the walk on Sandymount strand (perhaps in a fight at Westland Row?). Although the second interpretation is possible, it faces a number of difficulties. First, two passages in "Eumaeus" suggest that Bloom and Stephen are sitting in the cabman's shelter *before* midnight (16: 712, 1525). Second, after the time in the shelter, the walk to Eccles Street, the conversation in the kitchen, Bloom's account of his day, and well into Molly's monologue, she hears St. George's church bells ring for 2 a.m. (18: 1231–2). Third, given Stephen's inebriated condition, together with his indifference to the details of his surroundings, it's hard to envisage him recognizing that a new day has begun.

that study. Yet even when readers have appreciated this conception, it is far from clear what this all amounts to.

Far from clear to the reader—*and, equally evidently, obscure to Stephen himself.* Insignificance pervades Stephen's wandering meditations, forcing itself on him as well as upon us. It is, he realizes, a performance.[17] Whether he identifies with Hamlet (3: 14–6) or recalls his efforts to "dress the character" (3: 174), he conforms to Mulligan's characterization of him—he is "the loveliest mummer" (1: 97–8). Behind the artificiality of his intellectual efforts, he recognizes the press of raw feelings. Sexual lust belies not only his attempts at holiness but his philosophizing as well (3: 128–34). Reality breaks in as he fears the dog will attack him (3: 294–5). Momentarily, these impulses focus his perceptions and direct his actions. By contrast, his ventures at flying higher are fruitless, the would-be erudite reflections dwindling into banalities or unresolved questions. At the climax of the episode, they return him to earthy urges with a crash. From musing on Berkeley's theory of vision (3: 416), two words—"flat" and "back"—connect to sex, and to a flash of memory, an encounter that signaled to his starved sensuality the possibility of "a pickmeup" (3: 430). Now he dismisses the thought as absurd: "Talk about apple dumplings *piuttosto*. Where are your wits?" (3: 433–4). Suddenly aware of the gap between his intellectual posturing and his unsatisfied emotions, he poses the question that haunts all his self-interrogations—"What is that word known to all men?" (3: 435).[18]

17. As he will view his own performance in interpreting *Hamlet* in "Scylla and Charybdis" (9: 158, 465, 484, 761–2, 849, 941, 1067–9).
18. Again, Joyce apparently leaves a decision to the reader. Stephen engages in some release of bodily fluid—"Better get this job over quick" (3: 456). Does he masturbate (as Bloom does several hours later in the same place)? Or does he urinate? But this is not something we need to know. The question of the word known to all men recurs at important later moments when Stephen is central. See 9: 261 and 15: 1491–2.

Without an answer, Stephen is directionless. His feet lead him (3: 158–9, 487–8). Looking back as he leaves the beach, he observes a ship, deliberately steered, moving against the current, "homing" (3: 505). The perception serves as a contrast to his own wanderings— and as an emphatic reminder of his own self-estrangement. The great achievement of the chapter lies in bringing us close to his aimlessness, in permitting us to rehearse with Stephen the hollow performances. The attempts to philosophize, or to make sense of how his life should continue, peter out, leaving stale dissatisfaction in their wake. Trailing into insignificance, they confront him—and us with him—with the raw urges that go unsatisfied. To ask what exactly Stephen *does* as he lies "back over the sharp rocks" (3: 437) is to pose the wrong question. Because those empty, obscure, disjointed sentences catch his desolate mood, the sense of alienation is *felt*. What it is to be Stephen, at this moment in his life, is completely clear and sharp, brought into focus as we listen to his voice and enter his consciousness. A foreign perspective becomes, for an interval, our own.

* * *

The abstractions of "Proteus" contrast starkly with our introduction to "Mr Leopold Bloom" (4: 1). Bloom's world is one in which perceptual details matter. All his senses are alert. He appreciates the "fine tang" of a kidney, the unevenness of the "humpy tray," the "gelid light" of the morning kitchen (4: 4–6). Equipped with his creator's aural sensitivity, he discerns ever more complex sounds in the cat's mewing (4: 16, 25, 32). Naïvely, we might conclude that, unlike Stephen, who struggles to construct his world on the plan of an eclectic scholasticism, Bloom takes the world for what it is.

Joyce is profoundly skeptical about the idea of a "ready-made world" awaiting and potentially judging our efforts to fathom its structure—indeed one of the deep points of "Ithaca" is to offer an ironic *reductio* of that proposal.[19] To be sure, most readers of *Ulysses* feel relatively at home in Bloom's world, appreciating the kinds of connections he makes and understanding his jumps from topic to topic. Moreover, Joyce is rightly celebrated for his skill in capturing the rhythms and truncations of the inner speech that runs through everyday consciousness. Nevertheless, it would be a mistake to overlook the fact that, like Stephen's, Bloom's world is thoroughly and idiosyncratically constructed, or to suppose that the words on the page are always those of Bloom's inner monologue.

As he sets out to buy his breakfast, Bloom's thoughts wander. He imagines the possibility of visiting an eastern city:

The shadows of the mosques among the pillars: priest with a scroll rolled up. A shiver of trees, signal, the evening wind. I pass on. Fading gold sky. A mother watches me from her doorway. She calls their

19. The phrase "ready-made world" descends from an important article by Hilary Putnam, "Why There Isn't a Ready-Made World," in *Realism and Reason: Philosophical Papers Volume 3* (Cambridge, UK: Cambridge University Press, 1983), 205–28. Ultra realists, who think of the world as organized independently of human thought and human purposes, tout the possibility of objective reporting that captures that prior order. "Ithaca" is a sly answer to ultra realists, and those among them who echo Molly's morning reproach to Bloom: "Tell us in plain words." "Very well," answers Joyce, "here are objective answers to some questions you might have about Bloom's homecoming." Of course, like the authors of the books on which he modeled "Ithaca," Joyce has the privilege of choosing the questions. Less obvious is the fact that he can also dictate what should count as an answer. The early question, "Had Bloom discussed similar subjects during nocturnal perambulations in the past?" (17: 46–7), might be addressed in any number of ways: with a simple "yes," with the identification of topics or even by giving topics plus the gist of the conversation, or, as is actually done, by simply referring to the people and places. In fact, given any finite spatiotemporal segment of the actual world (or of any fictional world) there is a large infinity of true sentences that might be offered about it. Given any causal process, its history can be partitioned and presented in an infinite number of ways. The ordering of any world has to be the product of human decisions about what is important and valuable. Part of the high comedy of "Ithaca" is the wonderful whimsy of Joyce's choices. The deep point of that comedy is to debunk the idea of a single complete objective description. Reality does not speak for itself. (For more on this theme, see my discussions in chapter 4 of *Science, Truth, and Democracy* and chapter 5 of *Preludes to Pragmatism*.)

children home in their dark language. High wall: beyond strings twanged. Night sky, moon, violet, colour of Molly's new garters. Strings. Listen. A girl *playing one of those instruments* what do you call them: dulcimers. I pass. (4: 92–8, my italics)

How much of this consists of a stream of words running through Bloom's consciousness? Most of it, I suggest, in the passages I have italicized, consists of visual and aural images. Bloom imagines the shadows, the mosques, the priest, the trees, the wind on leaves and skin. He hears the mother's call, and the sound of the strings. As the moon rises, he compares the color of the night sky to that of Molly's garters. Perhaps some of these images and sounds are accompanied by words. As he envisages the woman on the threshold, he may utter, in inner speech, "A mother watches me from her doorway." But some of the phrases are suspiciously rhythmical, too "poetic" or literary for Bloom. "The shadows of the mosques among the pillars: priest with a scroll rolled up" has the cadence of a sophisticated authorial ear; "Fading gold sky," "shiver of trees," "dark language" might occur in the inner speech of poets, but they are unlikely candidates for Bloom's words.[20] To be sure, he would endorse them as descriptions of what his inner senses perceive. For all of us, there's a gap between language we recognize as apt, as made up of *les mots justes*, and the terms we use to describe what we experience.

Is Joyce then falling back into the trap that confined Dujardin and Schnitzler, as they falsified inner speech out of a misplaced respect for the coherence of thought? I think not. Bloom's inner life is a mixed-media affair. Perhaps, in the internet age, a novelist could develop interior monologue by mingling images and sounds (touches? tastes? smells?) with the words of inner speech. Joyce was confined to words on a page. So he allowed another narrative voice to enter.

20. Bloom's conception of poetic language is on display at 8: 62–3 and 17: 396–401, 413–7.

A reporter records—at this stage, probably faithfully—the qualities of the images and of the sounds. Sometimes, in bringing those images and sounds to the reader, the most accurate and vivid presentation requires literary language. Faithful narration goes beyond Bloom's words, providing characterizations he would accept—and probably admire.[21]

As we follow Bloom's thoughts through subsequent episodes (particularly, 5, 6, 8, 11, and 13), the idiosyncrasies of his world become ever more evident. They are apparent in his habit of bringing his own education to bear on the situations he confronts. His (often inaccurate) attempts to use the categories presented to him in the science classes of his schooldays serve as a (comic) counterpart to Stephen's applications of his Jesuit training.[22] Far more significant, because of the import for his own identity and for his relations with Molly, is the web of associations constructed around the East, the Moors, and Spain, all seen as exotic and in tension with the lives of Dubliners.[23]

That web is part of what distinguishes Bloom's world from the worlds of the men with whom he interacts during his long day. For Simon Dedalus, Joe Hynes, John Henry Menton, Lenehan, "Professor" MacHugh, and their ilk, even for Jack Power and Martin

---

21. The narrative voice may already be playing a more creative role at the beginning of this passage. Bloom imagines a large man sitting outside a carpet shop, and the figure is immediately connected to the pantomime character, Turko the terrible (4: 89). Perhaps Bloom's mental image reminds him of a stage performance. But Turko has already been invoked in a scene from which Bloom was absent (1: 258), in Stephen's recollection of his mother, and her visit to the pantomime. Moreover, the allusion will be taken up in Bloom's recollection of a dream (13: 1240–1) and in passages in "Circe" (e.g., 15: 298). Even at early stages in Bloom's inner monologue, there are interesting complexities about how to connect the words on the page with his consciousness.

22. For abortive efforts to understand the everyday world in terms of physics, see, for example, 4: 79–80; 5: 39–42.

23. Two imaginative episodes with strikingly different resonances occur already in "Calypso." See 4: 201–13 and 4: 219–28.

Cunningham, there is a proper order of society. It is one in which adult Irish males gather together in public spaces (typically in public houses). These gatherings strengthen the ties binding them to one another. They lament the oppression of their country and wax nostalgic for the past. The moral order they share emphasizes loyalty to the closely knit group, while fostering suspicion of outsiders. Indeed, the wants and needs of the band of brothers can permissibly be satisfied by exploiting those who do not belong. So, for example, Paddy Dignam's widow is to be protected by taking advantage of a legal loophole.

Bloom is recruited to help with this scheme, and is plainly uncomfortable about participating in it. His own moral predilections are cosmopolitan rather than partisan; universal, not parochial. As soon as we see him in company (at the beginning of "Hades"), Cunningham's forms of address reveal Bloom's status as an outsider.[24] Indeed, Bloom is temperamentally unsuited to the limited sympathies of the boys' club. His thoughts wander to distant places—not only to Gibraltar and the Near East, but also to Africa and China. He wonders how missionaries explain their values to their putative converts, people embedded in very different traditions (5: 325–30). Closer to home, he pauses to sympathize with local urchins, whom the band of brothers would probably pass without a thought (5: 5–9).

His cosmopolitanism has another dimension—his preference for mixed society and his interest in the lives of women. While his male peers constantly refer to other men, the wives are almost entirely absent: May Dedalus figures in a moment of self-indulgent sentimentality (6: 645–6) and in her widowed husband's reproof of

---

24. "Come on, Simon" (6: 4); "Come along, Bloom" (6: 8). None of the characters living on June 16, 1904, uses Bloom's given name (or, as Hynes might say, his "christian name" [6: 881]). Molly, of course, prefers "Poldy" to "Leopold."

his daughters (10: 682); Mrs. Dignam (first name unknown) enters solely as the object of fraternal male protection. The one woman who receives sustained attention is Molly—perhaps because she has a public role as a singer, perhaps because Menton's question about her choice of husband is widely shared (6: 704–5), perhaps because pointed inquiries and scurrilous gossip provide occasions for needling Bloom or for expressing disdain toward outsiders (6: 212–24; 11: 496–7).[25]

By contrast, Bloom shows genuine respect and sympathy for the women of his acquaintance—for Mrs. Breen, for Mina Purefoy, and for Nurse Callan. The male bonding apparent among the middle-aged Dublin males is recapitulated in embryo at the lying-in hospital, where the raucous exchanges among the young men (together with the chameleon, Lenehan) largely ignore the admonitions of the nurses (14: 168, 318) or the plight of the women they attend. Bloom's distaste for the carousing is equaled by his sympathetic concern for the mothers. Among the "medicals" and their friends only Dixon shows any trace of such sympathy (14: 818–35)—and it is fitting that, during the Nighttown interrogation of Bloom, Dixon speaks in defense of Bloom as "a finished example of the new womanly man" (15: 1798–9).

In doing so, he recalls the Citizen's verdict on Bloom. After Martin Cunningham has arrived to seek Bloom in Barney Kiernan's, the assembled "band of brothers" exchange (more or less venomous) characterizations of him. Reflections on Bloom's supposed Jewish identity combine with anti-Semitic stereotypes, inspiring Ned Lambert to recall a meeting, late in Molly's pregnancy with Rudy,

---

25. Dedalus' caustic remark employs the same form of address chosen by Boylan: "Mrs. Marion Bloom" (4: 244–5) instead of the conventional "Mrs. Leopold Bloom." In both instances, the substitution hints at the charge expressed by Bella Cohen's fan—"Petticoat government" (15: 2759–60).

when Bloom was shopping for "a tin of Neave's food" (12: 1651–2; compare 8: 949–52). The Citizen draws the consensus conclusion, crudely and directly: "Do you call that a man?" (12: 1654).[26]

Bloom's world is organized along different moral lines and in accord with different views of a functional society (and of the proper roles of its male members) than the shared world of the men with whom he has to interact. To the extent that they recognize these differences, his male contemporaries react with disdain or even savage contempt. Intimate access to Bloom's perspective, and the moral order embedded in it, enables readers to begin to appreciate his virtues.

* * *

Plainly, the device of interior monologue opens up for Joyce's readers the worlds of Bloom and Stephen (and, eventually, of Molly). Yet, for almost half of *Ulysses*, from the end of chapter 13 to the end of chapter 17, that technique is abandoned, in favor of further stylistic experiments (or, as disgruntled students might propose, stylistic extravagances). Why? After Bloom's orgasm and subsequent brief nap on Sandymount strand, why does Joyce withhold further access to his consciousness?

Interior monologue, when presented with Joycean skill, is immensely powerful. Joyce does not lavish it on all his characters, but he uses it, apparently whimsically, for a few minor figures. We never enter Mulligan's head, but we are granted small amounts of access to Father Conmee, Tom Kernan, Master Patrick Dignam, the typist Miss Dunne, and, more extensively, to the anonymous Thersites figure who narrates much of the scene in Barney Kiernan's. Blazes Boylan's consciousness speaks three short words (10: 327), enough

---

26. The question is posed, and answers to it canvassed, in a central episode in "Circe" (15: 2750–3499).

to convince anyone that it isn't a place to linger. Why these, and not others?

Because Joyce expands the concept of a perspective, freeing it from any necessary attachment to the consciousness of one of his characters, and even from anything we would normally view as an individual subject. The most obvious examples of the transcendence of an individual mind occur when Joyce allows for the contents of one mind to enter the consciousness of another. More generally, he creates new perspectives by deforming or augmenting the perspective of an individual character, to bring out more clearly particular traits or themes. Finally, there can be perspectives that seem to go beyond the limits of the human, that organize the world in ways quite distinct from ours, finding connections and saliences members of our species would find bizarre and unmotivated, even some that would violate well-established generalizations describing physical nature.[27]

To ask after the point of this expansion is entirely legitimate. What, if anything, is gained? Is Joyce simply flaunting his learning and teasing his readers (setting traps for all those hapless professors)? The complaint deserves a better answer than the obvious, if shallow, rejoinder that many of the perspectives introduced in the later chapters contain passages that are funny and even uproariously comic. I aim to show that there is a deeper, more significant point.

First, though, my thesis that Joyce expands the concept of perspective should be connected with one of the most brilliant and seminal pieces of Joycean scholarship. In commenting on "Cyclops," David Hayman called attention to an important aspect of Joyce's narrative technique. Although the dominant voice of chapter 12 of *Ulysses* is that of a scathing, splenetic Dubliner, its characteristically

---

27. These are particularly prominent in "Circe" and deserve more attention than I can give them here.

caustic comments are punctuated by passages of very different styles. These "burlesque asides," as Hayman dubbed them,

> belong to a nocturnal decorum generated by a single impulse if not a single persona, a resourceful clown of many masks, a figure apparently poles apart from the self-effacing narrator. This figure may be thought of as an arranger, a nameless and whimsical-seeming authorial projection.[28]

Hayman goes on to recognize the presence of the Arranger long before chapter 12, citing "Aeolus" and the insertion of "mock-headlines."[29]

I suggest liberating ourselves from the idea of "an Arranger" and focusing on the products of this alleged persona's work. Think instead of arrange*ments*. The stylistic innovations that pervade the later chapters of *Ulysses* are analogues of the worlds of experience already developed for Stephen and for Bloom. They are *potential* worlds, organized according to different principles for grouping elements of those worlds together, alternative ways of treating some aspects as foreground and relegating others to the rear, diverse in their appreciation of what is salient for what. Sometimes their connections do violence to features of our own world that we take for granted. An arrangement, then, is an alternatively organized world, or a fragment of such a world.

---

28. David Hayman, "Cyclops," in Clive Hart and David Hayman, eds., *James Joyce's* Ulysses, *Critical Essays* (Berkeley: University of California Press, 1974), 243–75, at 265. Despite my enormous admiration for Hayman's essay, I view the epithet "self-effacing" in the passage quoted as ill-chosen. To be sure, the narrator takes pains to avoid revealing his name, but he is hardly inclined to suppress his opinions or his personality.

29. Ibid., 266. The capitalized titles given to the various sections of chapter 7 were, in fact, late additions to the novel. So, as far as "Aeolus" is concerned, the Arranger may have entered only once Joyce had deployed him on a grander scale in the later chapters. Hayman does, however, also allude to features of chapters 8–11, although he doesn't specify just which passages he has in mind.

The general answer to complaints about Joyce's bumptious conceit in his own erudition is now easy to formulate. Juxtaposition of perspectives, proliferation of arrangements, intensifies the power of works of fiction. It is a device for helping readers to see things in very different ways, and thus to reconstruct their own worlds. Dewey's point about the record of literature in advancing ethical life is amplified. In its radical expansion of perspectivism, Joycean modernism can coax those who engage with *Ulysses* into reflections that modify their ethical categories and change the worlds in which attentive readers live. The rich and strange perspectives of the later chapters develop further the work of earlier interior monologues. Nor is the humor incidental. Wit helps to expand horizons and to disclose new possibilities.[30]

If this general answer is to be at all convincing, we shall have to look in detail at some examples. Although my principal focus will be on two of the places ("Sirens," "Oxen of the Sun") where the extension of the idea of a perspective challenges readers, it will help to start with more limited introductions of exotic arrangements. To repeat, Joyce is a skilled teacher. It is worth following his *gradus ad Parnassum*.

* * *

Commentators on "Aeolus" have failed to find a satisfactory label for the capitalized passages preceding individual sections. The obvious journalistic designations won't do. "Headline" is sometimes apt (7: 963), but most often not (7: 14, 326, 781). Similarly, "picture caption" occasionally works (7: 38–9, 195, 443), but usually fails (7: 221, 370, 871). Most importantly, any mundane term is at odds with the whimsy of many instances (7: 337, 938, 1014, 1021–2, 1032–4,

---

30. Here I recapitulate a theme developed by Martha Nussbaum, in her compelling account of how Joyce's humor can reconcile us to what has been seen as taboo. See her chapter in this volume.

1069–71), especially toward the end of the chapter. Increasingly, the capitalized passages appear to call attention to themselves and to the ways in which they—almost perversely—play against the content of the paragraphs to which they are attached. The arrangement exemplified in the chapter is a vivid display of disruption. From the moment when Stephen begins his "parable" (7: 921), the exuberance crescendos. The increasingly hilarious headlines underscore the pretentiousness and artificiality of the conversation as the (entirely male) company drifts toward its natural destination—a nearby pub. In doing so, they reinforce our sense of Stephen's desolate directionlessness, as he participates in another hollow performance.[31]

"Aeolus" is by no means the first moment in *Ulysses* at which the possibility of arrangement is raised. Recall Bloom's meditation on life in the East, as he sets out to do his breakfast shopping (4: 88–98). The language of the apparent interior monologue is not, I suggested, all Bloom's own. It is, rather, a faithful recording of the aural and visual images that run through his consciousness. Once that point is appreciated, it's reasonable to ask if the device is sometimes extended—if Joyce employs words that Bloom would neither use nor even accept to describe his subjective experience. That kind of deformation might, nonetheless, be true to the character of that experience, highlighting aspects of mood or emotion that Bloom resists acknowledging.

Arrangement appears to enter Bloom's interior monologue in chapter 5. After discovering the flower Martha Clifford has enclosed with her letter, Bloom reflects on the "language of flowers" (5: 261). As he walks, he re-reads what she has written, "murmuring here and

---

31. The mocking headlines undercut his storytelling, just as the comments of his audience will later puncture his efforts at interpreting *Hamlet*. "Aeolus" thus develops further the mood of "Proteus," as Stephen continues the wandering course that will lead him to Nighttown and the altercation with the soldiers.

there a word. Angry tulips with you darling manflower punish your cactus if you don't please forgetmenot how I long violets to dear roses when we soon anemone meet all naughty nightstalk wife Martha's perfume" (5: 264–7). How many of these words are Bloom's, and which are the ones he murmurs? The names of the flowers do not occur in the letter, but *most* of the other words do (the exceptions are: "soon," "all," "Martha's," and "don't"—Martha signs off in the nominative, not the genitive, and doesn't contract "do not"). Moreover, the terms common to sentence and letter occur in different orders, belying the thought of the sentence as expressing a singular consecutive reading. So the idea of Bloom's reading the letter, pronouncing individual words from it out loud, while the flower names are products of inner speech in the intervals of silence, will not do. Nor is the reading improved by supposing that images of particular flowers punctuate the murmurings. The sentence is neither one that Bloom produces, partly overtly, partly tacitly, nor a faithful account of the sequence of words and images in his consciousness.

Of course, the selection of flowers is itself odd. What do manflowers and nightstalks look like?[32] Both "manflower" and "nightstalk" suggest the closing image of the chapter, in which Bloom, looking forward to his bath, imagines the water lapping his penis (5: 570–2). "Tulips" is phonically close to "two lips," "violets" to "violence," "cactus" to "cock"; the romantic significance of "forgetmenot" is evident, and "anemone" suggests "anonymity." Arrangement has already entered *Ulysses*, bringing before the reader Bloom's half-desires and sexual uncertainties as he ponders the letter. The immediate impact of his sexually charged reverie is "weak joy," followed by distaste for the "usual love scrimmage" and "running around corners" (5: 268, 271).

---

32. As I learned from Google, "manflower" is urban slang for an unpleasant-sounding sexual act. The term seems to post-date *Ulysses*.

Bloom doesn't murmur the sentence attributed to him. Suppose, however, he did. Imagine the intonation pattern. It conveys—vividly, brilliantly, intimately—Bloom's mood at this moment. To read the sentence to oneself, as Bloom might say it, is to *feel* the growing sexual excitement, as well as the moments when it is held back by recognition of the effects that would likely follow.[33] Taken as a faithful rendering of his inner speech, this arrangement would be inaccurate. Regarded instead as a presentation of his emotions and of his mood, it is entirely faithful—more so than the pallid commentary (the "weak joy").

The arrangement contains further riches. First, "tulips" recapitulates a theme from "Calypso," Bloom's comparison of Milly's "sweet light lips" with those of her mother: "Full gluey women's lips" (4: 448, 450). Those lips will figure again in his bittersweet recollection of a pivotal moment in his courtship of Molly (8: 906)—and, as "sticky gumjelly lips," they will be juxtaposed immediately to flowers (8: 909, 910). Moreover, almost at the climax of her monologue, as she recalls that episode and that kiss, Molly will recall "one true thing" Bloom said to her, when he called her "a flower of the mountain" (18: 1577, 1576). That memory is embedded in her own catalogue of flowers, and her final affirmation is sparked by a modification ("mountain flower") of Bloom's perceptive phrase (18: 1606–9).[34] The sentence of the arrangement, the sentence Bloom does *not* murmur, thus expresses the sexual personality of a man who, when he makes love, speaks a language of flowers.

* * *

33. Here I offer an example of the effect discussed by Vicki Mahaffey and Wendy J. Truran (this volume). Readers *feel* the emotional mixture in Bloom's thoughts.
34. Of course, Molly's entire monologue, as well as the exchange preceding it (17: 2249ff.), qualifies as "nightstalk."

Fragmentary arrangements, like the brief excursions into the consciousnesses of minor characters, are not the main point of narrative
innovations. Perspectives are built on a larger scale in chapters 10, 13,
and 16—and even more ambitiously in "Sirens," "Oxen of the Sun,"
and "Circe." I shall continue to build from the relatively simple to the
complex.

"Wandering Rocks" is a *tour de force*, both of geographical precision and of brilliant misdirection.[35] It provides an account of the
doings of many figures during parts of the early afternoon. Those
featured include major characters and many minor personae, some
of whom appear only in this chapter. Dublin is conceived as a gigan-
tic organism, in which individual parts—cells, organs, intra-cellular
material—interact to produce unexpected effects. The perspective
offered is a view from the city, as if Dublin itself were writing a fragment of its biography.

This unusual author perceives, as unwary readers cannot, what
is occurring at each moment within its boundaries. It appreciates
the parallel arcs traced out by the "hayjuice arching" from Corny
Kelleher's mouth and the coin "flung" from Molly Bloom's generous hand (10: 221–3). It understands very well that Dignam's court
(10: 60) has nothing to do with the Dignam family, and that Father
Conmee is thinking only of the stubble in the Clongowes fields as he
walks across Dublin.

But what is the point? No Homeric parallel compelled Joyce to
include this chapter. Homer's hero was offered a choice between
braving Scylla and Charybdis or navigating through the wandering
rocks—and Odysseus elected the first option. The structure of the

---

35. Joycean scholars have documented the many ways in which the chapter's juxtapositions
mislead readers who lack detailed knowledge of Dublin geography. Clive Hart's "Wandering
Rocks" (in Hart and Hayman, *James Joyce's Ulysses, Critical Essays*, 181–216), pioneered
the enterprise, imaginatively using a stopwatch while retracing the various routes.

chapter helps explain its significance. We start and end with the grand personages. A long opening section takes us into the thoughts of "[t]he superior, the very reverend, John Conmee S.J." (10: 1), and a shorter close follows the cavalcade of the viceregal party. In between, we walk with "the little people," Bloom and Stephen among them. Dublin, the author, is a great egalitarian, for whom each of these individual lives is no more and no less significant than any of the others. For the grandees in the closing cavalcade, these little people are simply figures in the passing show, whose appropriate greetings are graciously acknowledged (10: 1201). The superior Father Conmee, with his shallow and repellent Panglossianism, is slightly puzzled by the apparent waste of so many "souls of black and brown and yellow men" (10: 143–4), but views all lives as designed to fulfill the Creator's providential purposes.[36]

For Conmee-Pangloss, human lives are significant only insofar as they contribute to some ineffable divine plan (and some, evidently, contribute much more than others). The closing vision of the viceregal party offers a hierarchical secular view: there are important lives, devoted to the nation's business, and many others whose doings possess only ephemeral significance. Dublin, the egalitarian author, treats its constituent parts more tenderly. Readers are invited to think of the many other novels, equally probing, that might be written about this ordinary day, books in which Tom Rochford or Dilly Dedalus might occupy the foreground.

"Wandering Rocks" expands the concept of perspective by providing a non-human point of view, one that opens up the possibility of exploring the lives of other Dubliners in the depth Joyce brings

---

36. Including the placement of turf in bogs, "whence men might dig it out and bring it to town and hamlet to make fires in the houses of poor people" (10: 105–6). Conmee's casual conclusion about the wastage of souls foreshadows Stephen's later, sharper judgment about the "Godpossibled souls that we nightly impossibilise" (14: 225–6). Even when very drunk, Stephen is a more rigorous thinker than his one-time schoolmaster.

to Bloom and Stephen. The possibility is signaled by the fragments of interior monologue. They are crucial to the chapter's function. To omit them would leave us with a view from outside the human. With the fleeting visits to the minds of Conmee and Boylan, Miss Dunne and Tom Kernan, Master Dignam and Gerty MacDowell (10: 1209–11), however, the view from Dublin contains, in embryo, a myriad of human worlds.

***

So far, I have attempted to show how Joyce's extension of the immediacy made possible by multivocality enables him to conjure perspectives beyond those generated by the use of standard interior monologue, creating great intimacy with his central characters, and thus inviting readers to reflect on their own organization of the world of experience (including its moral order). The passages on which I have focused *begin* his revaluation of values and his transfiguration of the commonplace. I now turn to two of the most ambitious expansions of the concept of perspective, found in the sections of *Ulysses* that cause the greatest difficulty and inspire charges that Joyce is showing off. The prose of "Sirens" plainly recapitulates music. An overture introduces motifs (11: 1–63) to be developed in the ensuing text. The divergence from any standard musical form is, however, clear. No composer has ever attempted to work with so many themes.[37] Yet the general ideas of development and recapitulation enable Joyce to deepen yet further readers' understanding of Bloom and his predicament.

Any attentive reader of "Sirens" could produce a "straight" third-person-narrative account of what happens in the bar of the

---

37. Without the printed page the numerous connections would be untraceable by all except the most talented musicians (those who conduct Mahler symphonies without a score, for example). It would require an extraordinary memory to recognize the recurrence of musical material in any piece of corresponding complexity.

Ormond Hotel and in the adjacent dining room. What is added in Joyce's musical version? A first obvious extension: further passages taking us into Bloom's consciousness. Equally evidently, the interior monologues and narrative descriptions are punctuated and some-times structured by repeated phrases—"bronze" and "gold" in close association, "jingle," "tap" are the most obvious examples. The jux-taposition of these motifs with passages revealing Bloom's thoughts suggests that sounds from afar can be heard within the Ormond, that information about other parts of Dublin becomes available. We are invited to compare two different worlds. One organizes Dublin in the afternoon of June 16, 1904, much as our "straight" narrator would. The other allows events and sounds that would normally be inaccessible to enter Bloom's consciousness. One instance of this occurs when words Stephen has uttered to himself apparently intrude into Bloom's reflections on Shakespearean wisdom (9: 651–2; 11: 907–8). Another occurs when the croppy boy's curse takes on a particular form, recalling the words used by the blind piano tuner, words nobody in the Ormond has heard (11: 1041, 1098; 10: 1120).

In meditating on Shakespeare's twenty-year separation from Anne Hathaway ("poor Penelope in Stratford" [9: 641]), Stephen conjures up the bard in London, dissatisfied with his own sexual adventures, sadly conscious of the affairs of his adulterous wife. "Sirens" portrays phrases from Stephen's inner speech as running through Bloom's thoughts. Bloom appreciates the Bard's everyday significance:

> Quotations every day in the year. To be or not to be. Wisdom while you wait.
> In Gerard's rosery of Fetter Lane he walks, greyedauburn. One life is all. One body. Do. But do.
> Done anyhow. (11: 905–9; cf. 9: 651–2)

The first line is plainly part of Bloom's interior monologue—as is the last. Just as surely, the intervening sentences are not. They are Stephen's privy thoughts, and they outrun Bloom's knowledge and his vocabulary. The apparent connection—from "do" to "Done"—is, however, misleading. "Done anyhow" records Bloom's ambivalent feelings as he blots the letter he intends to send to Martha Clifford.[38]

Joyce invites us to consider an arrangement in which Bloom not only utters Stephen's words, using them smoothly to connect two lines of thought, but feels the wealth of associations present in that part of Stephen's reflections on *Hamlet* from which the words derive. Aging Shakespeare walks in London, sourly musing, as Bloom does, on "scortatory love and its foul pleasures" (9: 632). Bloom, however, is struggling *not to be conscious* of the impending adultery in Eccles Street. He wants to blot out what his own "poor Penelope" is "doing behind the diamond panes" (9: 649–50). The arrangement thus conveys to us what is *banished* from inner speech, together with the anguish that threatens to well up and the firmness with which it is resisted.[39]

One major point of the arrangements pervading "Sirens" is to provide readers with intimate knowledge of the intensity of Bloom's pain and of the steadfastness with which he confronts it. Throughout the chapter signals from the source of that pain seem to

38. In refining my views about this important passage and about "Sirens" generally, I am greatly indebted to David Hills.
39. Throughout the day, he has been attempting to avoid Boylan, trying to put out of his mind thoughts of what will happen just after 4 p.m. "At four she said" (11: 188). In fact, Molly didn't specify a time in the exchanges recorded in "Calypso." Apparently, Bloom had already begun his determined efforts to suppress the thought. As the day continues, however, more details start to intrude. "He's coming in the afternoon" (6: 190).

Cutting off Bloom's train of thought as it veers toward Boylan has been Joyce's principal way of emphasizing the depth of Bloom's anguish over the foreseen adultery in Eccles Street (6: 190–1, 200; 8: 1168–72, 1176–9). As the jaunting car approaches its destination, Bloom explicitly formulates his strategy of avoidance: "Wish they'd sing more. Keep my mind off" (11: 914).

impinge—magically—on his consciousness. Thus, the "jingle" motif tracks Boylan's progress as the jaunting car takes him from Ormond quay to Eccles Street and the assignation with Molly. Bloom hears the departure—"a jing, a little sound" (11: 457). The sound comes again, down the quays (11: 498), along the river where Bloom previously walked (11: 606; 8: 1, 6), into Dorset Street (11: 812), by Dlugacz the butcher (11: 883), now in an extended form, as Boylan approaches his goal. Bloom apparently follows the journey ("Car near there now" [11: 912]). Boylan passes Larry O'Rourke's (11: 952–3) and dismounts in Eccles Street (11: 977–8). Now the music changes to recapitulate and develop a theme previously associated with the jingle motif (11: 496, 498, 500):[40] "One rapped on a door, one tapped with a knock, did he knock Paul de Kock with a loud proud knocker with a cock carracarracarra cock. Cockcock" (11: 986–8).

The odd intrusion of "tapped" picks up the "tap" motif, tracking the movements of the blind piano tuner, as he heads toward the Ormond. Boylan's further progress will be charted by the "cock-carra" motif (11: 1048, 1118). Punctuated by "tap," it interweaves with Dollard's performance of "The Croppy Boy." At the climax of the ballad, the yeoman captain, who has posed as a priest and heard the boy's confession, exposes the betrayal—and the boy delivers his curse (11: 1097–9). As Bloom prepares to leave the Ormond, Miss Douce's hand fondles the beerpull, with her thumb and finger,

> a cool firm white enamel baton protruding through their sliding ring.
> With a cock with a carra.
> Tap. Tap. Tap. (11: 1117–9)

---

40. Simon Dedalus, in the bar and out of Bloom's earshot, has referred to "Mrs Marion." The jingle motif intervenes, followed by Bloom's recollection of his wife's reference to Paul de Kock.

Betrayed Bloom exits; past the "fondling hand" slowly goes "soft Bloom, I feel so lonely Bloom" (11: 1134, 1136–7).

This arrangement, the musical organization of Bloom's world, involves radical departures from the events a conventional novel would describe as occurring in the bar and the dining room of the Ormond Hotel. Nobody hears the jingle of the jaunting car or the tapping of the blind piano tuner's cane (until he enters the bar). The crowing of the cock doesn't come into anyone's head. Yet we are invited to enter Bloom's consciousness as if all these impossible things happened in the world of his experience. Apparently, it is idealism on steroids—with the flow of his thoughts and emotions dictating the course of events. The rhythms of the motifs and of the thoughts they punctuate set the tempo of what goes on in other parts of Dublin. It would take no more than a few seconds for the jaunting car to go from Dlugacz's to Larry O'Rourke's. During the seventy lines (11: 883, 952–3) separating these events, Bloom's consciousness covers many topics: he associates the "punish-ment" threatened (promised?) by Martha Clifford with the servant girl whose heft he admired that morning in Dlugacz's; he finishes his letter to Martha and addresses the envelope; he meditates on Shakespeare; he considers the disagreeable visit to Dignam's; he tries to attract the attention of Pat the waiter; he watches Miss Douce use a seashell as a prop in flirting with a customer; he thinks about sunburn and ways of covering the skin; and he considers why people seem to hear the sea when they hold shells to their ears. In striking contrast to the meticulous organization of simultane-ous and successive events in "Wandering Rocks," "Sirens" seems to use Bloom's subjective states to determine the rate at which Boylan proceeds to his goal. His observation of Miss Douce's fondling hand appears to signal to him a further stage in the adul-tery in Eccles Street—the betrayal that brings home his deep loneliness.

Suppose, though, that Bloom did hear the jingle of the jaunting car informing him accurately of Boylan's progress; suppose that, at the moment of arrival in Eccles Street, the words "One rapped on a door" forced themselves into Bloom's head; suppose, too, that, as Boylan enters Molly, Bloom knows of that event by observing Miss Douce at the beerpull. If the world were so arranged, the agony of his thought and experience would be palpable. Were he to say it to himself, the jabbing rhythms of the sentence "One rapped on a door, one tapped with a knock, did he knock Paul de Kock with a loud proud knocker with a cock carracarracarra cock" would stab his consciousness. Even though the world of *Ulysses* lacks such magical connections, it is illuminating to view them from this (impossible) perspective. For, in doing so, the depth of Bloom's suffering and the strength he shows in fighting against it become parts of our intimate awareness. We feel with Bloom.

The betrayal to come pervades the entire episode. Simon Dedalus sings an air from *Martha*, whose title—"All Is Lost Now"—seems to sum up Bloom's predicament. The music is audible in the adjacent dining room, where Bloom is sitting. As he listens, he thinks of Molly's song, of Boylan's, of love and sex, of his own past with Molly (both on Howth Head and at one of their early meetings [11: 705–9; cf. 8: 899–916; 11: 725–32; cf. 14: 1362–78; 13: 1105–7]), and, at the high point of the air, of the possibility of renewal. The language used in describing the vocal climax foreshadows the description of the orgasm on Sandymount Strand (11: 745–50; 13: 736–40). At the consummation, Simon Dedalus and Leopold become expressions of the operatic hero: "Siopold!"[41] (11: 753) invites us to think

---

41. His friends often refer to Simon Dedalus as "Si." But there is another reading: *si* is Italian for "yes," affirming the possibility of return here, and anticipating Molly's famous closing phrases. Moreover, as Joyce almost certainly knew, *si* occurs prominently at the close of the principal Italian opera devoted to Ulysses, Monteverdi's *Il Ritorno d'Ulisse in Patria.* The final duet between Penelope and Ulysse ends with the lines "Sì, vita, sì / Sì, core, sì."

of the final cry—"Come to me!"—as issuing from Bloom's throat as well. It throbs with a sense of loss—and a hope of return, shared by both men. Dedalus has lost his wife and is in danger of losing a son he loves (6: 74); Bloom has lost a son and is in danger of losing his wife. After the moment of hope, the reality of the threat is brought home as the "jingle" motif recurs (11: 761–66).

The second musical performance, Ben Dollard's "trenchant" (11: 1148; cf. 6: 147) rendition of "The Croppy Boy," exposes a betrayal, and thus elicits a curse. In the arrangement of the chapter, though not in the text of the song, that curse takes on a very particular form: "you bitch's bastard" (11: 1098).[42] Those words were uttered in the previous chapter, as the unheeding Cashel Boyle O'Connell Fitzmaurice Tisdale Farrell brushed against a "blind stripling" outside "Mr Bloom's dental windows" (10: 1106–20). Nobody now in the Ormond was present at that incident. Nevertheless, the arrangement makes a double connection. Farrell's carelessness contrasts with the solicitude shown by Bloom (Leopold, not the dentist) as he helped the blind boy cross the street (8: 1078–131).[43] Further, as Miss Douce has already informed Dedalus (and the reader), the

---

42. Earlier, in confessing to the supposed priest, the boy includes among his transgressions a threefold curse—echoing another betrayal, Peter's denial of Christ (11: 1041). Here, too, the curse takes the same form, "You bitch's bast." The full curse is given earlier, as part of the identification of the Blind Stripling as the tuner of the Ormond piano (11: 285). Interestingly, the croppy boy's other confessed sin involves failing to pray for his dead mother (11: 1042–3), thus forging a connection to Stephen (cf. 1: 91–2).

43. Bloom's interior monologue during this passage reveals his capacity for empathy, as he tries to imagine the boy's experience. His conjecture about compensatory enhancements of other sensory abilities—"Tune pianos"—is prescient. Furthermore, Bloom's sympathetic response occurs as he is engaged in one of his periodic attempts to avoid thinking about Boylan (8: 1083–4). During the course of giving aid, Bloom is suddenly aware of a name (Penrose) he previously struggled to recall (8: 178–9, 1114); as we later learn, Penrose was the first of the men who aroused Bloom's jealous suspicions after his marriage to Molly (17: 2133). In bringing together both the first (the harmless Penrose) and the most recent and disturbing (Boylan), the web of connections here foreshadows the arrangement of "Sirens."

JOYCE'S ULYSSES

blind boy had tuned the Ormond piano earlier that day (11: 280–1). Now, as Boylan approaches Eccles Street, the arrangement introduces the tap motif, as the piano tuner makes his way back to the Ormond Hotel to retrieve the tuning fork he has left there (11: 933).

The increasing insistence of the motif, as the boy approaches his destination, tracks the movement of the song toward its climax. Identified through the curse as the croppy boy, the Blind Stripling is betrayed and condemned. As the tuner and "exquisite player" (11: 278), he *succeeds* in his arduous journey through Dublin, reaching the Ormond and collecting his tuning fork. Bloom, whose sympathy for the boy reminds us of his own unusual capacity—the ability to take up the perspectives of others—also figures doubly in the arrangement of "Sirens." Apparently defeated, as he leaves the Ormond, he has had to face the triumph of Boylan, hailed by Lenehan as "the conquering hero" (11: 340). Yet Bloom is almost immediately characterized as "unconquered hero" (11: 342).

As indeed he becomes in a coda to the chapter. In making his lonely way along Ormond quay, apparently despised and rejected as a sexual partner (11: 1284; cf. 11: 138–9, 169–70, 180), he views a "gallant pictured hero" (Robert Emmet) in a shop window (11: 1274). Musing on Emmet's last words, he makes his own protest, breaking wind in an extended fart (11: 1286, 1288, 1293). The last piece of arrangement in this complex chapter connects that gesture with the defiance of other rebels, with Milton's Satan and Dante's Malacoda (9: 32–4).[44] Bloom has been in his own kind of hell, tormented

44. In the last line of Canto XXI of the *Inferno*, Malacoda registers his protest by "making a trumpet of his arse." Stephen's allusion to this, and the juxtaposition with Milton, can be read (in the context of chapter 9) as his own assertion of defiance against the "deities" of Irish literature, A.E. prominent among them. Its deeper significance is to prepare for the reconceptualization of Bloom's fart, continuing the cross-chapter connections between chapters 9 and 11 that contribute to the arrangement of "Sirens." Although my focus has tended to emphasize a particular arrangement internal to a chapter, a more extended discussion of my main theme would recognize how interactions among chapters produce

240

with a musical equivalent of boiling pitch and prodding tridents. He responds by reaffirming his refusal to capitulate. Like Emmet, his epitaph is not yet written.

The net effect of the arrangement of "Sirens" is to bring home to us, alongside Bloom's extraordinary moral sympathy, the intensity of his suffering and the strength of his firmness in coping with his predicament. For all his efforts at drowning it out, the jabbing pain of Molly's infidelity surges again and again through his consciousness. The "sirens" of the chapter are not any of the people in the bar (whether they sing or not). They are the voices that would prompt him to some immediate action, whether a last-minute attempt to forestall the copulation in Eccles Street, or a turning away to some sexual alternative (Martha Clifford), or simply accepting the end of his marriage. Like Odysseus bound to the mast, he must suffer in resisting, and commit himself to a wise resistance. Like both Odysseus and the blind boy, he must make a difficult journey, and, at this stage, he can only hope to discover a way back to Molly. That concluding fart expresses his determination to try.

* * *

I turn now to the second of my two principal examples. Anthony Burgess characterized "Oxen of the Sun" with high praise: "[O]f all the episodes of *Ulysses*, this is the one I should most like to have written."[45] Burgess' judgment is easy to understand, for, as he remarks, chapter 14 is "a writer's chapter."[46] Joyce's sequence of parodies has attracted commentators, leading to discussions of how he achieved

distinctive arrangements. The present chapter has space for only limited gestures at that. Bloom's release of gas also connects to the close of chapter 4. The new Homeric hero, challenged by a rival, responds, not with an aggressive counter, but rather by repairing to the privy—where he produces a perfect bowel movement. This, too, is an expression of defiance.

45. Anthony Burgess, *Re Joyce* (New York: W.W. Norton, 1968), 156.
46. Ibid.

his many successes—and how he occasionally failed.[47] The development of English prose is, of course, supposed to parallel the development of the embryo. Yet, however much we learn about the intricacies of the styles Joyce imitates and however much attention is lavished on comparisons with embryology, a skeptical voice remains unanswered. To be sure, it is all very clever, and often extremely funny— but does it have any function in a novel ostensibly about a long day in Dublin?

Almost all the chapter focuses on events within the lying-in hospital, where Mina Purefoy eventually gives birth to her ninth child. Up to the point at which all the assembled men have left for the pub (14: 1439), Joyce presents a sequence of arrangements, differing not only in style but also in the moral orders they affirm. Some are abstractly secular, focusing on the intelligent achievements of social institutions (14: 7–32), others religious, either in simple piety (14: 93–110) or in allegorical presentation of Puritan values (14: 429–73). The Mandeville and Malory pastiches recognize the chivalric virtues of courage, comradeship, and conviviality (14: 123– 276). Pepys offers the moral perspective of the prominent-man-about-town (14: 474–528); Swift satirizes the conventional moralism of the eighteenth century (14: 581–650); Sterne continues the mocking of prudery and celebrates sensual pleasures (14: 738–98); Burke counters with a moderate defense of propriety, while Junius savages the hypocrisy of those (like Bloom) whose moral practices are at odds with the precepts they avow (14: 905–41). Lamb offers nineteenth-century sentimentalism (14: 1038–77), while Huxley presents the view from the latest science (14: 1223–309). Victorian

---

47. The Pepys pastiche (14: 474–528) is often criticized as especially weak. Joyce worked from an anthology, *English Prose from Mandeville to Ruskin*, whose editor, W. Peacock, "ruthlessly" edited Pepys (see J. S. Atherton, "The Oxen of the Sun" in Hart and Hayman, *James Joyce's Ulysses, Critical Essays*, 313–39, at 324). Atherton's essay is a fine example of the main line of critical discussion of chapter 14.

morality reaches its zenith with Dickens (14: 1310–43), on which Pater (14: 1356–78), Ruskin (14: 1379–90), and Carlyle (14: 1391–439) play distinctive (and more elaborate) variations.

The champions of these various moral perspectives are at odds with one another along many dimensions. Virtues celebrated by some are seen in very different lights by others. Wisdom, piety, courage, generosity, magnanimity, freedom, companionship, gentleness, temperance, modesty, constancy, honesty, honor, obedience, public-mindedness, and attentiveness to facts all receive disparate rankings in the diverse moral orderings of the world. Within the seeming cacophony of voices, however, some themes return again and again. The first, and most obvious, is the shared enthusiasm for human reproduction, coupled with frequent denunciations of those who fail to produce descendants. (This theme underlies the tortured syntax of the Sallust imitation, is celebrated gravely by Bunyan and exuberantly by Swift, and reaches its high point in the thunderings of Junius and Carlyle [14: 929–31, 1421–2]). The second values human sympathy for those who suffer (and for those who minister to suffering). This theme emerges early in the Anglo-Saxon prose (14: 60–70, 93–106), in praise of Bloom's kindliness (14: 182–6), and in Nurse Quigley's reprimand to the carousing company (14: 318–33). It is voiced by Burke (14: 865–70) and recurs in Carlyle (14: 1403–6).

We might think of these as *invariants* within the moral conversation.[48] The command to be fruitful and multiply serves as a constraint on the maxims espoused even by the most pious and puritanical. The value of sympathy for suffering similarly checks those who celebrate vitality, sensuality, and freedom—even though the check may be overridden in the overflow of exuberance, the breach is a violation of the moral order, not an expression of it. The loud carousers are

---

48. An idea developed by Robert Nozick, *Invariances* (Cambridge, MA: Harvard University Press, 2001), chapter 5.

muted as they enter the "antechamber of birth" (14: 1380). Drunken Stephen breaks the solemn mood with his call to the pub (14: 1391), but in doing so, the "*flair* for the cruder things of life," already noted by Bloom (14: 1359) violates his settled attitudes.[49]

The first of these shared moral judgments lends itself to condemnation of Bloom. Junius and Carlyle, relatively shallow in their application of moral maxims, find it easy to accuse Bloom for his failure in his "marital duties" and his recourse to extra-vaginal sex (including the masturbation witnessed on Sandymount Strand). Yet their moral authority is dwarfed by a passage I have not yet mentioned, Joyce's exquisite imitation of the prose of a writer he greatly admired. In a sequence of pastiches, the Newman paragraph (14: 1344–55) stands out for the respect paid to the original.[50]

Newman focuses not on Bloom's moral failures (his "sins" [14: 1344]), but on the role played by the memory of those misdeeds in the "sinner's" consciousness. The function of these memories is not to "insult" (in the manner of Junius and Carlyle), but to stimulate reflection, to prepare for psychological change through the recollection of the past and of what has been lost. Bloom has apparently been absorbed in a reverie (contemplating a bottle of Bass ale [14: 1182–3]), and Pater, admirably suited to foster moral awareness through meditation on an aesthetically appealing past, describes how Bloom's troubled awareness of what his life once was is focused by recalling a scene from the days in which he courted Molly.[51] Newman's grave

---

49. The passage runs parallel, in my view, to the eruption of raw impulses in "Proteus" and their disruption of Stephen's abstract theorizing. See above p. 217.

50. In *A Portrait of the Artist as a Young Man*, Stephen hails Newman as the greatest English prose author. There is reason to think that Joyce not only had great respect for Newman as a stylist when he wrote *Portrait*, but that this attitude persisted through the period in which he wrote *Ulysses*.

51. Apparently, the episode is the one in which Bloom upstaged Menton at a game of bowls (6: 701, 1010–12). The memory is triggered by a sudden recognition of Stephen: he is seen as the young boy whom Molly and her friends played with on that evening (14: 1366–75).

counsel urges Bloom to face the facts without blinking, to compare what has been with what is present, to understand clearly what has been lost. It crystallizes Bloom's own inchoate resolve to find his way back to Molly, present at earlier crucial junctures (8: 899–917; 11: 725–55), and recurring now as he recalls the scene from his courtship. To emphasize the importance of Newman's judgment, Pater closes by echoing Newman's characterization of the visions from the past (14: 1355, 1377–8).

Newman stands apart from the voices that present the other moral perspectives.[52] He does not offer explicit principles or maxims. Instead of outlining a moral order, emphasizing some values and rejecting or downplaying others, he proposes a method for renewing or refining one's attitudes and commitments, through the sustained consideration of the flaws and blotches that inevitably mar a human life. Rather than attempting to sketch his vision of the good, he aims to help those who wander (in "the middle span of our allotted years" [14: 859; 9: 831]) to find their way.[53]

Moral counsel can be conceived in two different ways. Many religious teachers and secular philosophers focus on presenting some body of principles, to be applied by their advisees as they confront different situations. A different approach is to regard the moral agent as already equipped, through socialization from childhood on, with a collection of concepts and rules of thumb; what the agent needs is advice on how to apply them and how to refine them in difficult situations. All adequately socialized adults carry a moral toolbox. Sometimes, however, they require better tools or more training in how to use the tools they already have. Wise moral counsel offers *methods* for moral practice and moral progress.

52. I am grateful to Martha Nussbaum for helping me to clarify the discussion in the remainder of this section.
53. Stephen's version, in "Scylla and Charybdis," cites Dante in the original.

Dewey conceives moral discussion in this way, and so does Joyce's version of Newman. Both turn away from emphasizing principles or celebrating dominant virtues to commend processes of reflection.[54] Newman's advice focuses on what Bloom has, almost always throughout *Ulysses*, shied away from doing: namely to face squarely the past events that have generated his current predicament. "Sirens" has made abundantly clear the suffering entailed in doing that, and pain surely oppresses him as he communes with the bottle of Bass. Although he has resolved to find his way back to Molly, he remains in need of direction. Yet Newman's suggestion is incomplete. How exactly does confrontation with the "sins" of the past promote moral growth? How should Bloom's meditation proceed?

Here, I suggest, the invariances among the diverse moral orders point the way. The accusing voices tell him *where* to focus: on his sexual withdrawal from Molly, and on the wounds underlying it. Bloom must recognize his own failure to come to terms with Rudy's death, and what it has meant, for him and for others. The emphasis on sympathy and its importance is complementary. His task is to extend his capacity for adopting the perspectives of others—a capacity developed in him to an unusually high degree—to the painful events and situations he has scrupulously suppressed. "Oxen of the Sun" is thus a moral accounting of Bloom, of his strengths as well as his failures.

The coda to the chapter reacts to the sequence of disparate moral practices, with their divergent priorities about genuine virtues, in a cruder way. Instead of seeking invariances and looking for methods of moral advance, it initially rejects the moralizing enterprise. Outside

---

54. Dewey's development of this approach is prominent in *Human Nature and Conduct*, volume 14 of *Middle Works* (Carbondale: University of Southern Illinois Press, 1983) and in the later chapters of *The Quest for Certainty*, volume 4 of *The Later Works* (Carbondale: University of Southern Illinois Press, 1984). My *Moral Progress* (forthcoming) attempts to sharpen Dewey's insights.

the hospital, liberated from the constraints appropriate to that setting (14: 1381–3), the language of the carousing band descends into
chaos. The moral order dissolves as well. As the perspectives of the
past are, one and all, rejected, anything goes. Ever drunker, the voices
acquiesce in the impulses of the moment. Nothing has any value
except insofar as it satisfies a momentary desire.

But there is a last voice, an equally crude final moralistic reaction.
A poster glowers at the roistering crew as they head toward Nighttown.
Blunt relativism is matched by the blunt morality of old-time funda-
mentalism. J. Alexander Dowie speaks the closing words, warning the
sinners of the future costs of their misdeeds (14: 1588–91).

Bloom follows the revelers. In doing so, he expresses in embry-
onic form the wisdom of Newman's counsel and the invariances of
the chapter. Not only is he moved by a sympathetic wish to protect
Stephen. He also knows, inchoately, that it is not yet time to return to
Eccles Street. Before he can join Molly in the marriage bed, he must
begin to come to terms with the painful events of the past (including
those of the afternoon). The many arrangements of "Circe" will begin
that confrontation.

* * *

"Circe" juxtaposes strange arrangements with the fictional world
Joyce has presented to his readers, a world constituted by the events
of a recognizable day in a recognizable city. Interior monologue,
brilliant as it may be for illuminating aspects of a character, is left
far behind in the profusion of apparently bizarre alternatives. Those
kaleidoscopic presentations take us further into Bloom's thoughts
and feelings as he begins the process of self-examination. They continue the process of undermining moral prejudices. We no longer
view Bloom as pusillanimous, weak, lecherous, and deceptive—
as we might well be inclined to characterize a figure from another
novel who performs very similar actions—but as someone whose

fortitude, strength, suffering, integrity, and capacity for sympathy are genuinely admirable. In short—as a hero. Like Odysseus, he must undertake a difficult and dangerous journey, without map or compass to guide him.

Does this appraisal of Bloom go too far in importing an optimistic tone into *Ulysses*? Have I perhaps indulged two of my principal enthusiasms—for Dewey and for Joyce—in a misguided effort to link these two (remarkably different) writers?[55] I don't think so. Dewey is no providentialist, believing, with Dr. Pangloss and Father Conmee, that all is bound to come right in the end. He builds on a point more eloquently expressed by William James, whose early writings are pervaded by the thought that we cannot know in advance whether our efforts to achieve various goals—to attain knowledge, to act well, to find a basis for our value judgment—are either guaranteed success or are doomed to failure.[56] In our ineluctably uncertain situation, the best we can do is to try to achieve the aims that survive reflective scrutiny, using the tools we judge most suited to the job. The meliorism shared by James and Dewey—and by Joyce, too—is no jaunty confidence that all will be well, but a considered commitment to go on, hoping for improvement. Dewey's special emphasis on method issues in proposals for how to assess ends and means. His notoriously dull prose (which often seems to have the smell of wet wool) begins to elaborate a method of moral inquiry centered on sympathetic engagement with rival perspectives.[57] That too is *shown* in *Ulysses*. Bloom's capacity for perspective-sharing, coupled to

55. I am much indebted to the reader for OUP for posing versions of these questions. They deserve answers.
56. This theme runs through many of the essays in *The Will to Believe*, particularly "The Sentiment of Rationality," "The Moral Philosopher and the Moral Life," and (in its most famous epistemological form) the title chapter.
57. In my judgment, Dewey only begins this task. In *Moral Progress*, I try to carry it further.

his acceptance of Newman's counsel, leads to a moral vision recognizably superior to the conventional chumminess of his fellow Dubliners.

No reader of *Ulysses* can dare to predict what will happen to Bloom and Molly in the subsequent weeks, months, and years—or even what June 17 will bring. Whether finding their way forward depends on renewing their marriage, and whether that will occur, are both radically uncertain. The novel leaves us with Bloom's first efforts to explore the terrain from different perspectives, and with the ebbs and flows of Molly's soliloquy. In their different ways they have started to deploy the method Dewey outlines and that Joyce shows us.[58]

The showing invites us, Joyce's readers, to try it ourselves, to reassess the values we have, often casually, absorbed from the ambient society. To tender that invitation, and thus potentially to bring about a "revaluation of values," Joyce needed to reform the novel. He extended narrative technique, using many different perspectives, or arrangements, to jolt us into new understandings. I have attempted to understand some of the ways in which his reforms were accomplished and to explore their philosophical significance.

However, *Ulysses* was not the end either of his narrative innovations or of his philosophically significant writing. The initially bewildering polyphony of *Finnegans Wake* extends the approach of "Circe," proliferating fictional worlds on a cosmic scale. The anchoring fictional world disappears—the guiderails have vanished—leaving a space unoccupied by anything to which readers have

---

58. Dewey's remark that writers of fiction have done more than the philosophers to advance moral practice (cf. my n6) applies to himself (and to me). Joyce's vivid depiction of the perspectival method has more impact than discursive accounts. Philosophers, however, can sometimes help others to look in the right places and to recognize what is there. In my judgment, this conception of a philosophical role runs through the approach to philosophy in literature inaugurated by Cavell.

"straight" narrative access. How can that be? Echoing the Citizen, we might ask, "Do you call that a novel?" The answer, teasingly offered in Joyce's mode of address for his readers—"gentlewriter" (FW 63: 10), "drear writer" (FW 476: 21)—is that the fictional world to be contrasted with these alternatives is one we must construct, from scratch, for ourselves. Out of our own experiences and the elements of Joyce's kaleidoscope,[59] we build the fiction to extend, refine, and illuminate our conception of our lives and their meanings.

Ulysses points the way, revealing the complexity of ethical life and the depth of what might easily be dismissed as quotidian. Through its assembly of perspectives it turns the wandering of a middle-aged Dubliner into an Odyssey, transfiguring the commonplace. Everyday experience becomes something rich and strange. In *Finnegans Wake*, Joyce takes a further step. He invites us to become authors, to reflect on the idiosyncrasies of our own lives, and to reconstruct the world for ourselves.

BIBLIOGRAPHY

Atherton, J. S. "The Oxen of the Sun." In Clive Hart and David Hayman, eds., *James Joyce's* Ulysses, *Critical Essays*. Berkeley: University of California Press, 1974, 313–39.

Burgess, Anthony. *Re Joyce*. New York: W.W. Norton, 1968

Dewey, John. *Experience and Nature*. Volume 1 of *The Later Works*. Carbondale: University of Southern Illinois Press, 1981.

Dewey, John. *Human Nature and Conduct*. Volume 14 of *Middle Works*. Carbondale: University of Southern Illinois Press, 1983.

---

59. For an extended defense of this image as appropriate for *Finnegans Wake*, see my *Joyce's Kaleidoscope: An Invitation to* Finnegans Wake (New York: Oxford University Press, 2007); a subsequent article, "Collideorscape: *Finnegans Wake* in the Large and in the Small," *Joyce Studies Annual* (2009): 188–211, provides a more detailed reading of the passage (143: 3–28) in which Joyce characterizes the Wake as a "collideorscape."

Dewey, John. *Logic.* Volume 12 of *The Later Works.* Carbondale: University of Southern Illinois Press, 1991.

Dewey, John. *The Quest for Certainty.* Volume 4 of *The Later Works.* Carbondale: University of Southern Illinois Press, 1984.

Dujardin, Édouard. *Les lauriers sont coupés.* Paris: Flammarion, 2001.

Goodman, Nelson. *Ways of Worldmaking.* Indianapolis, IN: Hackett, 1978.

Hart, Clive. "Wandering Rocks." In Clive Hart and David Hayman, eds., *James Joyce's Ulysses, Critical Essays.* Berkeley: University of California Press, 1974, 181–216.

Hayman, David. "Cyclops." In Clive Hart and David Hayman, eds., *James Joyce's Ulysses, Critical Essays.* Berkeley: University of California Press, 1974, 243–75.

James, William. *Pragmatism.* Cambridge, MA: Harvard University Press, 1975.

James, William. *The Principles of Psychology.* Volume I. Cambridge, MA: Harvard University Press, 1981.

Kenner, Hugh. *Joyce's Voices.* Berkeley: University of California Press, 1978.

Kitcher, Philip. *The Advancement of Science.* Oxford: Oxford University Press, 1993.

Kitcher, Philip. "Collideorscape: *Finnegans Wake* in the Large and in the Small." *Joyce Studies Annual* (2009): 188–211.

Kitcher, Philip. *Joyce's Kaleidoscope: An Invitation to* Finnegans Wake. New York: Oxford University Press, 2007.

Kitcher, Philip. "Putnam's Happy Ending? Pragmatism and the Realism Debates." *Graduate Faculty of Philosophy Journal* 38, no. 2 (2018): 431–42.

Kitcher, Philip. *Science, Truth, and Democracy.* Oxford: Oxford University Press, 2001.

Mendelson, Edward. *The Things That Matter.* New York: Anchor Books, 2007.

Nozick, Robert. *Invariances.* Cambridge, MA: Harvard University Press, 2001.

Putnam, Hilary. "Why There Isn't a Ready-Made World." In *Realism and Reason: Philosophical Papers Volume 3.* Cambridge, UK: Cambridge University Press, 1983, 205–28.

Schnitzler, Arthur. *Leutnant Gustl.* In *Meistererzählungen.* Berlin: Fischer, 2003, 51–84.

INDEX OF NAMES

Page numbers followed by n indicate footnotes.

INDEX OF WORKS

Page numbers followed by n indicate footnotes.